Clinical Practice at the

Laura Smith
Editor

Clinical Practice at the Edge of Care

Developments in Working with At-Risk Children and their Families

palgrave
macmillan

Editor
Laura Smith
London

ISBN 978-3-319-82858-9   ISBN 978-3-319-43570-1   (eBook)
DOI 10.1007/978-3-319-43570-1

This Palgrave Macmillan imprint is published by Springer Nature
The registered company is Springer International Publishing AG
The registered company address is: Gewerbestrasse 11, 6330 Cham, Switzerland

Foreword

As a social worker the most difficult decisions I made, and the most challenging work I did, were with children and families where entering care was a real possibility. I can still vividly recall struggling with how to make what seemed to be impossibly difficult decisions about whether children should remain at home or be removed, and I agonised about how to work with families to prevent children being removed while feeling that they were safe (or at least "safe enough"). To this day I wonder what happened to many of these children: Did I make the right decisions? Did I help the child and their family? Could I have done more?

When doing this work, I found remarkably little research or theory that was helpful. There was not much written on these issues, and it was difficult to apply the rather general prescriptions from research to the specific circumstances of the child and family I was working with. I was fortunate to have some wise and patient supervisors who helped me think through these issues, yet, even so, there was not much of a framework for doing this complex work.

If anything, the importance of developing good practice in this area has grown since I practiced in the 1990s. There are record numbers of children entering care, with a particular spike in the use of care proceedings. And therefore, the focus of this book—on how we can work effectively with such children and their families—is incredibly timely. Never has it been so important for us to explore whether we are providing the most effective help for these children. Like most researchers and many others, I am deeply concerned about the huge rise in children entering care, particularly as a result of court proceedings. Obviously care is sometimes the right option for children—but it is difficult to see any objective reason why we are seeing a 250 % increase in children subject to care proceedings today compared to 30 years ago. (In 1995 there were 5027 care applications; in 2015 there were 12,741; and in 2016 a further massive increase is being reported.) The factors we know that cause children to enter care—poverty and deprivation or serious parental problems such as drug or alcohol problems or mental illness—have not increased on this scale, and it is therefore hard to believe there is a need for such an increase in the numbers entering care.

In this context we need urgently to address what can be done to reduce the need for care. Taking children into care who do not need it is unethical, not just because it is wrong for the child but because we know the consequences are appalling for the parents. I remember myself taking two young children into care just before Christmas one year, and as I drove away from court with the toddlers in the back of my car, I stopped and watched as their bereft mother pushed an empty double buggy across the dark road in front of me and back to her flat. In that instance, I am fairly confident that the decision was the right one, but I am far from convinced that the help I gave was as good as it should be.

Yet the importance of this book stretches far further than the crisis in the over-use of the care system we currently face. For the expertise presented herein speaks to a deeper need for reform in Children's Services. This book, for me, represents a contribution to a wider movement that aims to rediscover the essential purpose of Children's Services. This movement is born out of a conviction that child and family social work has taken a wrong turning: for many years now service development and delivery have taken a managerialist and bureaucratic approach to the delivery of services. As a result, even well-intentioned changes have too often resulted in a proliferation of forms, new computer systems and less time spent with families and children. And many of the reforms have been poorly thought-through and counter-productive.

Yet rolling back this approach is not straightforward. And in part, it is difficult because for too long we have not thought and written and researched about what actually happens when we meet people and how we can make a difference. That is the focus of this book.

A particular strength of the book is that the chapters are written by people who have direct experience of this challenging and complex area of work. The contributors are, without exception, leading practitioners: people who have worked with families and understand the complexities, challenges and ambiguities inherent in the work, and who are sharing the things that help them to do this work well. The contributors include some of the most skilful helpers of families that I have come across.

This does not mean that the book is always an easy read. Many of the chapters introduce concepts and language that can seem foreign to which we are used to. This is not accidental. Often our "common sense" language conceals assumptions about the nature of problems and how they can be assessed or worked with; developing new languages can help us to see problems differently and can allow us to be creative in how we approach working with people.

The different chapters introduce a wide variety of insights and approaches that may be helpful in developing the way we work with children on the edge of care. As such they offer an opportunity for us not just to reduce the need for children to enter care but more fundamentally to rethink the ways that we deliver services. For they represent a commitment to developing skilled and wise practice with families and children through listening to and learning from excellent practitioners.

I am therefore delighted to have the opportunity to write this Foreword. This book is full of insights that anyone working in this field will find helpful. I wish that I had been able to read it 25 years ago when I started working in this field; I have no doubt it would have helped me undertake better assessments and provide more effective help for children and their carers. I can therefore only urge those who are interested in helping families to read this book and benefit from the distillation of skill, knowledge and experience that it represents.

Donald Forrester
Professor of Child and Family Social Work,
Cardiff University, Wales, UK

Acknowledgements

The editor and contributors would like to thank Nicola Jones, Sarah Busby, Sharla Plant, Eleanor Christie and Cecilia Ghidotti at Palgrave Macmillan for all their guidance and support.

We are, as ever, grateful to those who have supported the development of our clinical thinking and practice and who have offered their encouragement and suggestions: Ruksana Ahmed, Tessa Baradon, Roland Casson, Elaine Farmer, Naomi Fisher, Glenda Fredman, Julia Harrop, Fran Hedges, Richard Holland, Emma Gamble, John Launer, Pam Ledward, Sasha Long, Josie Lynn, Tina McElligott, Vivien Norris, Nick Pendry, Jenny Taylor, Pam Tower, David Trickey and Rachel Watson.

We would also like to acknowledge the personal and practical support received from our families and friends, including Lenny Fagin, Dee Fagin, Jessica Fagin, Louise Goligher, Luke Hanson, Mark Jaeckel, Chris Mercer, Richard Murray, Aoife Murray, Marcie Murray, Adrian Read, Elliot Smith, Ava Smith, Gregory Swann and Fadime Tiskaya.

Finally, we would like to thank the families that we have worked with for their support, generosity and inspiration and for trusting us with their stories, wishes and future hopes. We are particularly grateful to those who have allowed us to share their (anonymised) experiences through quotes and case studies.

Contents

Notes on the Contributors

Heleni-Georgia Andreadi is a UKCP registered Systemic Psychotherapist and Supervisor. She is a Clinical Supervisor for the Hackney CYPS Clinical Service and Principal Systemic Psychotherapist in the Rehabilitation and Recovery Service for Camden and Islington NHS Foundation Trust. Heleni has developed and delivered postgraduate systemic training and has a special interest in developing Multi-family Group Therapy within Children's Social Care and Adult Mental Health Services.

Stella Christofides is a HCPC registered Clinical Psychologist and BABCP accredited Cognitive Behavioural Psychotherapist. Stella has held senior positions within Children's Social Care and Specialist CAMHS teams, including a Youth Offending Team and a Transition Service linking child and adult provision. She currently works in private practice, providing individual therapy and assessments of children, adolescents and parents for the family courts.

Abel Fagin is an HCPC registered Counselling Psychologist and is currently employed at the Anna Freud Centre Parent-Infant Project and the North East London NHS Foundation Trust Perinatal Parent-Infant Mental Health Service. He previously worked within Hackney CYPS, where he led various parenting groups, provided specialist parent-infant interventions and completed assessments for the family courts. Abel's current roles involve direct parent-infant work, clinical supervision, delivering training in parent-infant psychotherapy and the further development of the New Beginnings programme.

Jeremy Greenwood is a UKCP registered Systemic Psychotherapist. He has designed and delivered training for Morning Lane Associates and for Frontline. He has held senior clinical posts at the Anna Freud Centre and in several local authorities and was Clinical Lead within London Borough of Harrow Children's Social Care. He is currently working in private practice and with Morning Lane Associates.

Elly Hanson is a HCPC registered Clinical Psychologist who specialises in the field of abuse and trauma. She also has a particular interest in adolescence. Currently her work with local authorities, law enforcement and the voluntary sector focuses on child sexual abuse and exploitation. This includes consultation, training and research with the CEOP command of the National Crime Agency and the NSPCC.

Elizabeth Mensah is a UKCP registered Systemic Psychotherapist and Supervisor. She has delivered Multi-family Group Therapy in a range of contexts, including Children's Social Care, where she has also led family therapy clinics and provides specialist systemic assessments. She has extensive experience working with individuals, families, couples and groups in the UK and Africa, with an additional area of specialism in the assessment and treatment of psychosocial effects of female genital mutilation. She currently works for the Hackney CYPS Clinical Service and in private practice.

Pamela Parker is a HCPC registered Clinical Psychologist. She currently works as Psychology Lead for the Cambridgeshire Children's Social Care Clinical Service and in private practice. Pam has a special interest in working with children with disabilities and their families, Looked After Children and in developing psychologically healthy and high functioning teams.

Caroline Pipe is a UKCP registered Systemic Psychotherapist and Supervisor. She is currently Head of Clinical Practice for Hammersmith and Fulham Children's Social Care, providing training and supervision for social work practitioners alongside leading a team of clinicians focusing on edge-of-care interventions. Caroline has previously developed and delivered specialist systemic training for the Institute of Family Therapy.

Andrea Shortland is an HCPC registered Clinical Psychologist and Associate Fellow of the British Psychological Society. Andrea has held senior clinical posts within Multi-Dimensional Treatment Foster Care, Children's Social Care and Looked After Children's CAMHS teams. She is an associate with ASSIST Trauma Care. Her private practice is focused on trauma-focused intervention with parents, children and families. She also provides expert witness reports for the family courts in England and Northern Ireland.

Laura Smith is a HCPC registered Clinical Psychologist and Associate Fellow of the British Psychological Society. She is currently Clinical Lead for Hackney CYPS and leads the CYPS Clinical Service. Her areas of specialism are the development and delivery of services to address child abuse and neglect, and psychological and systemic assessment and intervention with Looked After children.

Abbreviations

AAI	Adult Attachment Interview
ADHD	Attention Deficit Hyperactivity Disorder
AF-CBT	Alternatives for Families—Cognitive Behavioural Therapy
AIM2	Assessment, Intervention, Moving On (2nd Edition)
ASC	Autism Spectrum Conditions
BSP	Brainspotting
CAI	Child Attachment Interview
CAMHS	Child and Adolescent Mental Health Services
CAT	Cognitive Analytic Therapy
CBT	Cognitive Behavioural Therapy
CDC	Child Dissociative Checklist
CMM	Co-ordinated Management of Meaning
CRIES	Children's Revised Impact of Event Scale
CSE	Child Sexual Exploitation
DBT	Dialectical Behaviour Therapy
DDP	Dyadic Developmental Psychotherapy
DES	Dissociative Experiences Scale
DM-ID	Diagnostic Manual—Intellectual Disability
EMDR	Eye Movement Desensitisation and Reprocessing
FCASE	Families and Communities Against Sexual Exploitation
FFT	Functional Family Therapy

GAD7	Generalised Anxiety Disorder 7-Item Scale
GP	General Practitioner
HNC	Helping the Non-compliant Child
IES	Impact of Event Scale
IQ	Intelligence Quotient
ISTSS	International Society for Traumatic Stress Studies
LGBTQ	Lesbian, Gay, Bisexual, Trans, Queer or Questioning
MAC-UK	Music and Change—UK
MFGT	Multi-family Group Therapy
MIM	Marshak Interaction Method
MST	Multi-systemic Therapy
MST-BSF	Multi-systemic Therapy—Building Stronger Families
MST-CAN	Multi-systemic Therapy—Child Abuse and Neglect
MST-PSB	Multi-systemic Therapy—Problem Sexual Behaviour
NHS	National Health Service
NICE	National Institute of Clinical Excellence
NSPCC	National Society for Prevention of Cruelty to Children
ODD	Oppositional Defiant Disorder
PBS	Positive Behaviour Support
PCG	Parent Child Game
PCIT	Parent–Child Interaction Therapy
PDI	Parent Development Interview
PHQ	Patient Health Questionnaire
PIRAT	Parent-Infant Relational Assessment Tool
PLO	Public Law Outline
PSI	Parenting Stress Index
PTS	Post-Traumatic Stress
PTSD	Post-Traumatic Stress Disorder
RAD	Reactive Attachment Disorder
RD/EF	Risk Detection/Executive Functioning
SFAI	Safety First Assessment Interview
SL/F	Social Learning/Feminist
SMART	Specific, Measurable, Agreed Upon, Realistic, Time-Limited

TF-CBT	Trauma-Focused Cognitive Behavioural Therapy
ToL	Tree of Life
TSCC	Trauma Symptom Checklist for Children
TSCYC	Trauma Symptom Checklist for Young Children
VIG	Video Interaction Guidance

List of Figures and Tables

Figures

Tables

List of Boxes

1

Introduction

Laura Smith

Children and Young People at the Edge of Care

For children, young people and their families, being at the edge of care is associated with psychological distress, disruption, loss and the risk of immediate and/or long-term harm. Situations and cohorts where this term is used, both in practice and clinical research, are highly variable. However, it is generally applied to:

- Children and young people considered to be in need of becoming Looked After, as they are at risk of, or experiencing significant harm
- Children and young people who are in care and for whom long-term placement decisions have yet to be made

L. Smith (✉)
London

© The Author(s) 2016
L. Smith (ed.), *Clinical Practice at the Edge of Care*,
DOI 10.1007/978-3-319-43570-1_1

1

- Children and young people who are returning home following a period in care, either to live with their birth families or other primary caregivers.

Working to support families at the edge of care can therefore involve considering a large number of possible presenting difficulties, caregiving contexts and wider situational factors. The ages of children and young people, developmental issues and immediacy of risk issues are also key influences. As a consequence, practice in this area involves a combination of assessment and intervention with the child and their system, along with risk management.

Policy and service development in relation to edge-of-care practice has been a growing area of focus in recent years. In the UK, reviews of child protection social work (Munro 2010, 2011), youth justice (Taylor 2016) and family justice (Norgrove 2011) have made recommendations that services be reshaped. Innovative practice in edge-of-care settings has also been encouraged and taken forward (UK Department for Education 2014). Research in applied settings has focused on developing the evidence base for different approaches, within and across the fields of child and family social work, psychology and psychotherapy. This has led to a growing body of literature that attempts to define best practice relevant to edge-of-care contexts, as well as opportunities for practitioners to benefit from lessons from research.

Considerable variation remains in the local provision of generic and specialist services for at-risk children and their families, meaning that there are significant geographical differences in the quality and range of support available. Whilst, in the UK, legal responsibility for ensuring children's welfare and overseeing the effective delivery of services for children lies with Local Authorities (UK Children Act 2004), this is to be undertaken in partnership with others and may be commissioned locally and nationally. Within this context, edge-of-care work is commonly undertaken by Local Authorities, the NHS, voluntary providers and practitioners in private practice. Some is delivered through national and international programmes that are being formally evaluated, whilst some falls within the remit of well-established or more recently developed local models of delivery. An aim of this title is therefore to bring together clinical considerations and developments in such a way that these can be thought about in range of practice settings and local circumstances.

Clinical Considerations

Increasing attention has been paid in research and practice to the contribution of clinical practice to achieving positive outcomes for children and families at the edge of care. This may be provided by practitioners from a range of professional backgrounds, such as Clinical and Counselling Psychology, Psychiatry, Nursing, Occupational Therapy, Psychotherapy (including Systemic Psychotherapy) and Social Work. Family support work and social pedagogy may also support the delivery of clinical interventions.

What defines clinical practice in this area is a breadth of focus informing the direct and indirect application of theory and models of assessment and intervention. This is a developing field, where a number of orientations and methodologies are potentially relevant. However, psychological and systemic approaches have been prominent, arguably as they have the capacity to both describe and inform understanding of a variety of presenting concerns at the edge of care. These include issues affecting the emotional wellbeing, behaviour and development of children as well as the assessment of current and future risk.

The knowledge and skill set needed by practitioners delivering clinical assessments and interventions does not only relate to theory, relevant research and clinical skills. As this is a developing field, clinicians also benefit from becoming part of a learning culture, which includes taking a curious and critical position in relation to their work and its outcomes.

The overall aim of this title is therefore to draw together research, theory and applied practice considerations to illustrate key perspectives in the field of clinical work at the edge of care. It is hoped that these will resonate with practitioners' experiences, will prompt critique and debate and will lead to further development of ways forward in service delivery with children, young people and their families.

Chapter Outlines

. *Chapter 2: Interventive Assessment* focuses on the conceptualisation of assessment as an interventive activity, the theoretical and research base for taking this approach in edge-of-care practice, recommended models and methods of interventive assessment and specific considerations for trial interventions. Examples are given of systemic and cognitive-behavioural techniques in practice and of ways to combine specialist assessment tools with interventions. Conditions for the implementation of interventive assessment practices are also discussed.

Chapter 3: Influencing Systems considers the relevance of the theory and practice of systemic consultation to understanding and influencing edge-of-care contexts. Issues relating to power, patterned responses and the need for reflective and reflexive practice are discussed. Ways of putting theory into practice are described, including methods of consultation with teams, managers and case-holding front-line practitioners. Examples are given of risk and decision-making issues arising in children's social care and similar contexts, where indirect systemic work can support greater effectiveness and positive outcomes. A case study also illustrates how direct and indirect clinical work can be combined.

Chapter 4: Evidence-Oriented Practice supports the idea that edge-of-care clinical practice can usefully include a range of approaches, in the context of emerging research demonstrating the effectiveness and potential of various types of intervention. An overview of relevant interventions and their evidence base is given, on the basis that clinicians and services can draw on these to take forward practice in local contexts. It is argued that multi-component interventions are likely to be more effective than those used in isolation. In addition, attention is drawn to the evidence that interventions are more likely to be effective if attention is paid to robust case conceptualisation, sequencing of strands of intervention and goal-orientation and engagement issues. Case examples illustrate ways that evidence-oriented interventions might be put into practice in edge-of-care settings.

Chapter 5: Attending to Infant Mental Health focuses on how infant mental health issues can arise in edge-of-care contexts, why these should be prioritised and how they might best be addressed. Theoretical conceptualisations of how infants become "at risk" are discussed. A three-stage methodology for assessment is proposed, including the use of formal and informal assessment measures and consideration of engagement issues with families and professional systems. In addition, general considerations and specific options for effective intervention are described. An extended case study illustrates how infant mental health-focused work can reduce risk and achieve positive outcomes.

Chapter 6: Safeguarding Children with Disabilities outlines particular risk issues for this cohort at the edge of care, drawing on relevant theory and research into UK child protection outcomes. A family life-cycle framework is proposed for understanding how difficulties leading to risk of harm may arise. Key issues in assessment and formulation are discussed; including engaging with families and children with disabilities, sharing formulations, the significance of developmental histories, differential diagnosis and diagnostic overshadowing. Ways of working indirectly with professional networks and options for direct intervention with children and families are further described, including more in-depth discussion of the applicability of Theraplay and Systemic Family Therapy.

Chapter 7: Late Entries into Care addresses challenges for clinical practice with adolescents at the edge of care, their families and wider systems. The particular presenting needs and risks associated with this age and stage are discussed, along with the usefulness of psychological assessment and formulation within the domains of adolescent development, family life and community contexts. Considerations for direct and indirect clinical intervention, including lessons from research and developments in practice, are highlighted; including multi-component, residential-based and multi-professional approaches. A case example describes how these ideas can be applied to achieve better outcomes.

Chapter 8: Working with Trauma highlights the need for trauma to be considered as a key presenting concern underlying risk issues within families at the edge of care. Further, the importance of differentiating between post-traumatic stress (PTS/PTSD) and developmental/complex trauma is discussed. Methods for the identification and assessment of trauma symptoms are also summarised. A three-stage framework for intervention is proposed, in line with the evidence base and alongside considerations for the appropriateness of undertaking trauma-focused therapy in edge-of-care contexts. Child and parent-focused case studies illustrate how this can be delivered in practice.

Chapter 9: Multi-family Group Therapy describes the relevance and application of this methodology to edge-of-care practice, drawing on theory-, research- and practice-based learning. The core components and practice of multi-family work are outlined, along with specific considerations for their implementation with families at the edge of care. It is proposed that mentalisation-based therapy techniques, social learning theory-oriented approaches and collaborative narrative practices are particularly relevant. Organising principles, establishing a safe and effective therapeutic context and the role of the clinician are discussed in detail. Case examples further link theory and methods described to clinical practice, whilst giving an insight into service user experiences of multi-family groups.

Chapter 10: Understanding and Preventing Re-Victimisation discusses risk factors and contexts for children and young people re-experiencing abuse and significant harm, with a focus on re-victimisation following childhood sexual abuse. Processes contributing to re-victimisation are discussed, including psychological, systemic and societal factors. Assessment approaches and clinical interventions to prevent further sexual abuse and exploitation are suggested, in line with the evidence base and clinical practice developments that support individual children and young people, parents and caregivers, and their wider systems.

Chapter 11: Safe Returns from Care considers the usefulness of systemic theory and practice when applied to achieving positive outcomes in family rehabilitation. Risks and opportunities for change in this context are discussed, along with systemic understandings of how these might arise and be addressed in clinical practice. Ways of responding clinically to support both planned and unanticipated returns from care are described. It is argued that practitioners may usefully attend to dialogical processes between professionals and families and embed the use of "Anticipation Dialogues". Systemic approaches to preparing parents and children for reunification are also discussed. Practice examples illustrate how systemic interventions can be helpfully integrated into wider casework.

Conclusion

Whilst by no means exhaustive in their scope, the chapters that follow aim to capture how developments in clinical practice can contribute to the field of edge-of-care work. It is important to note that the psychological and systemic focus of this book does not preclude the need for a range of perspectives and approaches to be brought to bear in this task. Arguably, the topics that are discussed in each chapter represent key areas where clinical approaches can make a significant difference to both edge-of-care processes and outcomes.

Common themes include the importance of considering assessment and intervention as interlinked and mutually informed processes; the engagement and involvement of children and families; the usefulness of multi-faceted interventions; and the need for a reflective practice stance towards using theory, research and clinical methodologies to address the challenges and risks that commonly arise in edge-of-care contexts. In addition, the complexity and potential of applying an emerging evidence base are foregrounded across different areas of concern. Recommendations for further learning and steps towards best practice are also identified. It is hoped that these will both challenge and encourage future clinical practice developments.

References

Munro, E. (2010). *Munro review of child protection part 1: A systems analysis.* London: UK Department for Education.

Munro, E. (2011). *Munro review of child protection final report: A child-centred system.* London: UK Department for Education.

Norgrove, D. (2011). *Family justice review.* London: TSO.

Taylor, C. (2016). *Review of the youth justice system.* London: UK Ministry of Justice.

UK Children Act. (2004). London: TMSO.

UK Department for Education. (2014). *Overview report: Department for education children's social care innovation programme.* London: UK Department for Education.

2

Interventive Assessment

Heleni-Georgia Andreadi and Laura Smith

Introduction

The concept of interventive assessment describes a process whereby information gathering and analysis is joined with therapeutic action—either simultaneously via the application of procedures that serve both functions or via the strategic combining of assessment and therapeutic tools and methodologies. The theory and practice of interventive assessment is in accordance with philosophical paradigms and therapeutic approaches currently referred to as "post-modern": Second-order cybernetics, post-Milan systemic therapy, social constructionism, narrative and other collaborative practices.

These approaches inform different ways of thinking about the function and purpose of assessment and intervention within the context

H.-G. Andreadi (✉)
London, UK

L. Smith
London, UK

© The Author(s) 2016
L. Smith (ed.), *Clinical Practice at the Edge of Care*,
DOI 10.1007/978-3-319-43570-1_2

9

of clinical practice. Informed by Bateson's interpretations of systems theory as applied to human interaction and communication, second-order cybernetics calls for a shift away from thinking about assessment, observation and intervention as neutral and objective processes. Instead, these are considered to be informed by mutual influence and co-creation between the different members involved in a system (Bateson 1972; Becvar and Becvar 2006; Hoffman 1985). The impact of the observer (assessor) on the system and the reciprocal nature of their interaction and influence are recognised. These ideas provide the basis for alternative understandings of the role and actions of professionals engaged in working with families.

Consideration of interventive assessment processes is particularly relevant to clinical work in edge-of-care contexts, where it is often felt necessary to begin to intervene, even whilst further assessment is needed. In such circumstances, assessments and interventions serve the purpose of gathering robust and rich information to inform risk management and decision-making, whilst at the same time addressing presenting concerns wherever possible.

Towards Interventive Assessment Practices

Systemic and narrative practitioners have critiqued traditional forms of health and social care assessment as focusing too heavily on problems, inadequacies and their history. Likewise, clinicians operating in various mental health and social care contexts have noted the power differentials inherent in traditional assessor-assessed relationships—especially when working across social difference, including those associated with socioeconomic status, race, culture, gender, class, sexuality and ability (Burnham 2013). These can reinforce the continuous development and internalisation of negative stereotype and thin descriptions of iterative failure (Madsen 2007; Singh and Clarke 2006).

From an earlier post-Milan systemic therapy discourse, Lang et al. (1990) introduce the need for practitioners—whether a therapist, psychologist, social worker or other—to "constantly question how to make a judgement such that the possible outcome will allow for greater opportunities for the future in terms of change and growth through elaboration and reconstructions". Almost two decades later, the need for an integrated approach to "ongoing, iterative assessment that pays attention to the weave of content and process, mediated by shared and reflective observation" is reaffirmed by Vetere (2006), who further states that "assessment is not a one-off activity".

Post-modern paradigms advocate assessment and intervention models that promote resource-based, solution-focused developments, based on the assumption that people live "in relationship with" rather than "being" their problems. Madsen (2007) therefore proposes that assessments are informed predominantly by narrative, collaborative understandings that place assessor and the assessed in more equal positions, collaborating to investigate the impact that problems have in their lives, to identify resources and preferred actions and to plan ways of introducing and sustaining change. He notes: "Interactions around the telling and witnessing of these stories influence the development of therapeutic relationships and the way in which work together unfolds".

To this end, Singh and Clarke (ibid.) specifically describe a more egalitarian and culturally aware approach to the assessment of families at the edge of care. They suggest that such an approach can be more conducive to the formation of collaborative therapeutic relationships, shown to be a significant predictor of effective outcomes (Hubble et al. 1999). They give examples of their assessments of "abusive" families—usually from a different culture, race, class and ability to theirs—and the impeding challenges traditional assessment methods can pose to practitioners, families and the potential for change.

Interventive Assessment Approaches

There are various specific interventive assessment models and techniques that are relevant to edge-of-care practice. Those selected for discussion here have the potential to be applied and adapted across a range of family circumstances, with children of different ages and their parents across a range of abilities, situations and cultural contexts. Whilst some relevant approaches constitute programmes of intervention in themselves, others are clinical tools or techniques. Both may be considered to offer both assessment and interventive potential, as means to progress the engagement of a family and address difficulties, whilst at the same implicitly gaining a richer understanding of their psychological and relational circumstances.

The Writtle Wick model (Barratt 2012) involves multi-family group work, drawing on the Marlborough Model (Asen et al. 2001), with a cohort of families whose children are either in care proceedings, subject to child protection plans or at the pre-proceedings stage of the Public Law Outline (PLO). Children may be living at home or placed in foster care. Parents referred to the Writtle Wick programme tend to have complex problems themselves; including histories of abuse and neglect in their own childhoods, experiences of domestic violence and drug and alcohol issues. The multi-family group programme that forms the core component of the model runs for 6 days and involves psycho-education sessions, family activities and shared mealtimes. These allow an opportunity for the programme facilitators to observe and assess family functioning and its amenability to change over an intensive and supportive intervention period. Closeness to the family over an extended period provides direct access to knowledge about their patterns of interaction and how these might be shaped, particularly in relation to parenting. For example, facilitators may find themselves drawn into responding to children at key points in group sessions, due to their parent's lack of emotional availability. This level of insight would be much less possible if relying solely on families' self-report or shorter, non-interactive observations and assessment tools. As with other interventive assessment approaches, feedback from families at Writtle Wick is reportedly very positive. It is inferred that this is due to parents finding the multi-family framework to be collaborative and that receiving feedback based on "real-life" shared experiences is more readily acceptable and meaningful.

The Parent Child Game (PCG) is similarly applicable to edge-of-care practice, in that it offers an intervention programme that allows for close observation of family interactions whilst simultaneously promoting change through the live coaching of parenting skills. A key feature of PCG is that it has an embedded means to quantify progress, via the use of baseline and follow-up ratings of "child-directive" vs. "child-centred" parenting behaviours (McMahon and Forehand 2003). This makes it well suited to be used as a trial intervention with families who have relevant presenting concerns—primarily child behavioural difficulties and attachment-related difficulties. Within PCG, baseline and follow-up ratings, and the rationale behind some parenting behaviours being promoted over others, are shared explicitly with parents at the start of the programme. This degree of transparency means that it is clear to parents what is being asked of them. At the same time, practitioners offering live coaching to the parent gain a very immediate sense of their capacity to take on new ideas and how the parent is able to manage the emotional and practical demands of doing things differently. The model also requires that "homework" focused on skills practice is completed between sessions. Whether this is completed or not, and other issues arising when homework is attempted, can offer useful insights into parents' capacity to generalise in their day-to-day lives and wider issues influencing their situation. For example, it may be discovered that a parent living with their children in overcrowded accommodation is (understandably) struggling for practical reasons.

With a further focus on family relationship issues, during the transition to and through adolescence, the Safety First Assessment Intervention (SFAI) model (Bickerton et al. 2014) draws on generic systemic theory and more specifically on Attachment-Based Family Therapy (Diamond and Stern 2001). It therefore conceptualises children's mental health difficulties as relational and within the context of trans-generationally developed patterns of relating and communication. The ultimate aim of the model is to offer an interventive assessment framework that addresses severe mental health crises in adolescents in the community, prevents hospitalisation and minimises the subsequent risk of out-of-home placement, institutionalisation and/or the development of problem-saturated and pathologising narratives about young people and their families. It is particularly relevant as the significant impact of mental health distress and acute crises on family (and other) relationships and the capacity to care for others has been widely evidenced, with mental health concerns often being a key issue in families at the edge of care.

The SFAI model is described as a journey for the young person and their family through five different levels and processes: "… (the five levels) move from the establishment of safety to formulation of the issues in a relational context, developing a shared understanding of the problem, collaborative planning and referring for longer term specific therapies as required" (Bickerton et al. 2014). The model further encourages practitioners to continuously hold the young person's safety in mind whilst vigorously assessing family dynamics, risk and the wish and capacity to care and to change.

SFAI draws on similar principles to those underlying the Open Dialogue approach to acute mental health crises, currently being used in Early Intervention mental health contexts (Seikkula et al. 2003). Within an Open Dialogue framework, acute mental health crises (including first-episode psychosis in adolescence) are assessed within a relational context. The involvement of all systems—family, community, medical and social care networks—is fostered through dialogue and the use of the reflecting team paradigm (Andersen 1987). The effectiveness of the model is partly attributed by its founders to the dialectical involvement of all potential stakeholders, as well as the integration of the traditionally distinct processes of diagnostic formulation, risk assessment, assessment of pharmacological and medical and psychosocial needs. These are drawn together within a multi-systemic, collaborative interventive framework, which holds both the sustainability of the individual's supportive familial and social connections and their recovery at the centre of case conceptualisation.

Several promising interventive assessment tools constitute interviewing processes, which aim to develop understanding of a child, parent or family's difficulties whilst creating potential for change.

Influenced by post-modern communication theory, and the therapeutic applications of the Coordinated Management of Meaning (CMM) model, Tomm's series of papers on Interventive Interviewing (Tomm 1987a, b, 1988) provide both a theoretical framework and a practice tool for the practitioner undertaking systemically framed interventive assessments. Tomm based his development of different question categories on his observations of the impact his and his colleagues' interviewing had on their clients' progress, the therapeutic process and relationships. In the first of a series of papers, Tomm (1987a) describes his movement from a first- to a second-order conceptualisation of the therapeutic process, from assessment to intervention, in a way that reflects the way that an assessment process can become interventive: " ... many questions do have therapeutic effects on family members, (directly) through the implications of the questions and/or (indirectly) through the verbal and non-verbal responses of family members to them ... it would be more coherent and heuristic to regard the whole interview as a series of continuous interventions".

Tomm (1988) further describes four broad categories of questioning, depending on the practitioner's intent on using them: linear, circular, strategic and reflexive. Even though all of these can be relevant and helpful in influencing the therapeutic process, reflexive questions seem to be the most coherent with the process of interventive assessments. The term "reflexive", as understood in a post-modern systemic context, refers to one's ability to move and make connections between pre-existing, preferred and emerging beliefs, cognitions, emotions and actions. One's capacity to do this with others' beliefs and actions is described as relational reflexivity (Burnham 2005). Reflexivity, self and other, is often the focus of assessments in edge-of-care situations. Reflexivity also refers to the meaning-making process that is understood within the same paradigm as inherent to human interaction and communication. Tomm (1987b) supports the use of reflexive questioning with "the intent to facilitate self-healing in an individual or family".

There are many different types of reflexive questions, each with different interventive functions. In Table 2.1, we have set out the categories that are most relevant to edge-of-care practice, with some of the intentions of their use as outlined by Tomm (1987b) alongside some of our own clinical examples.

With a similar focus on interviewing as the basis for identifying key information and for promoting new ways forward, motivational interviewing (MI) has increasingly been utilised in edge-of-care and child

Table 2.1 Reflexive questioning in edge-of-care practice

Question category	Intent
Future oriented *Which aspects of your parenting would you like your child to have when they become parents?* *How do you think your relationship with your daughter might be different when she is a teenager in a couple of years?*	• To cultivate family goals • To explore anticipated outcome • To highlight potential consequences • To explore and/or introduce hypothetical possibilities • To suggest future action • To pose dilemmas • To instill hope and trigger optimism
Observer perspective *If your baby could tell us how he feels, what do you imagine he would say about how you and your partner are caring for him right now?*	• To enhance self and/or other-awareness • To explore interpersonal perception and interaction
Unexpected context change *If your daughter became more independent and started going to school again, what would you do with your free time?* *How long do you think you can continue having the same argument with your mother before she gives in?*	• To explore opposite content, context and/or meaning • To explore the fear of change and/or the need to preserve homoeostasis • To introduce paradoxical confusion
Embedded suggestion *If you were to take responsibility for the things that have made it difficult for your parents to trust you in the past, how would that change their mind about what you can and can't do now?*	• To embed a reframe or an alternative action • To embed a volition, an apology or forgiveness
Normative comparison *Do you think the way John sometimes talks back at you is similar or different to what other teenagers do?*	• To draw a contrast with a social, developmental or cultural norm • To effect social, developmental and inclusive normalisation
Distinction clarifying *Who do you think in your family is the least affected by this assessment process? What makes you think that?*	• To clarify causal attributions, dilemmas or sequences of action • To separate or connect elements of patterns • To introduce metaphors or hypotheses • To invite uncertainty where beliefs and patterns have become rigid and entrenched

protection practice. In essence, MI seeks to identify barriers to change whilst promoting shifts in attitudes and behaviour. This is acheived via the use of different types of strategically focused open questions, applied within a conversational context that supports engagement and build rapport—for example, through the use of active listening skills and the use of reflective summary statements (Miller and Rollnick 2012). As a methodology, MI has been extensively developed and researched in substance misuse work and other areas of mental health practice (Hettema et al. 2005). There has been a growing interest in using MI where there are concerns about child abuse and neglect, due to its applicability to working with parents who do not necessarily agree with or share professionals' concerns about their family life and/or do not fulfil what is being asked of them (e.g. being asked to access mental health support or domestic violence support services). The intention of MI in this context is to identify and address resistance and ambivalence whilst maintaining a focus on the impact of concerns in relation to the child or children (Forrester et al. 2012). MI has successfully been used with substance misusing parents whose children are at risk of coming into care, as part of the Option 2 Intensive Family Preservation Programme in Wales (Forrester et al. 2008).

Another potentially useful psychological approach, which similarly seeks to simultaneously identify, explore and address sources of stasis, is Socratic questioning, also known as "guided discovery" (Padesky 1993). This is a key component of cognitive-behavioural therapy (CBT), which involves the therapist taking a deliberately curious stance in questioning. The strategic intention of Socratic questioning is to identify and collaboratively examine the underlying beliefs, feelings and intrapsychic processes that are getting in the way of the client achieving adaptive changes. In edge-of-care work, this might involve a therapist-client dialogue about a child's behaviour or the parent-child relationship, which seeks to identify and challenge underlying views that are leading to difficulties such as conflict and emotionally harmful parental responses. An example is given in Box 2.1, in which Socratic questioning is used to help the parent identify possible ways forward for themselves.

Box 2.1 An example of Socratic questioning at the edge of care

Parent: I just can't deal with her anymore. She has no respect for me. You all just think I'm "emotionally abusing" her—but what am I meant to do? She does my head in, I'm sorry.

Therapist (clarification): You're feeling angry with her? How long have you felt like that?

Parent: More and more, since her Dad moved out. She doesn't care about me or my home anymore. She thinks she can do what she wants now.

Therapist (probing assumptions): She doesn't care? That's tough on you. What exactly does that mean for you?

Parent: She comes in late and hardly speaks to me anymore. It makes me feel really upset, yeah, you know?

Therapist (questioning perspectives): Can you be sure it's because she doesn't care? I wonder if there are other ways of looking at that you've thought about?

Parent: Well, she is trying to stay out of my way as she wants to avoid me having a go at her. I know I've said some really terrible things to her when I'm angry. Yeah, she doesn't want the hassle. She will wait till I'm nearly asleep and then come into my bed though. She knows I will just give her a cuddle then, even though she's really too old for it.

Therapist: (probing implications and consequences): So you've noticed that sometimes you are close and sometimes you are on bad terms with her? That perhaps she stays away because of how you react?

Parent: It's like, we're not close like we used to be, the more it goes on. She is just growing up so fast. I'm worried she will end up in trouble.

Therapist (clarification): You've been worried about her. And it sounds like you'd like to feel closer again?

Parent: Yeah, but I'm not sure if there's anything I can do about that. It's down to her as well, you know.

Therapist (summarising): You think it would be difficult, but you'd both need to do things differently?

Parent: Well, yeah, she'd need to agree to some of my ground rules at home. I know I need to keep my temper with her, but it's hard at the moment. That's why I've been saying she can't live with me.

Therapist (probing information): Have you noticed what helps you keep your temper?

Parent: I'm calmer when I know where she is—when she lets me know where she is and what time she'll be back, then I don't get so wound up and stressed.

Therapist (encouraging alternatives): Have you any ideas about how you could get there?

Parent: I guess I could check in with her when she's not come home.

Therapist (synthesising): It sounds like you've got an option there to help you feel calmer and closer together, things that are important to you both. How could you test out whether that helps?

Drawing on similar collaborative principles, Bertrando and Arcelloni (2006) build on the original views and practices of systemic hypothesising and propose the sharing of the practitioner's formulations around relational dynamics and patterns—with the system in focus at an early stage of the assessment process. They consider hypothesising as dialogue, and within that framework, they advocate the informative potential of assessment and formulation in enabling change and the co-creation of preferred stories.

The usefulness of sharing a hypothesis can be illustrated by taking the clinical example of a young person placed urgently with a foster family, following her mother's acute psychotic episode. In this case, it was the sharing of the clinician's formulation that enabled a shifting of positions that both the mother and the young person had unhelpfully adopted. As part of an assessment of the mother's ability to reflect and empathise with her daughter's emotional distress and need for containment, the clinician decided to share his evolving hypothesis that fighting seemed to have become the main way of expressing difficult feelings and concern for others in the family. The clinician also wondered how helpful and effective this pattern had and/or continued to be now that the mother was out of hospital and the young person was due to return to the family home. Following the sharing of this hypothesis, both mother and daughter asked for some time to think about this and their preferred ways of being with each other. They subsequently asked whether their joint sessions with the practitioner could focus on helping them to develop new ways of sharing their thoughts and feelings and communicating without "hurting" each other.

Collaborative practices, as described above, can at times pose dilemmas for professionals in edge-of-care contexts who are often requested to assess and plan interventions with and for families where there is suspected, but not proven, abuse. There is often ambiguity and uncertainty around the nature and circumstances of the abuse and/or the identity of the perpetrator(s). More recently, and with the evolution of internet and gang-related abuse, it is important that clinicians develop interventive assessment practices that ensure the young person's safety in wider contexts, as well as considering their experiences within their family. Systemic practitioners have explored ways of working with children and young people presenting with symptoms/behaviours that indicate possible experiences of abuse—such as self-harm, suicidal attempts, acting out and harmful sexualised behaviours—but where no explicit disclosures have been made and there is not conclusive evidence of what has happened. These situations can often create heightened fear, concern and suspicion amongst professional systems, especially when they are asked to find ways to support young people in talking or taking action.

To address such issues, Lang and McAdam (1996) present their ideas as a framework that is intended to effectively work with families and professional systems around assessing the risk for the young person. This includes consideration of disclosure and non-disclosure and the development of intervention plans with all relevant stakeholders in the young person's safety and wellbeing. Known as the "Beyond Risk and Above Suspicion Interview", their model aims to keep all members of the system safe from abuse and accusations accordingly. Lang and McAdam go as far as recommending the inclusion of the suspected perpetrator in this interventive assessment practice, especially in situations where they are closely connected to the young person's network and there is no evidence (or admittance) that would suffice their removal from this position.

The "Beyond Risk and Above Suspicion Interview" itself involves conversations that assess different adults' position and role in the young person's life; identify the safe, protective adults; and explore patterns and circumstances that might place the young person at risk or increase vulnerability. The young person is often interviewed confidentially and on their own initially; and they are reassured that any decision, such as to disclose or not, will not interfere with involved adults' responsibility and commitment to keeping them safe. The next stage of the interview itself focuses on specific actions and measures that adults can take to ensure that the young person remains safe and the "suspected" perpetrator remains above suspicion in the future. For example, in a situation where one of the parents is suspected of abusive behaviour, both parents are interviewed and asked to contribute to a safety plan. The protective parent may suggest that they monitor contact or become responsible for ensuring that a third reliable person (themselves or another safe family member) is present at all times.

Assessment Tools Combined with Interventions

Another way to approach interventive assessment is to strategically combine relevant assessment tools with time-limited trial interventions, in order to target presenting concerns and gauge potential for change. Benefits of this approach are that trial interventions can be focused in a more bespoke way to meet parents', children's or families' needs and their impact can be evaluated and evidenced. The usefulness of specialist psychological assessment tools in edge-of-care work is widely recognised—although these not always made available in a timely way, and the evidence base for the contextual validity of particular tools is at an emerging stage (Farmer and Lutman 2012; Shemmings and Shemmings 2014). Therefore, particular care needs to be taken in providing clear and well-reasoned assessment plans. It is helpful if these take into account how and when assessment tools are to be applied. For example, cultural contexts may require that assessments are adapted or presented in particular ways, in order to be relevant and acceptable to the family. If interventions are being undertaken in parallel, rather than beginning once assessments are completed (often necessitated by the need to address risk issues), whether these are therapeutically oriented or otherwise, it may be part of the clinician's role to agree how assessment and intervention strands of the work will inform one another and how any ongoing feedback is communicated.

A full discussion of specialist assessment options is outside of the scope of this chapter. However, examples of the use of assessment tools combined with interventions in edge-of-care settings might include the following:

- Completion of a Parenting Assessment Manual Software (PAMS) assessment (McGaw 2016), before and after delivery of a parenting skills and attachment-focused intervention
- Use of the Child Attachment Interview (CAI) and Parenting Stress Index (PSI) tools (Shmueli-Goetz et al. 2008; Abidin 2012) pre- and post-completion of Video Interaction Guidance and parental substance misuse interventions (Kennedy et al. 2012; Forrester et al. 2008)

- Completion of a Child Abuse Potential Inventory (CAPI) screening (Milner 2004; Ondersma et al. 2005) to inform risk management during a Parent Child Game intervention, delivered alongside trauma-focused psychological therapy with a parent (NICE 2005).

Assessment tools may be selected according to several criteria. Their reliability and validity should be considered, including cross-cultural validity and, where relevant, reliability when used with particular client groups such as parents or children with intellectual disabilities, autistic spectrum conditions and those who have experienced trauma. Tools need to be relevant to identified areas of concern or risk (including relevance to concerns held in the family itself and in different parts of the professional system). It is useful if there is potential to triangulate with other sources of information. Ethically, it is also important to be informed by the principal of doing the minimum necessary, in order to avoid unnecessary intrusiveness and the risk of an iatrogenic effect on coping. In edge-of-care work, this can occur when assessment processes evoke or intensify feelings of being scrutinised and/or judged.

Trial Interventions

There are a number of factors that need to be taken into account when deciding whether or not a trial intervention is viable or appropriate. Firstly, the plan of work needs to be agreed by both the family and professionals and coordinated with other aspects of care planning. The rationale for interventions needs to be oriented to both presenting concerns and prospects for engagement and success. Within an interventive assessment context, it remains ethically important to avoid setting families up to fail and to avoid "start again syndrome" (Brandon et al. 2008), particularly given that problem recognition and intention to change are not in themselves predictive of readiness to change in relation to child abuse and neglect (Littell and Girvin 2005).

Therapeutic engagement with trial interventions is less likely to be problematic than with stand-alone assessments, as families find interventive assessment approaches more acceptable, supportive and meaningful

(Harris 2012; Barratt 2012). However, the shift to an interventive assessment approach is likely to reposition existing practitioner-client relationships, especially if these were previously focused solely around the provision of therapeutic support. This may be helpfully considered in the context of reflexive discussion of the therapeutic relationship. Similarly, information sharing, limitations around confidentiality and agreed methods and types of feedback should also be discussed in a transparent and collaborative way wherever possible, whilst acknowledging and adhering to constraints or requirements of the wider system, including those linked to legal or statutory processes. These may also influence and limit timescales around a trial intervention plan and therefore what options are available. Likewise, time constraints may result from consideration of the child's developmental timescales. Within these contexts, consideration may usefully be given to what expectations are held about what is achievable, on the part of the family, professionals and wider systems.

Risk management alongside the provision of trial interventions may include the short-term provision of additional support to mitigate the impact of particular concerns—for example, through the provision of intensive home-based parenting support whilst parenting skills issues are addressed. It is also helpful to set out in advance the conditions under which the intervention should be discontinued or reviewed.

Recommendations for Practice Development

Interventive assessment as a framework and approach within edge-of-care contexts presents practitioners with multiple affordances, as well as some challenges that invite further dialogue and service development. These types of practices sit well within a collaborative context and can promote inter-agency partnership working, service user involvement and co-production.

A helpful model for considering challenges to the implementation of interventive assessment is provided by Lang et al. (1990). They describe the different domains of action and meaning-making that practitioners alternatively inhabit and operate from at different times, depending on the context, expectations and specific tasks of their role and position. Applied to edge-of-care work, these three domains of "production", "explanation" and "aesthetics" may refer to (1) the statutory tasks and rules set by the organisational, social and legal systems; (2) the curious and exploratory position a practitioner might adopt in their conversations with families in order to facilitate the development of new stories; and (3) the ethos of one's professional practice and the ways one chooses to enact their professional role at any given point.

The three domains can likewise provide a helpful conceptual framework for undertaking interventive assessments with edge-of-care families, as it recognises the need for constant move between positions of authoritative action, investigative processes and curious collaboration. It also highlights the importance of remaining reflexive about our moral and ethical positioning whilst making and enacting our clinical judgement.

For interventive assessment practices to be more widely applied and effective, a further culture shift within edge-of-care settings is required, so that the focus moves from crisis-led interventions to more integrated assessment and intervention practices that foster prevention and/or sustainable change. Tangible organisational developments to bring this about require resources, time and creativity, as well as commitment from practitioners, managers and commissioners—particularly in order to develop the necessary theoretical knowledge base and skill set for practitioners to proceed effectively and to maximise the potential of existing services.

Further evaluation, focusing on longitudinal outcomes and comparison of different approaches, may usefully provide the evidence that will make such practice paradigms more established and influence policy and decision-making.

References

Abidin, R. R. (2012). *Parenting stress index* (4th ed.). Lutz, FL: PAR.

Andersen, M. D. T. (1987). The reflecting team: Dialogue and meta-dialogue in clinical work. *Family Process, 26*, 415–428.

Asen, E., Dawson, N., & McHugh, B. (2001). *Multiple family therapy: The Marlborough model and its wider applications*. London: Karnac.

Barratt, S. (2012). Incorporating multi-family days into parenting assessments: The Writtle Wick model. *Child and Family Social Work, 17*, 222–232.

Bateson, G. (1972). *Steps to an ecology of mind.* Chicago: University of Chicago Press.

Becvar, D. S., & Becvar, R. J. (2006). *Family therapy: A systemic integration.* Boston: Allyn and Bacon.

Bertrando, P., & Arcelloni, T. (2006). Hypotheses are dialogues: Sharing hypotheses with clients. *Journal of Family Therapy, 28*, 370–387.

Bickerton, A., Ward, J., Southgate, M., & Hense, T. (2014). The safety first assessment intervention: A whole family approach for Young people with high risk mental health presentations. *Australian and New Zealand Journal of Family Therapy, 35*, 150–168.

Brandon, M., Belderson, P., Warren, C., Howe, D., Gardner, R., Dodsworth, J., et al. (2008). *Analysing child deaths and serious injury through abuse and neglect: What can we learn? A biennial analysis of serious case reviews 2003–2005.* London: Department for Children, Schools and Families.

Burnham, J. (2005). Relational reflexivity: A tool for socially constructing therapeutic relationships. In C. Flaskas, B. Mason, & A. Perlesz (Eds.), *The space between: Experience, context and process in the therapeutic relationship.* London: Karnac.

Burnham, J. (2013). Developments in social GGRRAAACCEEESSS: Visible-invisible, voiced-unvoiced. In I. Krause (Ed.), *Cultural reflexivity.* London: Karnac.

Diamond, G. S., & Stern, R. (2001). Attachment based family therapy: Facilitating re-attachment. In S. Johnson (Ed.), *Attachment and systems therapies.* New York: Norton.

Farmer, E., & Lutman, E. (2012). *Effective working with neglected children and their families: Linking interventions to long-term outcomes.* London: Jessica Kingsley Publishers.

Forrester, D., Pokhrel, S., McDonald, L., Copello, A., & Waissbein, C. (2008). How to help parents who misuse drugs or alcohol: Findings from the evaluation of an Intensive Family Preservation Service. *Child Abuse Review, 17*(6), 410–426.

Forrester, D., Westlake, D., & Glynn, G. (2012). Parental resistance and social worker skills: Towards a theory of motivational social work. *Child and Family Social Work, 17*, 18–129.

Harris, N. (2012). Assessment: When does it help and when does it hinder? Parents' experiences of the assessment process. *Child and Family Social Work, 17*, 180–191.

Hettema, J., Steele, J., & Miller, W. R. (2005). Motivational interviewing. *Annual Review of Clinical Psychology, 1*, 91–111.

Hoffman, L. (1985). Beyond power and control: Towards a "second order" family systems therapy. *Family Systems Medicine, 3*, 381–396.

Hubble, M., Duncan, B., & Miller, S. (Eds.). (1999). *The heart and soul of change: What works in therapy.* Washington, DC: American Psychological Association.

Kennedy, H., Landor, M., & Todd, L. (Eds.). (2012). *Video interaction guidance: A relationship-based intervention to promote attunement, empathy and well-being.* London: Jessica Kingsley Publishers.

Lang P., & McAdam E. (1996). Beyond risk and above suspicion. Pre-publication manuscript.

Lang, W. P., Little, M., & Cronen, V. (1990). The systemic professional: Domains of action and the question of neutrality. *Human Systems: The Journal of Systemic Consultation and Management, 1*(1), 39–57.

Littell, J. H., & Girvin, H. (2005). Caregivers' readiness for change: Predictive validity in a child welfare sample. *Child Abuse and Neglect: The International Journal, 29*(1), 59–80.

Madsen, W. (2007). Working within traditional structures to support a collaborative clinical practice. *The International Journal of Narrative Therapy and Community Work, 2*, 51–61.

McGaw, S. (2016). *Parenting assessment manual software (PAMS) 4.0.* Truro: Pill Creek Publishing.

McMahon, R. J., & Forehand, R. L. (2003). *Helping the non-compliant child: Family-based treatment for oppositional behaviour* (2nd ed.). New York: Guilford Press.

Miller, W., & Rollnick, S. (2012). *Motivational interviewing: Helping people change* (3rd ed.). New York: Guilford Press.

Milner, J. S. (2004). The child abuse potential (CAP) inventory. In M. L. Hilsenroth & D. L. Segal (Eds.), *Comprehensive handbook of psychological assessment: Vol. 2. Personality assessment* (pp. 237–246). New York: John Wiley & Sons.

NICE. (2005). CG26: *Post-traumatic stress disorder management.* Retrieved from https://www.nice.org.uk/

Ondersma, S. J., Chaffin, M. J., Mullins, S. M., & LeBreton, J. M. (2005). A brief form of the child abuse potential inventory: Development and validation. *Journal of Clinical Child and Adolescent Psychology, 34*(2), 301–311.

Padesky, C.A. (1993). Socratic questioning: Changing Minds or guiding discovery. *European Congress of Behavioural and Cognitive Therapies*, London, UK.

Seikkula, J., Alakare, B., Aaltonen, J., Holma, J., Rasinkangas, A., & Lehtinen, V. (2003). Open dialogue approach: Treatment principles and preliminary results of a two-year follow-up on first-episode schizophrenia. *Ethical Human Sciences and Services, 5*, 163–182.

Shemmings, D., & Shemmings, Y. (Eds.). (2014). *Assessing disorganised attachment behaviour in Children: An evidence-based model for understanding and supporting families*. London: Jessica Kingsley Publishers.

Shmueli-Goetz, Y., Target, M., Fonagy, P., & Datta, A. (2008). The child attachment interview: A psychometric study of reliability and discriminant validity. *Developmental Psychology, 44*(4), 939–956.

Singh, R., & Clarke, G. (2006). Power and parenting assessments: The intersecting levels of culture, race, class and gender. *Clinical Child Psychology and Psychiatry, 11*(1), 9–25.

Tomm, K. (1987a). Interventive interviewing: Part 1. Strategising as a fourth guideline for the therapist. *Family Process, 26*, 3–13.

Tomm, K. (1987b). Interventive interviewing: Part 2: Reflexive questioning as a means to enable self-healing. *Family Process, 26*, 167–183.

Tomm, K. (1988). Interventive interviewing: Part 3: Intending to ask lineal, circular, strategic, or reflexive questions? *Family Process, 27*, 1–15.

Vetere, A. (2006). Commentary: The role of formulation in psychotherapy practice. *Journal of Family Therapy, 28*(4), 388–391.

3

Influencing Systems

Jeremy Greenwood

Introduction

Clinical practice in edge-of-care contexts often involves working indirectly with families, via offering consultation to practitioners, teams and organisations. Although clinical consultation can draw on a variety of theoretical orientations, systemic approaches to this type of work have become increasingly prominent in recent years (Aggett 2015; Pendry 2011). Arguably, this is due to their congruence with thinking about and intervening with complex families and their surrounding relationships, including professional systems. In general, it is useful to thoughtfully consider indirect clinical practice and consultation, as these have been identified as key ways to influence the quality of work provided by mental health and social care teams (Onyett 2007). Looking closely at systemic clinical consultation in edge-of-care settings therefore provides an opportunity to examine its contributions, strengths and applicability.

J. Greenwood (✉)
London, UK

© The Author(s) 2016
L. Smith (ed.), *Clinical Practice at the Edge of Care*,
DOI 10.1007/978-3-319-43570-1_3

Systemic clinical consultation has the explicit aim of bringing new information into the system as a whole, through exploration of views as well as the offering of new perspectives (Gross 1994). Thus, it offers a potential means to enhance practice with children and families and contribute to decision-making. General principles and examples of systemic clinical consultation in edge-of-care settings, as delivered to social workers and other professionals carrying out direct work with families, have now been established. Likewise, learning has also developed around consultation to those in management positions within organisations. These will be discussed further below.

One of the proposed strengths of a systemic perspective is that it pays attention to the wider context and understands that the culture, resources and orientation of organisations set an important tone that can either support or hinder the workforce in carrying out effective work with families. These have been identified as significant factors in risk management and decision-making in child protection practice (Broadhurst et al. 2010; Munro 2010b). Systemic consultation may thus help to identify where interventions should be directed (Daniel 2005). Systemic conceptualisations also allow for organisational and family processes to be thought about in parallel (Rivett and Street 2009). Ideas in relation to power, patterned responses and how to create change through feedback and reflexivity are some of the key systemic contributions to supporting and thinking about organisations undertaking edge-of-care work, and these will therefore be discussed in more detail below.

Power

Power in relationships is always seen as central within systemic thinking. Therefore, the systemic approach to influencing edge-of-care practice begins with an appreciation of how power operates within organisations and between individuals. This is related to the understanding that a belief in one's own power is an epistemological error (Bateson 1972). Power is considered to reside in the system as a whole and not in any one part. The implication for systemic consultation is that power is viewed as mutable and as something that can draw the system towards supporting some outcomes over others. Taking account of hierarchical power in an organisation, or the power attached to practising in different ways, is used to enhance thinking about ways to achieve positive changes in working culture and practice. Likewise, a perspective that comprehends the systemic nature of the organisation can lead to decisions that have greater coherence within the whole. This might mean supporting actions within edge-of-care systems that allow front-line workers to spend more time with families, engage in supervision and access high-quality consultation, or promoting evidence-based approaches in such a way that these are empowered. In addition, a variety of starting points, strategies and consultative approaches might be used in different organisational contexts, depending on the current distribution and operation of power that might affect or inhibit change. When consultation is focused on direct work with families, who may be disempowered at both legal, societal and personal levels in edge-of-care situations, consideration of power dynamics is also essential (Fruggeri 1992; Jones 1994).

Patterned Responses

Systemic approaches offer an understanding of repetitive patterns in families and professional systems. These are considered to exist between and within people, as influenced by the social environment (Bateson 1972, 1979) through complex feedback loops (Bateson 1972, 1979). The concept of "cybernetic feedback" further extends this idea (Tomm 1985). Full consideration of these ideas is beyond the scope of this chapter. However, they are considered relevant to edge-of-care work where family situations are often entrenched and complex, as the recognition of patterned responses opens up the possibility that these might be described, reconsidered or reorganised. Describing a significant part of a pattern can lead to a change in how meaning is ascribed, which can in turn lead to other significant changes. In a child protection context, this might mean that front-line practice can be reconsidered and, hence, possibilities opened up for improvement. For example, a social worker might be thought to be making rash or reactive decisions, whilst their manager might criticise their reports for a lack of analysis. Taking those actions in isolation risks failing to appreciate that the same social worker might fare differently operating in a system where they felt more supported, where administrative processes were re-allocated so they had more time to process their work with families, and where they were in receipt of thoughtful supervision and consultation. Systems change can therefore make a material difference to the way in which practitioners perceive and respond to the families they are working with (Forrester et al. 2013).

In the process of ascribing meanings to patterns, at some point a punctuation point needs to be reached (Campbell and Huffington 2008) and action needs to be taken. In the above example, a systemic approach might suggest that some material changes be made to the social worker's working environment and then tested to see what kind of difference this made to outcomes for children and families.

Reflective Practice and Reflexivity

Reflective practice privileges professionals' ability to consider the information they are presented with by grappling with the intellectual and emotional dimensions of the work, rather than overly relying on following case management procedures or assumptions. A focus on the importance of reflective practice is not unique to systemic thinking. However, systemic approaches offer some relevant ideas that are particularly applicable to supporting those working with at-risk children and families. These include encouraging professionals to utilise multiple perspectives and the use of a "not knowing" (Anderson and Goolishian 1992) position, when having to face difficult decisions that have important implications for children's future wellbeing and safety. "Not knowing" in this context involves acknowledging the limitations of knowledge and opinions that might be held and reflecting on influences on (often) varied and conflicting views about how risk might best be managed.

A related systemic concept is reflexivity, described as "the capacity of any system of signification to turn back on itself" (Lax 1992) and as reflection that requires considered action in the context of feedback from relationships (Tomm 1987, 1988; Dallos and Draper 2010). Reflexivity has a close relationship to reflective practice in child safeguarding practice

(Aggett 2015), as it supports the generation of alternatives to emotionally reactive, crisis-driven and task-focused casework. These have been identified as particular issues of concern in edge-of-care work—where a context of risk, pressure on resources and professional anxiety often champions a search for quick solutions, with case throughput and decision-making viewed erroneously as evidence of problem resolution (Munro 2010a). Taking a reflexive stance allows for complexity and protects against bias and decisions that lack objectivity. This reflects the reality of working within complex relationships, where a great number of variables need to be taken into consideration and outcomes cannot be easily predicted. Supporting reflexivity encourages a movement between inward- and outward-focused curiosity, between self and other, where the practitioner's focus moves between what they are bringing to an interaction and its impact and what the other is bringing, in such a way that encourages the taking of responsibility for one's way of interacting (Oliver 2005). Practitioners can also usefully support reflexivity in their clients—as, when families start to become more reflexive towards one another at crucial times, this is often an indicator of their capacity for long-lasting change. For instance, a parent who is supported to see their adolescent child's point of view when they are engaged in risk-taking behaviour may, in turn, be more able to adapt their own responses to reduce conflict and improve the child's compliance with limit-setting. Likewise, a parent who makes negative assumptions about their child's disruptive behaviour after school might be encouraged to wonder what sort of day they have had, rather than falling into habitually perceiving such behaviour as proof of their selfishness.

Another systemic idea that can applied to encouraging reflective practice is that of "safe uncertainty" (Mason 1993), which places an emphasis on the importance of curiosity and holding in mind that our ideas are constructions that may or may not be useful, rather than containing absolute truths. The concept of "safe uncertainty" also draws practitioners' attention to the need to hold a balance between remaining curious and acknowledging that they may have some helpful knowledge and expertise to draw upon. This ensures that risk management remains open to new ideas, whilst ensuring that uncertainty does not lead to vagueness and never taking a position. Moreover the concept of "authoritative doubt"—defined as the ownership of expertise in the context of uncertainty—can be understood as the stance a practitioner needs to take in order to move towards a position of reflexivity (Mason 1993). When these ideas are used to inform consultation, it becomes a means to support a balance between facilitating the case holder's own knowledge and the offering of some expertise that they can make use of. Similarly, thinking about work with families who have complex difficulties requires utilising different positions and sources of experience and expertise in the family and professional system. These perspectives can be used to inform thinking about how to proceed when they are elicited and considered explicitly; so that relationships become characterised by mutual influence (Mason 2005).

Box 3.1 Case example: Cicely

Cicely (4) lived with her mother Karen and was subject to a Child Protection Plan due to significant neglect. Karen's longstanding mental health issues had a significant impact on her day-to-day functioning and had led to several hospital admissions, during which Cicely was placed in foster care. Professionals working with the family hypothesised that mother and daughter had got into a kind of negative feedback loop due to these separations, which was impacting on their attachment relationship. It was hypothesised that Cicely had emotionally withdrawn from Karen, which she in turn experienced as rejection. This led Karen to feel hurt and in turn to withhold affection. A referral was made for attachment-focused therapeutic work, which was quickly deemed to have a positive outcome. Concerns in the professional system were reduced, due to an assumption being made that they had overcome the main obstacle to achieving change. However, systemic consultation promoted the idea of holding onto positions of "safe uncertainty" and "authoritative doubt". This led to consideration of other important impeding factors, such as Karen's pre-occupation with her relationship with her partner, Jesse, who was in and out of the family's life.

A further systemic contribution to embedding reflective practice is through supporting practitioners to consciously foster and develop a sense of relational responsibility. This involves shifting the way in which developments (and decisions) in practice are made, towards dialogue and reflection amongst professional groups rather than acceptance of a context of isolated personal responsibility (Gergen and McNamee 1999).

This can potentially lead to different way of practitioners working with one another, as attempts to made to warm a context for collaboration, for example, by demonstrating a respectful curiosity about preferred models and ways of talking (Burnham 2005). Relational responsibility is particularly significant to complex edge-of-care practice, as new and creative ideas can emerge from a sense of connectedness, something of crucial importance when the professional system requires us to make decisions in relation to risk. Taking relational responsibility also guards against the issue identified in several UK Serious Case Reviews of single worker bias/error (Munro 2008; Nuffield Foundation 2013; Duncan and Miller 2014).

Making decisions when children are deemed to be at risk is a difficult task, where different options have significant negative as well as positive aspects. For example, a child coming into care may be provided with with safety, but also experience disruption, separation and loss. Decision-making dilemmas can lead to professional systems becoming "stuck". Indications that this is happening might include strongly held differences of opinion remaining unresolved within professional and family networks; a practitioner focusing exclusively on procedural tasks and ceasing to think in detail about what is presently occurring in the family; and/or people holding fixed and certain views that only take into account information that confirms their pre-existing viewpoint. In such scenarios, systemic thinking aims to create a process of reflexivity that encourages an appropriate and helpful balance between thinking and action and a space to question one's biases and prejudices (Cecchin et al. 1994). Being aware of our own assumptions is also a starting point for being more curious about the views of others, especially when they are very different to our own (Daniel 2005). In the context of consultation, this might involve asking reflexive questions that embed some new ideas and encourage curiosity about other perspectives. For example, where a professional holds the view that a family is responding defensively or not taking on board statutory concerns, a consultant might ask the following:

- What if the family was able to see you as a potential resource rather than as a threat?
- Is there anything you need to do differently to help aid that process?

- If you consider how much power you have (in the family's eyes or in actuality), how does that influence your thinking?
- If you were to think of these parents as wanting the best for their children, how might you understand their actions?
- How can you continue to be empathic towards this parent in such a way that is inclusive of the impact of their situation on the children?

If permission is given to more closely explore interactions with families in the spirit of self reflexivity (Tomm 1988), systemic consultation can also be helpful to normalise the idea of becoming biased and emotionally reactive in high pressure situations. Often, a simple acknowledgment that this is occurring can lead to a helpful exploration. A practice example might be an occasion where a social worker is thought to be reacting somewhat negatively towards a family, including speaking in a raised voice with a parent during a telephone call. The development of this kind of dynamic between professionals and families at the edge of care, and its implications, has been identified and explored helpfully in recent research (Forrester et al. 2013). In this particular scenario, it might be that the social worker's response appears disproportionate to the situation, unhelpful to the family, and is not congruent with how they relate generally to others. Exploring this in clinical consultation could involve using circular questions to explore what might be similar or different about the social worker's experience with this family, compared to others. For example, it might be that the situation is reminiscent of other cases where the presenting problems were similar in nature, and there were poor outcomes. Supporting front-line workers' capacity to recognise these kinds of responses can further develop reflective practice.

Systemic consultation can also support a context where increased thought and reflection might lead to better decision-making, without directly contradicting the "pressure to act" that is commonly felt in high-risk child protection work. Where discussions about casework and organisational values tend to be task and action focused, it can be helpful for clinical consultation to offer and discuss some tangible ideas and possibilities. For example, it can be helpful to reframe "wondering about" or "reflection" as "gaining more ideas" and "planning" and to invite a conversation about multiple solutions, options and their anticipated consequences. This in turn can generate space and capacity for reflection, so that better decisions are made with greater clarity (Aggett 2015).

Consultation to Managers

Consultation to those holding management positions in child protection settings has become a focus for systemic practice in this area. There is a growing body of evidence that demonstrates how organisations tasked with child protection need to change in order to prioritise reflective practice above processes (Munro 2010b), rather than engaging in strengthening organisational defences, including the use of bureaucratic processes to engender an illusory sense of control and certainty and as a substitute for professional decision-making (Ofsted 2011).

Clinical consultation that supports those with management and service development responsibility can help services as a whole, by identifying what to prioritise and achieving a better understanding of which types of cases are not progressing towards positive outcomes and are holding up the workflow. This is significant, as higher case loads mean it becomes much harder to do the kind of thoughtful work that is required to make a difference to families.

Systemic approaches may include the provision of group supervision to support managers to reflect on their practice. This typically involves bringing people together to map out and making sense of an identified issue. Through working in a group context, multiple perspectives and positions can be usefully represented and explored. For example, managers overseeing edge-of-care services might share a genuine desire to embed a more thoughtful and skilled practice amongst their workforce, but find that staff training programmes are not having their desired impact. However, they might also describe themselves as being tasked by the service with the enforcement and monitoring of essential and time-consuming administrative processes. This type of situation has been conceptualised systemically as a "double bind" (Bateson et al. 1956; Bateson 1972). Supporting this kind of reflexive analysis can prove invaluable, as long as different positions (broadly) are considered, in this case the competing demands that are being placed upon both managers and workforce. Discussions might then lead on to exploring which demands and processes had become their "highest context" (their most significant influence) for action (Pearce 2009). This could eventually open possibilities for exploring alternatives and the suggestion of material changes to the demands placed on the front-line practitioners. There is growing evidence that these kinds of development make an important difference to the quality of practice (Forrester et al. 2013).

Likewise, the domains model (Lang et al. 1990) may be used to help managers explore complex organisational processes with one another, in order to assist a move away from fixed and habitual practices (Oliver 2005). After Maturana (1985), Lang, Little and Cronen describe how the different domains of "Production" (where there is one reality and version of the truth and there is an imperative to reduce complexity and make decisions), "Explanation" (where multiple realities and understandings are acknowledged and valued) and "Aesthetics" (consideration of morality and ethics related to accountability and responsibility) can be used to distinguish between different aspects of human actions (Lang et al. 1990) (Fig. 3.1).

Using the domains as an orienting structure for discussion, a topic of inquiry may be chosen that is important to the group. Three different conversations take place, each informed by of a different domain, so that the "rules" and remit of the conversation differ accordingly. This can ensure a great deal of clarity and purpose: Commonly, it is discovered

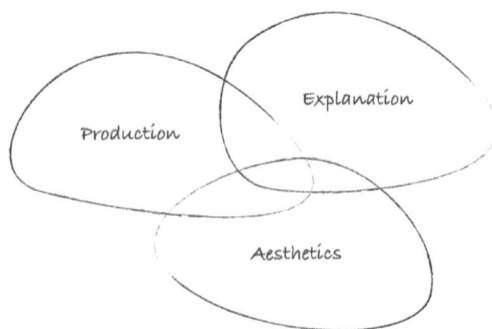

Fig. 3.1 Three domains of reflexive enquiry

that in usual circumstances, people talk to each other across domains and that this results in confusion. Within edge-of-care contexts, it is often useful to start within the domain of "Production", as that tends to be where practice gets "stuck". Within this domain, participants are asked to express strong opinions, to seek facts and establish truths. Within the domain of "Explanation", they are encouraged to explore options and possiblities as widely as possible, whilst demonstrating curiosity about each other's views. Finally, in the domain of "Aesthetics", the group are tasked with creating coherence and a mutually acceptable way forward from the previous two conversations (Oliver 2005).

For example, managers of a parenting support service, working in an edge-of-care setting, might be invited to reflect on organisational demands around case throughput and timely record-keeping. In the domain of "Production", some of the barriers to change might be explored and the competing demands they were under thought about in some detail. For example, it might be noted that case management deadlines could get in the way of having the time to think through and plan direct work with families. In the domain of "Explanation", options for how to manage competing demands and a desire to prioritise direct work with families might be discussed. Risk management procedures might also be considered, alongside managers' and practitioners' views of what is needed to feel safe enough to work effectively in a context of high risk. Concerns might be shared about who is being held accountable for what, if and when the wrong decisions are made. Finally, within the domain of "Aesthetics", managers might be invited to formulate how they might prioritise giving support to case management tasks in order to free up their practitioners to focus on the core business of effective safeguarding practice, whilst maintaining their focus and values. In discussion of how practice might be enacted differently, the need for more mutual support and respectful challenge might also be considered.

Practice-Based Consultations

Practitioners in edge-of-care contexts are often highly skilled at spotting dangers and risks to children and young people but may be less confident or resourced to find ways of intervening, which is a crucial component of discovering whether a family can make changes that prevent long-term significant harm to their children. Systemic approaches to consultation in such circumstances aim to enable the necessary transition from assessment to intervention and offer a space for the consideration of how risks can be worked with, better understood and reduced. Occasionally, clinical consultation can induce a change simply through offering an opportunity to come alongside, whilst taking a difference perspective. This fits with the systemic idea of joining and influencing systems as a vehicle for change (Minuchin 1974). Sometimes simply drawing up a genogram and tracing trans-generational patterns of beliefs and behaviours can support the creation of new narratives and hypotheses. Circular questioning (Selvini et al. 1980) or Interventive Interviewing approaches (Tomm 1987, 1988) used in discussion with the case holder can also galvanise practice in the direction of intervention. For example, a practitioner might be asked future-oriented questions about what children might end up learning about relationships from their family context, as they grow older. This serves the purpose of drawing out the impact of both risk factors (such as emotionally abusive exposure to domestic violence) and protective possibilities (such as the presence of supportive extended family).

Often, the complexity and multi-faceted nature of edge-of-care work with families means that professional time and effort is significantly taken up with co-ordinating with other services and professionals. This is particularly the case for those in social work case-holding roles, who additionally hold responsibility for pulling together the professional network within statutory frameworks. In this context, clinical consultation can help to draw focus and effort towards interventions and provide ways for case holders to focus the time they have with families and network partners most effectively. Systemic approaches to doing this could involve preparing case holders to ask relevant and powerful systemic questions at network meetings, supporting their use of therapeutic approaches in family sessions and supporting the formulation of risk issues.

It is important to emphasise that clinicians can do both direct work with families as well as offering consultation to others in relation to the same family; and that whilst this can be a complex process that requires a good deal of self reflexivity, it moves us away from the idea of intervention as a unitary "product" and more towards the idea that intervention consists of multiple components in a non-linear fashion (Wren and Daniels 2005).

Box 3.2 Case example: Peter

Peter, aged 14, was no longer living at home with his mother, Judy. A Family Therapist, Peter's social worker and other members of the professional system were tasked in various ways with establishing whether it was safe enough for him to return home and with undertaking preparatory work.

Through ongoing consultation with the Family Therapist, Peter's social worker was able to helpfully reinforce and add to the direct clinical work. For example, after a clinical session where Judy explored how difficult she found setting boundaries—especially given her own very chaotic upbringing—the social worker followed this up by supporting her to use targeted parenting strategies during contact sessions with Peter, which helpfully took the work forward. When progress was being made, the social worker took a very cautious position in relation to whether it was safe enough for Peter to return home, based on historical concerns that led to Peter being taken into care, which included Peter becoming violent towards Judy and missing school for long periods of time. On the whole, the Family Therapist held a more optimistic view, due to the way both Judy and Peter were managing their differences in the sessions and the fact that Judy in particular had recognised her part in the way their relationship had deteriorated, instead of taking a blaming view of Peter as she had done previously. By openly discussing this in consultation, each was able to reflexively acknowledge their different positions, which contributed to much more detailed discussions and better-informed case planning as they got closer to the time when Peter returned home.

Consultation in Team Meetings

There are certain systemic practices that can be particularly useful when helping to structure group case discussions in edge-of-care practice settings, be it in traditional team meetings or in what some UK local authorities refer to as a unit or pod meeting (Goodman and Trowler 2011). In units/pods, case responsibility tends to be shared so that each member of the small, multi-disciplinary team gets to know the families they are working with and cases are co-worked to a greater or lesser extent. Such practices can be supported by the integration of clinical consultation or coached so that the team is able to generate and sustain them independently.

These ways of working, which can be modified to suit preferences once the basic structure has been understood and used, begin with the case worker bringing a dilemma where they feel stuck in relation to their next meeting with the family or the professional system. Whilst the team are discussing the family, someone can draw a genogram that provides a point of reference for developing helpful questions. Genograms may include a wealth of information about the quality of relationships, cultural and community contexts, in a way that is accessible across different professional models and terminology (McGoldrick 1992). It is often helpful for whomever ordinarily leads the team (e.g. a Social Work Team Manager or Consultant Social Worker) to be tasked with monitoring whether questions being asked about the family are still relevant to the case worker's dilemma (as it is very easy to go off into numerous directions that can add to a sense of confusion, usually fuelled by an unhelpful underlying sense of responsibility or belief in the need to sort out everything at once). This also positions the team manager in an empowered and effective way in relation to the group. The team may then be invited to hypothesise in relation to the dilemma, whilst the case worker sits out, a principle that originates from the Milan team (Selvini et al. 1980), where participants are encouraged to explore multiple ideas rather than falling into collusive agreements around a dominant hypothesis. The case worker isn't invited to participate but just listens attentively, in line with how reflecting teams operate in family therapy (Andersen 1987). The chair needs to ensure that this is adhered to; for example, by reflecting that "they've done a lot of thinking already, so give them some time to hear you thoughts". Group members are encouraged to come up with different ideas in order to generate multiple perspectives, which serve to promote change (Watzlawick 1984). The case worker then chooses their preferred hypothesis. At this point, the clinician providing consultation or the chair helps the case worker to think through what it is that has drawn them to that particular hypothesis and, importantly, helps them find ways of testing out the hypothesis before their next meeting. Experience suggests that this part of the meeting often gets overlooked, sometimes due to the fact that this requires the highest level of skill. If testing out the hypothesis involves having a different kind of conversation with a family or other significant person in the system, this may be explored via role playing in the meeting, or the team may be helpful to the caseworker by generating questions and reflections about difficulties and opportunities that may arise in taking forward interventive action. Other sources of support for the practitioner may be identified. Here, the concept of reflexivity (Tomm 1987; Krause 2012) can remind us that becoming aware of something and even reflecting upon its usefulness is only the starting point of real change—as the actions required to actually practice differently usually take a great deal of time and effort, and there are usually a number of factors that can impede that process, including practitioners finding it hard to develop new skills that can take them into unknown territory. By encouraging and facilitating this process, taking on professional challenges (Forrester et al. 2013) and consideration of useful relational risk-taking is supported (Mason 2005).

In discussion of preferred hypotheses, and how these might be tested, it is important that the case worker isn't overloaded with too many ideas. As far as possible, these should relate directly to the needs of the family and evidence-based thinking. On many occasions, the case holder finds that the planned interventions to test out hypotheses take them in a different direction to that anticipated but that is an inevitable and sometimes helpful part of the process, as hypotheses should be thought about in terms of how useful they are, as opposed to whether or not they are true (Cecchin 1987). An additional role for the chairperson is to help tie the day-to-day testing out of the group's ideas to the overarching goal and reason for their involvement with the child and their family, which, in edge-of-care scenarios, always includes an updated understanding of risk and what needs to be done to lower it. Practice experience suggests that by the second or third week of meeting to discuss the same family using this methodology, a great deal of clarity in relation to the purpose of the work being undertaken is achieved. However, it is common that teams can get "carried away" with hypothesising and use of their curiosity. However, when teams embrace hypothesising *ad infinitum*, this often leads to a lack of coherence; and other parts of the system will understandably consider this to indicate a lack of effectiveness and poor risk management. Therefore, what is needed is "targeted curiosity", that is, curiosity that has a direct relationship to the dilemma being described. In systemic terms this involves combining the principle of curiosity with the understanding that context defines meaning. In edge-of-care practice, the context of safeguarding therefore needs to give overall shape to the use of curiosity in team working.

Conclusion

Systemic approaches offer a number of ways to influence and support practice and service development in edge-of-care work and to add value to challenging and potentially life-changing decision-making. These can potentially be used on their own on as part of wider clinical consultation processes. Clinicians who can offer a flexible and thoughtful approach to systemic consultation, potentially across different aspects of organisational systems, can therefore play an important role in embedding the kind of reflective and theoretically congruent practices that are needed in the complex task of safeguarding.

References

Aggett, P. (2015). A six step invariant consultation model: Helping family workers have new ideas for going forward. *Context: Working with Complexities, 139,* 19–21.

Andersen, M. D. T. (1987). The reflecting team: Dialogue and meta-dialogue in clinical work. *Family Process, 26,* 415–428.

Anderson, H., & Goolishian, H. (1992). The client is the expert: A not-knowing approach to therapy. In S. McNamee & K. Gergen (Eds.), *Therapy as social construction.* Newbury Park, CA: Sage.

Bateson, G., Jackson, D., Haley, J., & Weakland, J. (1956). Towards a theory of schizophrenia. *Systems Research and Behavioral Science, 1*(4), 251–264.

Bateson, G. (1972). *Steps to an ecology of mind.* New York: Ballantine Books.

Bateson, G. (1979). *Mind and nature: A necessary unity.* London: Fontana/Collins.

Bateson, G., Jackson, D., Haley, J., & Weakland, J. (1972). Toward a theory of Schizophrenia. In G. Bateson (Ed.), *Steps to an ecology of mind.* New York: Ballantine Books.

Broadhurst, K., White, S., Fish, S., Munro, E., Fletcher, K., & Lincoln, H. (2010). *Ten pitfalls and how to avoid them: What research tells us.*

NSPCC. Retrieved from https://www.nspcc.org.uk/services-and-resources/research-and-resources/

Burnham, J. (2005). Relational reflexivity; A tool for socially constructing therapeutic relationships. In C. Flaskas, B. Mason, & A. Perlesz (Eds.), *The space between: Experience, context, and process in the therapeutic relationship*. London: Karnac Books.

Campbell, D., & Huffington, C. (2008). Six stages of systemic consultation. In D. Campbell & C. Huffington (Eds.), *Organisations connected: A handbook of systemic consultation*. London: Karnac Books.

Cecchin, G. (1987). Hypothesising, circularity and neutrality revisited: An invitation to curiosity. *Family Process, 26*(4), 405–414.

Cecchin, G., Lane, G., & Ray, W. (1994). *Cybernetics of prejudices in the practice of psychotherapy*. London: Karnac Books..

Dallos, R., & Draper, R. (2010). *An introduction to family therapy: Systemic theory and practice*. Maidenhead: Oxford University Press.

Daniel, G. (2005). "Thinking in and out of the frame": Applying systemic ideas to social work with children. In M. Bower (Ed.), *Psychoanalytical theory for social work practice*. London: Routledge.

Duncan, A., & Miller, G. (2014). *Serious case review under working together 2013 in respect of Child D: Agreed at the serious case review panel May 2014*. Retrieved from http://www.haringeylscb.org/sites/haringeylscb/files/child_d_overview_report_final_march_2015_0.pdf

Forrester, D., Westlake, D., McCann, M., Thurnham, A., Shefer, G., Glynn, G., et al. (2013). *Reclaiming social work? An evaluation of systemic units as an approach to delivering children's services. Final report of a comparative study of practice and the factors shaping it in three local authorities*. Luton: University of Bedfordshire/Tilda Goldberg Centre for Social Work and Social Care.

Fruggeri, L. (1992). Therapeutic process as the social construction of change. In S. McNamee & K. Gergen (Eds.), *Therapy as social construction*. London: Sage.

Gergen, K., & McNamee, S. (1999). *Relational responsibility*. London: Sage.

Goodman, S., & Trowler, I. (Eds.). (2011). *Social work reclaimed: Innovative frameworks for child and family social work practice*. London: Jessica Kingsley Publishers.

Gross, V. (1994). Reflections on the practice of systemic management in the climate of the "contract" culture. *Human Systems. The Journal of Systemic Consultation and Management, 5*(1–2), 97–108.

Jones, E. (1994). *Family systems theory: Developments in the Milan-Systemic therapies*. London: John Wiley.

Krause, I. B. (Ed.). (2012). *Culture and reflexivity in systemic psychotherapy: Mutual perspectives*. London: Karnac.

Lang, W. P., Little, M., & Cronen, V. (1990). The systemic professional: Domain of action and the question of neutrality. *Human Systems: The Journal of Systemic Consultation and Management, 1*, 39–56.

Lax, W. D. (1992). Post-modern thinking in clinical practice. In S. McNamee & K. J. Gergen (Eds.), *Therapy as social construction*. London: Sage.

Mason, B. (1993). Towards positions of safe uncertainty. *Human Systems: The Journal of Systemic Consultation and Management, 4*, 189–200.

Mason, B. (2005). Relational risk-taking and the therapeutic relationship. In C. Flaskas, B. Mason, & A. Perlesz (Eds.), *The space between: Experience, context, and process in the therapeutic relationship*. London: Karnac Books.

Maturana, H. (1985). *Oxford conversations*. Conference jointly organised by the Kensington Consultation Centre, London, The Family Institute, Cardiff and the Charles Burns Clinic, Birmingham.

McGoldrick, M. (1992). Ethnicity and the family life cycle. *Family Business Review, 5*(4), 437–459.

Minuchin, S. (1974). *Families and family therapy*. Cambridge, MA: Harvard University Press.

Munro, E. (2008). *Effective child protection* (2nd ed.). London: Sage Publications.

Munro, E. (2010a). Learning to reduce risk in child protection. *British Journal of Social Work, 40*(4), 1135–1151.

Munro, E. (2010b). *The Munro review of child protection. Part 1: A systems analysis*. London: Department for Education.

Ofsted. (2011). *Edging away from care—How services successfully prevent young people entering care*. Retrieved from https://www.gov.uk/government/publications/how-services-prevent-young-people-entering-care-edging-away-from-care

Oliver, C. (2005). *Reflexive inquiry: A framework for consultancy practice*. London: Karnac Books.

Onyett, S. (2007). *New ways of working for applied psychologists in health and social care: Working psychologically in teams*. Leicester: The British Psychological Society.

Pearce, B. (2009). *Making social worlds. A communication perspective*. Oxford: Blackwell.

Pendry, N. (2011). Systemic practice in a risk management context. In S. Goodman & I. Trowler (Eds.), *Social work reclaimed: Innovative frameworks for child and family social work practice*. London: Jessica Kingsley Publishers.

Rivett, M., & Street, E. (2009). *Family therapy: 100 Key points and techniques*. London: Routledge.

Selvini, M. P., Boscolo, L., Cecchin, G., & Prata, G. (1980). Hypothesizing—circularity—neutrality: Three guidelines for the conductor of the session. *Family Process, 19*(1), 3–12.

The Nuffield Foundation. (2013). Making not breaking: Building relationships for our most vulnerable children. Findings and recommendations of the Care Inquiry. Retrieved from http://www.nuffieldfoundation.org/sites/default/files/files/Care%20Inquiry%20-%20Full%20Report%20April%202013.pdf

Tomm, K. (1985). Circular interviewing: A multi-faceted clinical tool. In D. Campbell & R. Draper (Eds.), *Applications of systemic family therapy: The Milan approach*. London: Grune and Stratton.

Tomm, K. (1987). Interventive interviewing: Part II. Reflexive questioning as a means to enable self-healing. *Family Process, 26*(2), 167–183.

Tomm, K. (1988). Interventive interviewing: Part III. Intending to ask lineal, circular, strategic, or reflexive questions? *Family Process, 27*(1), 1–15.

Watzlawick, P. (1984). *The invented reality*. New York: W.W. Norton.

Wren, B. and Daniels, G. (2005) Narrative therapies with children and their families: A practitioner's guide to concepts and approaches. In Vetere, A. and Dowling, E. (Eds.), *Narrative therapies with children and their families. A practitioners guide to concepts and approaches*. London: Routledge.

4

Evidence-Oriented Practice

Laura Smith

Introduction

Clinical practice with children and families at the edge of care has the potential to affect change at a fundamental level—whether through keeping families intact or supporting positive alternative care arrangements for children. Clinical interventions in this context are often required to address deep-seated and complex issues. These are likely to include a combination of difficulties, including those being experienced by the child or children themselves (such as emotional, behavioural or developmental concerns); parenting issues; issues with the parent's individual functioning such as mental health issues, learning disabilities and substance misuse issues; parental relationship issues and domestic violence; and family relationship problems (Cleaver et al. 2011; Ward et al. 2014). Families at the edge of care often experience co-occurring difficulties in different areas.

L. Smith (✉)
London, UK

© The Author(s) 2016
L. Smith (ed.), *Clinical Practice at the Edge of Care*,
DOI 10.1007/978-3-319-43570-1_4

It is well documented that children who are at risk of entering the care system experience higher rates of health problems, mental health difficulties, attachment-related difficulties and psychological distress (Milburn et al. 2008; Cleaver et al. 2011; Davies and Ward 2012). Likewise, their parents are likely to be experiencing additional social and economic difficulties and psychological legacies from their own previous life experiences. These may in turn combine to affect their engagement with support services (Reder and Fredman 1996; Fauth et al. 2010).

Therefore, practising in accordance with the evidence base is a challenge, as family circumstances tend to be unique and multi-faceted. These risk being oversimplified if mapped solely onto diagnostic categories or generalised conceptualisations of psychological distress. In addition, although there has been an increasing amount of research into clinical practice with at-risk children and their families, this has not definitively identified a preferred model or care pathway for achieving positive outcomes (Silver et al. 2015).

It is thus unsurprising that the edge-of-care interventions that have been found to be most effective are those that operate on a multi-modal basis, in order to address various presenting concerns in a co-ordinated way. However, the current evidence base suggests that best practice means doing more than deploying only systematised, multi-component approaches (Fraser et al. 2013; Farmer and Lutman 2012). This invites scope for clinicians and those developing services to orientate practice towards what is known to be effective, whilst holding in mind possibilities for developing modes of delivery suited to local contexts and to different children and families. Therefore, this chapter will consider systematised approaches alongside other relevant types of intervention, which may be used on their own or in combination to enhance a wider evidence-oriented intervention plan. Additionally, key features and qualities of successful clinical work in edge-of-care contexts, as identified in research and practice, will be discussed in more detail.

Contexts

A defining quality of edge-of-care practice is that it needs to sit effectively within specific statutory and legal processes, which set parameters to ensure the primacy of the welfare of the child and rights to family life (UK Children Act 1989; UK Human Rights Act 1998). It is also shaped by the issue of timeliness—in relation to individual case planning (discussed further below) and as a wider service delivery issue—in that edge-of-care interventions need to be co-ordinated and deployed to reflect levels of need and opportunities for change at different points in a family's life cycle or the trajectory of developing difficulties (Luckock et al. 2015). For example, as infancy is the highest risk period for child mortality related to child abuse and neglect, this should be considered when targeting interventions both within individual families and when prioritising service resources. Similarly, it is important to ensure that edge-of-care interventions are offered in time to achieve what might reasonably considered to be a positive outcome for the child. Rutter et al. (2007) thus caution that, "the longer maltreatment persists and the more intensive it is, the harder it will be to overcome the consequences".

It is also key that clinical practice in this context sits within effective clinical accountability and governance frameworks. In part, this is due to wider requirements for clinical services to demonstrate evidence-based practice and cost-effectiveness. However, within edge-of-care settings, governance is especially needed as interventions tend to be resource-intensive, to present challenges in terms of defining a "positive outcome," involve ongoing risk management and may be generative of a degree of professional anxiety and complex systemic dynamics.

Evidence-Oriented Interventions

Systematised Approaches

Currently, the most robust emerging evidence for effectiveness in edge-of-care contexts lies with systematised, multi-modal interventions. The most credible of these have already been subject to randomised controlled trails, have been widely disseminated and have received endorsement by governmental authorities and/or respected research and practice development institutions.

Homebuilders

The Homebuilders programme is one of the longest-established multi-component family intervention models, disseminated widely in the USA since its inception in the mid-1970s, with over 150,000 families completing the programme to date. Homebuilders is targeted at families whose children are considered to be at risk of coming into care and those where the intention is for children to return to live at home via family rehabilitation. Families are engaged in a 4–6-week schedule of intensive therapy, including 8–10 hours of direct face-to-face support. They also have access to round-the-clock telephone support. Interventions are provided by a qualified and experienced clinical team with small caseloads (of typically 2 families per therapist). These are delivered in the family home and community settings and are focused on preventing child abuse and neglect, reducing family conflict and ameliorating child behaviour problems. Key components include collaborative engagement with families, building motivation to change, assessment and goal-setting, crisis planning, risk assessment in areas of concern (such as domestic violence and suicidality), cognitive-behavioural therapy to support behaviour change, skills development using a "teaching-practice-feedback" cycle, the provision of concrete goods and services (whilst developing families' strategies to access these independently) and the co-ordination of wider professional systems (Kinney et al. 2004). There have been several adaptations of the Homebuilders model, including the promising Option 2 programme recently developed in Wales, focused on families where parental substance misuse is a primary presenting concern (Forrester et al. 2012).

Several studies have evaluated Homebuilders, with, initially, positive findings for its effectiveness. Two comparative studies found that children in families receiving the Homebuilders programme were significantly more likely to remain living at home, including those who were rehabilitated from foster care (Wood et al. 1988; Fraser et al. 1996). A long-term follow-up study found that Homebuilders families were more likely to have discontinued use of services, due to the family situation having stabilised (Walton 1998). However, more recently, further high-quality studies found Homebuilders to be no more effective than treatment as usual, in terms of the likelihood of children coming into care and achieving positive outcomes in other areas (USDHHS 2001).

Multi-systemic Therapy

Multi-systemic Therapy (MST) is, arguably, the best known intervention model currently applied to improving outcomes for young people who are at risk of entering custody or care. Established for over 30 years, with over 500 sites worldwide, it is a manualised, community-based programme that takes an intensive, multi-modal approach. A range of interventions are delivered by an single therapist to address difficulties at individual, family, school and community levels, via identifying and addressing problem drivers and harnessing strengths (Henggeler 2012). As with Homebuilders, there is a significant focus within the model on family engagement and on therapist flexibility, with interventions delivered on an outreach basis and families having round-the-clock access to telephone support. Adaptations to standard MST have been developed, including MST-PSB for young people presenting with problem sexualised behaviours, MST-CAN to address child abuse and neglect and MST-BSF for families with co-occurring parental substance misuse difficulties, physical abuse and neglect (developed through merging MST-CAN with Reinforcement-Based Therapy, an evidence-based substance misuse programme for adults).

There have been numerous research studies indicating the effectiveness of MST. A recent meta-analysis concluded that the model is most effective for young people under 15 years old, with small but significant MST treatment effects on rates of out-of-home placement, future offending, young people's mental health, substance use and family functioning. However, various moderator effects were identified, including study characteristics, sample characteristics and outcomes monitored (Van der Stouwe et al. 2014). A number of outcome studies have focused specifically on families where child abuse and neglect were the primary presenting issues. However, for this cohort, the evidence for MST relative to other interventions is mixed. In the initial evaluation of MST for child maltreatment, families randomly assigned to receive either MST or parent training achieved similar positive outcomes for progress in addressing referral difficulties, as well as improvements in parental mental health and reductions in parental stress levels. MST families achieved comparatively bigger improvements in the quality of parent-child relationships, but parent training was more effective in addressing wider social problems (Brunk et al. 1987). Similarly, a comparison of MST-CAN and parent training for families where children had been physically abused found that these approaches had similar results in some areas—including, crucially, the rate of re-abuse experienced by children at 16-month follow-up. However, children whose families received MST-CAN had reduced mental health symptoms, whilst their parents had reduced rates of emotional distress and presented fewer parenting behaviours associated with child maltreatment. Their children were also less likely to be placed outside of the family home at follow-up (Swenson et al. 2010). A pilot study of the most recent MST adaptation, MST-BSF, indicates that it has the potential to successfully reduce parental substance misuse and depression whilst reducing "psychological aggression towards the child," as well as reducing re-abuse incidents and the number of out-of-home placements compared to treatment as usual (Schaeffer et al. 2013).

Interestingly, process research examining mediators of change within MST have highlighted that improving family relationships is likely to be the mechanism via which positive outcomes are achieved (Huey et al. 2000; Dekovic et al. 2012; Tighe et al. 2012). Therefore, it is useful to consider the appropriateness of MST for particular families depending on whether parent-child and/or family relationship/parenting issues are assessed to be the main driver contributing to presenting concerns. However, for older children, it appears that better outcomes are achieved if MST focuses more on peer risk issues and school engagement (van der Stouwe et al. 2014). It is also worth noting that, for young people and their families with the most complex and severe difficulties, the current evidence base suggests that MST needs enhancing across a range of intervention domains and processes in order to succeed (Stambaugh et al. 2007).

Box 4.1 Case example: Jayden

Jayden, aged 12, lived at home with his mother Jody and 17-year-old sister Aliyah. Jayden had been excluded from school following numerous incidents of challenging behaviour and remained out of education several months later. There were concerns about his association with gang-affiliated peers, who would visit him at home and sometime stay overnight. Jayden

Box 4.1 (continued)

himself rarely left his bedroom but would demand money from Jody to spend on online gaming and takeaway food. There were longstanding concerns about the physical state of the family home and about high levels of conflict between Jody and Aliyah. This sometimes resulted in physical altercations between them. Jody had previously been diagnosed with a mild learning disability and depression. As a result of these concerns, Jayden had been made subject to a Child Protection Plan.

Jayden and his family were provided with MST over an initial nine-month intervention period, subsequently extended to 13 months. During this time, Jody regularly met with an MST therapist, at the family home and at a local cafe. She was provided with parenting skills training focused on the development of positive household rules, encouraging Jayden's engagement with family activities and home tutoring, and limit-setting. She was also provided with individual cognitive-behavioural therapy sessions to address low mood and motivation to change. A mental health and developmental screening assessment was proposed to Jayden, but he declined to co-operate with this.

At the end of the intervention period, little had changed in terms of Jayden's personal presentation and engagement with education. However, he was no longer visited at home by gang-affiliated peers, since Jody became better able to set limits around who could visit the house. Incidents of conflict between Jody and Aliyah had reduced. However, it was discovered that Aliyah was stealing money by using her mother's debit card without permission. It also became apparent that Jody struggled with budgeting and with maintaining household organisation at a reasonable level. It was therefore decided that a Legal Planning Meeting would be convened, to consider further assessments and interventions within the Public Law Outline.

Functional Family Therapy

Functional Family Therapy (FFT) is another of the longest-established, multi-modal intervention models currently used in edge-of-care contexts. Presently, FFT is delivered to more than 25,000 families per year, predominantly in the USA, but also across European and non-European settings worldwide. FFT is a staged intervention model, with a predominantly relational focus. Again, there is a strong emphasis on engagement at the commencement of therapy, followed by a sequenced use of both systemic and social learning-oriented intervention strategies—intended to affect change via increasing motivation, addressing high levels of family conflict, encouraging more functional cognitive attributions and emphasising relational skills-building. FFT also works towards families being able to generalise change across different situations. This typically involves delivering up to 30 hours of direct clinical input to families over a three-month period. As with MST and Homebuilders, interventions are provided by qualified clinicians or specialist social work/nursing practitioners holding small caseloads. To date, FFT has primarily been used with families where young people are engaged with the youth justice system due to significant conduct difficulties and/or criminal activity. However, it has been subject to several adaptations, tailoring the programme to different clinical populations and different age groups. Adaptations for families where there has been abuse and neglect, and those targeting families with younger children, tend to focus more on parental difficulties (such as addressing parental mental health and substance misuse) and parenting issues (Alexander and Robbins 2010; Sexton 2011).

The evidence base for FFT mostly relates to outcomes for young offenders. Several cohort studies of FFT have noted reductions in rates of out-of-home placement and improvements in emotional and behavioural difficulties, alongside reductions in recidivism for young offenders (Rist 2011; Thorgersen 2012; Sexton 2016). The extent of therapists' fidelity to the FFT model is associated with better outcomes (Graham et al. 2014). Of particular relevance to edge-of-care practice is one of three studies completed by Barton, Alexander and colleagues, which compared out-of-home placement rates for children whose families had received FFT vs. treatment as usual, in a US child welfare context. This concluded that FFT led to a significant reduction in children coming into care and also brought about a reduction in overall service use by families (Barton et al. 1985).

Alternatives for Families: A Cognitive-Behavioural Therapy (AF-CBT)

AF-CBT is another phased intervention programme, currently disseminated across a range of settings in the USA and Japan, which combines elements of CBT and family therapy with the aim of addressing child physical and emotional abuse and neglect. Areas of focus are child behavioural difficulties, trauma, parental self-regulation difficulties and family conflict (Kolko and Swenson 2002; Kolko and Kolko 2009). AF-CBT draws on cognitive, social learning and systems theory and psychological understandings of aggression and its interplay with victimhood. During therapy, parents and their school-aged children attend parallel and joint therapy sessions, once or twice per week for up to a year. Treatment is sequentially focused on engagement, individual skills development and relationship skills. It is designed to be delivered by clinicians or other specialist professionals who have experience and skills relevant to working with physically abusive parents.

There is promising research evidence for the effectiveness of AF-CBT, although this model has yet to be subjected to more rigorous evaluation. Foundational research looking at the CBT-oriented and Family Therapy elements of AF-CBT vs. treatment as usual found that the AF-CBT interventions were more effective (Kolko 1996a, b). Components of AF-CBT—including anger control training, cognitive restructuring and imaginal exposure—have also been found to be effective in reducing physical abuse risk and improving family functioning (Urquiza and Runyon 2010). In addition, practitioners trained in AF-CBT, and classified as using elements of the model in their work, were found to achieve better outcomes for families (Kolko et al. 2011).

Treatment Foster Care

Treatment Foster Care can take various forms—the most widely disseminated model currently being Multi-Dimensional Treatment Foster Care (MTFC), now known in the UK as Treatment Foster Care Oregon (TFCO). In MTFC/TFCO, children and young people spend a defined period of time (of around nine months) in a foster care placement, during which social learning theory-informed interventions are provided to the child themselves, their foster carers and their birth family. These are intended to bring about improvements in the child's wellbeing and behaviour and to increase the likelihood of them being able to live safely with their birth families or, where this is not possible, in an alternative long-term placement. MTFC/TFCO is delivered by a team with clearly defined clinical and non-clinical roles and responsibilities within the model, working intensively with a small cohort of children at any one time (Fisher and Chamberlain 2000; Moore et al. 2001).

There is a small amount of evidence to date that MTFC increases the likelihood of children and young people returning to live with their birth families subsequent to treatment, compared to treatment as usual (Biehal et al. 2011; Turner and Macdonald 2011). Additionally, research suggests that MTFC can be effective in addressing attachment-related difficulties in preschool-aged children and in improving psychological and behavioural outcomes for adolescents whose behaviour is rated as highly antisocial and/or aggressive (Chamberlain and Moore 1998; Fisher and Kim 2007; Westermark et al. 2011; Biehal et al. 2012). Significant limitations to research on MTFC to date have been identified, which may partly account for a lack of evidence for its effectiveness as an intervention towards family rehabilitation (Harold and DeGarmo 2014; Green et al. 2014).

Therapeutic Jurisprudence

Family Treatment Drug Court/Family Drug and Alcohol Court

The US Family Treatment Drug Courts model (FTDC), further developed in the UK as the Family Drug and Alcohol Court (FDAC), is an edge-of-care intervention for children and families where parental substance misuse is a primary cause for concern. This is the case in around two-thirds of care applications in the UK (Forrester and Harwin 2006). FTDC and FDAC bring together the judiciary, therapeutic and social work interventions as part of a collaborative, outcome-focused approach, which is delivered to families from the point at which care proceedings are initiated. Interventions offered within this model aim to address drug and alcohol misuse, relationship issues and parental mental health issues and include mentalisation-based therapy, cognitive analytic therapy (CAT) and couples therapy, as well as interventions focused on parent-child relationships such as Video Interaction Guidance (VIG) and systemic family therapy. These interventions are co-ordinated as part of an integrated care plan and reviewed via the court process (Bambrough et al. 2013). Within FTDC and FDAC, judges engage directly with families outside of court hearings, meeting with them regularly to review their progress and to direct plans to address issues of concern. Judges may use therapeutic approaches such as motivational interviewing to engage families and support progress.

An evaluation of the FTDC model, looking at outcomes for more than 2000 families, found that children were significantly more likely to remain living with their parents if family court proceedings went via this route. Proceedings for families where reunification was achieved tended to be significantly longer than usual. However, when it became apparent that parents were not able to resolve their substance misuse issues, then alternative permanency decisions for children were made more rapidly (Worcel et al. 2008). A recent UK pilot study looking at outcomes of the FDAC approach (comparing children whose families went through care proceedings via FDAC with matched comparison children in standard care proceedings) found that a significantly higher proportion of FDAC parents ceased misusing substances. However, there was not a statistically significant difference in the number of children who were able to remain living with or return to live with their parent(s). Where children were found by the courts to need alternative permanency arrangements, decisions were not reached any more rapidly for FDAC families. The majority of children in both types of care proceedings ended up with alternative carers. Further case factor analysis suggested that, where families had multiple problems at the point of entering care proceedings, there was a low rate of family reunification or stabilisation regardless of the type of court process they went through. However, a promising finding was that children in families who had gone through FDAC and achieved reunification experienced lower rates of further abuse and neglect at one year follow-up (Harwin et al. 2014).

New Orleans Intervention Model

Similarly to FTDC and FDAC, this model also involves interventions that are co-ordinated with aligned legal processes, with a view to making recommendations as to whether or not family rehabilitation is a realistic possibility. This approach is currently being piloted in the UK, following its development in the New Orleans Tulane Infant Team (Zeanah et al.

2001; Minnis et al. 2010; Pritchett et al. 2013). The model provides intensive, multi-modal support to children aged under 60-month old, their birth families and foster carers, with a view to addressing issues stemming from earlier abuse, neglect and trauma and enhancing the potential of caregiving relationships to build children's resilience and improve their developmental, health and psychological outcomes. Prior to the delivery of interventions, there is an intensive assessment phase comprising around 15–20 hours of direct contact with children and their carers, aimed at systematically evaluating the quality of current caregiving and identifying the child and family's intervention needs. Interventions that may subsequently be provided within the model include individual psychotherapy for parents and dyadic therapy with parents and children. Emphasis is also placed on engaging families in wider support systems (Larrieu and Zeanah 1998).

An initial study found that children in receipt of the New Orleans programme spent the same amount of time in care on average as a comparison group. Notably, significantly more of the children in the New Orleans group ended up in care. This is accounted for on the basis that the programme demands a more focused level of commitment and progress from birth parents than treatment as usual. The rationale is that without the level of progression demanded by the programme, families are not making significant enough shifts in the quality of relational experience offered to children to ensure good enough child outcomes. The potential of the New Orleans approach is shown in another finding of the initial model evaluation, which found that it led to a significant reduction in the relative incidence of abuse and neglect of children who returned home to live with their birth families. This was also the case for subsequent children born to mothers who had previously engaged in the programme, including those whose children were removed from their care (Zeanah et al. 2001).

Component Interventions

A large number of additional therapeutic interventions, with established or emerging research evidence, have the potential to be applicable in edge-of-care contexts—as part of a wider care package and in various combinations. Those considered here include family and child-focused approaches that aim to achieve improved psychological and developmental outcomes for the child, alongside stabilisation and improvements to family functioning. In addition, parent and caregiver-focused interventions are also potentially highly relevant—including those that address parental issues such as mental health difficulties, trauma, substance misuse, domestic violence, couple relationship issues and adaptive functioning skills (Cleaver et al. 2011). However, there is less robust evidence currently that solely parent-focused interventions have a direct impact on outcomes for children (Barlow and Schrader McMillan 2010).

Systemic Family Therapy

A number of the interventions described in this chapter may be considered to be fundamentally systemic in orientation or have systemic family therapy as one of their core or possible components. However, systemic family therapy in itself bears consideration, as it has a growing presence in edge-of-care practice in the UK and elsewhere. Systemic practice can take a wide variety of forms—involving short-, medium- and longer-term work, intensive and intermittent sessions and work with different configurations of a child's family and network of support. Similarly, there is a broad body of systemic theory that is relevant to the conceptualisation of family difficulties, to the ways in which presenting concerns are discussed in clinical sessions and the posited change process (Dallos and Draper 2015). Of particular relevance to edge-of-care work are developments that either adapt existing systemic ideas and practices to meet the needs of this clinical context (Pendry 2012) or focus on key presenting concerns common to high risk children and families. With respect to the latter, key areas of development have been systemic therapy with families affected by domestic violence (Cooper and Vetere 2005; Vetere and Cooper 2001; Vetere and Cooper 2003; Jenkins 2009; Aggett et al. 2015), attachment-related difficulties (Dallos and Vetere 2009; Crittenden et al. 2014), working with trauma (Smith 2013), sexual abuse (Carr 2000) and child behavioural difficulties and parent-child relationship difficulties (Carr 2009a; Keaveny et al. 2012). However, research to date indicates that systemic family therapy needs to be provided as part of a wider package of care in order to affect change subsequent to child abuse and neglect (Carr 2009a).

Video Interaction Guidance

Video Interaction Guidance (VIG) is a short-term intervention intended to enhance parent-child relationships, based on theories of intersubjectivity (Trevarthen and Aitken 2001; Cross and Kennedy 2011). It is one of a family of video-feedback-based interventions that have been developed in the UK, Europe and the USA over the past three decades. The focus of VIG is on creating an iterative process between the client, therapist and strategically chosen video clips, whereby attuned relationships are reflected on, promoted and generalised. VIG interventions are generally offered over 3–6 cycles, with each cycle comprising of a video session with the parent and child(ren) and a shared review session with the parent.

There is now significant evidence for the effectiveness of VIG and other similar video-feedback interventions, from a number of high-quality research studies. It has been demonstrated that VIG is a means to improve parental sensitivity, to promote secure attachment relationships between children and their parents and to reduce the number of disorganised attachment relationships between children and their parents (Klein and Velderman 2005; Fukkink 2008; Fukkink et al. 2012). Of particular interest to edge-of-care practice is a small-scale study undertaken with families who were subject to ongoing assessment in a residential unit during care proceedings, during which time decisions were being made about whether babies should remain in the care of their birth mothers. This found that VIG was effective in improving maternal sensitivity and in significantly reducing concerns about babies' relational experiences as measured by the CARE-INDEX (Kennedy, et al. 2010).

Parent-Infant Psychotherapy and Child Psychotherapy

Parent-infant psychotherapy (PIP) involves working therapeutically with a parent and their baby together, with the overall aim of supporting optimal infant development. PIP interventions may be short, medium or longer term and may be delivered in small groups, as well as with individual parent-infant dyads. The theoretical basis for most parent-infant psychotherapy is psychodynamic and representational, with an increasing focus on attachment and its emotional and behavioural correlates as key to understanding and addressing presenting concerns for the baby and their relationship with their primary caregiver(s). Similarly, child psychotherapy draws its theoretical framework from psychodynamic theory and models of practice, but generally involves longer-term, relatively frequent individual sessions being offered to the child, alongside feedback and support being provided to their parent or carer to support the child's progress.

In recent years there has been an increasing focus on bringing together the evidence base for parent-infant psychotherapy and child psycho-therapy, with systematic reviews finding evidence of their effectiveness to address a range of emotional, behavioural and developmental issues (Barlow et al. 2015; Kennedy and Midgley 2007; Midgley and Kennedy 2011). It is apparent that child psychotherapy has the potential to usefully address common presenting issues experienced by children at the edge of care, including the emotional and developmental consequences of early trauma, sexual abuse and neglect (Trowell et al. 2002; Boston et al. 2009; Heede et al. 2009). Similarly, parent-infant psychotherapy has been shown to be effective in addressing attachment-related concerns. For example, it has been shown to be effective in improving attachment security between depressed mothers and toddlers (Toth et al. 2006). However, the current evidence base does not yet offer a clear rationale for the mechanism of change through parent-infant psychotherapy. It is proposed that this could include improving parental sensitivity and reflective functioning. Another hypothesis is that parent-infant psychotherapeutic interventions can help to address unresolved issues from parents' own histories along-side inducing behaviour change (Cohen et al. 1999; Fraiberg et al. 1975).

Helping the Non-Compliant Child/the Parent-Child Game/ Parent-Child Interaction Therapy

Helping the Non-Compliant Child (HNC) and the Parent-Child Game (PCG) are interventions for children aged 4–9 and their parents based on behavioural, social learning and cognitive theory principles (McMahon and Forehand 2003; Jenner 1999). HNC was originally developed to address child conduct problems, but PCG has gone on to be applied in UK child protection and edge-of-care contexts with a growing remit towards addressing parent-child relationship difficulties and child abuse and neglect (Jenner 1997). Both HNC and PCG involve parents attending 12 or more weekly sessions with their child or children, during which they are offered live coaching to develop their parenting skills, delivered via an earpiece by therapists using a video link or positioned behind a two-way screen. Sessions focus on increasing parents' use of "child-centred" parenting skills and reducing their use of unhelpful "child-directive" behaviours, such as criticism or unnecessary commands. Homework is set between sessions, during which parents are expected to practice skills that have been developed.

Parent-Child Interaction Therapy (PCIT) is very similar to HNC and PCG, both in its theoretical orientation and in its mode of delivery, which includes the development of parenting skills via live coaching. However, its focus is different in that it is designed specifically for preschool children and their parents. PCIT also has the explicit intent to change the quality of parent-child relationships as well as addressing child conduct problems (Eyberg et al. 2008). Whilst a number of studies have shown that PCIT is effective in addressing child conduct problems, a randomised controlled trial has also demonstrated the effectiveness of PCIT for reducing child physical abuse recidivism (Eyberg and Bussing 2010; Chaffin et al. 2004).

Likewise, PCG has been well validated as an intervention to address child conduct problems via a large number of comparative studies, with strong long-term follow-up data and evidence of its effectiveness across diverse social, cultural and ethnic groups (McMahon and Forehand 2003; McMahon et al. 2010). There is also an emerging strand of the literature indicating its potential for addressing attachment-related concerns, which is significant given the interlinking of attachment and behavioural difficulties where there are complex family issues (Sutton 2001; Scott and Dadds 2009).

Choosing and Applying Interventions

Effective edge-of-care interventions share a number of key aspects, which may be considered fundamental to best practice. These are the defining features or ways of working that allow for maximum progress and timely use of resources in casework.

Case conceptualisation—drawing on relevant theory or model-specific frameworks—is essential in order to critically analyse and pull together an understanding of edge-of-care difficulties, their impact and interactions with one another. This needs to be more of a process than an event, one which is available and meaningful when shared across professional, family and wider systemic contexts (Weisz and Bearman 2008; Ward et al. 2014). At the same time, there may be tensions created in trying to prioritise case formulation processes whilst there is a perceived need to take action to address risks to children.

Sequencing—deciding which interventions to provide to whom, in what order, simultaneously or concurrently, and at what pace, is also highly relevant. As seen above, a common factor in the most well-researched interventions in edge-of-care contexts is that these involve multiple components delivered as part of a co-ordinated intervention strategy. This approach may also be taken when putting together bespoke packages of care for families. Case-co-ordination and review processes within professional systems are key to making this possible. This may mean that clinicians are required to participate more closely in care planning processes than might ordinarily be the case within traditional child and family mental health settings. Equally, local partnerships at service level need to be equipped to strategically co-ordinate casework, for example, when an adult mental health or substance misuse intervention is being provided in conjunction with parenting work and therapeutic support for a child or family. Alternatively, there is the option to develop local provision of multi-component services. For example, the Early Years Parenting Unit (EYPU) model brings together adult mental health and systemic knowledge and skills to offer an 18-month edge-of-care intervention programme for parents with personality difficulties and their young children, including individual- and group-based therapeutic support alongside multi-family and parent-child therapies (Daum and McLean 2015).

The timeliness of interventions also needs to be considered, in terms of whether positive outcomes can be achieved at the present time or "in time", within the child's developmental timescales. This is particularly relevant when considering whether to offer interventions to address longstanding and complex parental difficulties. Similarly, long-term child psychotherapy might be considered clinically appropriate to address the impact of trauma, but it might be necessary to address other issues first (such as family relationship concerns or peer-group risk issues) in order to create a stable enough context for this intervention to be useful.

Goal orientation is another key aspect of successful edge-of-care interventions. Goal-setting and orientation can take a number of forms. For example, in Video Interaction Guidance, goals are developed collaboratively with parents as "helping questions" and revisited during each cycle. In Multi-systemic Therapy, goal-setting follows on from the creation of formulation-like "fit circles," which set out how different issues contribute to difficulties and leads into mapping of how they will be addressed (Henggeler et al. 2009). Goal-directed interventions can be particularly helpful when accountability is driven by statutory and legal processes or thresholds. For families, a goal-directed framework also offers more transparency and clarity around expectations about what needs to change. Goal-setting processes also offer an opportunity for collaboration and the creation of a therapeutic relationship, as children and families' own concerns and priorities can be acknowledged and integrated into the frame of reference set for clinical interventions. Similarly, professionals are required to be respectfully "up front" about their intentions and focus.

Engagement of children and families in edge-of-care interventions has also been identified as a core component of successful edge-of-care models and methodologies (Fauth et al. 2010; Ofsted 2011; Scott and Barlow, 2010). The task of engagement in this context is inherently relational; including components such as building trust, being reliable and open, conveying empathy and acceptance, cultural competence and being persistent and available (Korbin 2007; Barlow and Scott 2010; Shemmings et al. 2012). Empathy is likely to be of particular importance in working with parents who have had adverse early experiences of caregivers who lacked emotional availability, sensitivity and responsiveness to their needs, experiences that are known to form the basis of a person's capacity to go on to develop mentalisation skills in relation to others (Fonagy et al. 2004). By providing empathic support to parents and other family members in edge-of-care contexts, practitioners are therefore offering an essential interpersonal scaffold towards both parental reflective functioning and the accessibility of therapeutic support. Providing empathy when parents or children are saying or doing things that put themselves or others at risk, or that convey attitudes that condone harmful consequences, requires a high degree of skill. In this context, rather than providing empathy for particular behaviours, providing "person empathy" is likely to be more appropriate and effective (Elliot et al. 2011). Empathic clinical practice needs to be supported by empathic and effective supervision for the practitioner themselves (Ferguson 2011). It is notable that therapist qualities have been shown to contribute significantly to outcomes in edge-of-care work (as elsewhere); as exemplified by some striking early FFT research, which looked at process variables and found that therapists' capacity for warmth, affect-behaviour integration and humour, as well as their ability to structure the intervention through being directive, were associated with over half of the variability in predicting FFT outcomes (Alexander et al. 1976).

On a practical level, clinical interventions may also be offered and organised in such a way as to maximise engagement, for example, by offering flexibility around the location and timing of appointments, supporting families to attend using reminders, offering transport to clinics and being sensitive to the level and impact of day-to-day demands being placed on a family. This is especially important when interventions are being offered as part of a statutory or legal process that means a family is required to attend clinical sessions (or face significant consequences). Taking into account practicalities not only helps promote attendance but also conveys more fundamental messages about accessibility and collaboration.

Furthermore, it may be necessary to consider the usefulness and sustainability of offering higher-than-usual levels of support to promote engagement. This can be helpful when families are being asked to engage intensively with time-consuming and emotionally demanding intervention plans. The feasibility of offering longer-term support to sustain progress may be an issue when parents' or children's difficulties are recurring or chronic, for instance, in the case of parents who have mental health issues with high rates of relapse or moderate to severe learning disabilities. In such circumstances, a family's wider engagement with community or other sources of support may usefully become components of intervention plans, especially for those experiencing high levels of social exclusion.

Alongside efforts to promote families' engagement with interventions, practitioners also need to be mindful of "disguised compliance" as a risk factor within edge-of-care contexts (Reder et al. 1993; Munro 2011). This is defined as occurring when "a parent or carer giving the appearance of co-operating with child welfare agencies to avoid raising suspicions, to allay professional concerns and ultimately to diffuse professional intervention" (NSPCC 2014) and has been identified as a feature of interactions between parents and professionals in a number of UK Serious Case Reviews. Professionals' awareness of the presence or absence of genuine engagement with interventions offered can be further complicated by dynamics in the system. These can include professional splitting and the development of systemic processes that make it harder for individuals to respond to, or address, issues arising (Furniss 1991). Therefore, clinicians in edge-of-care work need to be particularly mindful of how monitoring and tracking of progress may usefully inform ongoing risk assessment.

Box 4.2 Case example: Serena

Serena, aged 5, had recently started living full-time with her mother Esther. For two years previously, she had mostly stayed with her mother's ex-partner Marilyn during the week, whilst Esther worked shifts. However, Esther and Marilyn were on worsening terms as time went on and their co-parenting arrangements became highly conflictual, leading to Serena ceasing to be have any contact with Marilyn. Esther also reported long-standing psychological difficulties, which she traced back to her own childhood experiences of sexual abuse and neglect. Esther described struggling to bond with Serena, avoiding touching her or being touched, often losing her temper with her over small things, frequently shouting and swearing at Serena, feeling low in mood and experiencing trauma-related flashbacks. In turn, Serena was withdrawn and anxious at school, where staff described her as appearing fearful of Esther. A statutory Children's Social Care assessment concluded that Esther was emotionally abusive towards Serena. Little progress was made during an initial Child Protection Plan, and Esther was considered to be "hard-to-engage," as she repeatedly missed appointments and didn't appear motivated to follow advice that was offered by Serena's Social Worker.

There was a co-ordinated multi-agency response to these concerns. Esther was prioritised for individual psychotherapy by her local adult mental

Box 4.2 (continued)

health service, having previously been on a long waiting list. She and Marilyn were offered mediation sessions by a local voluntary sector agency supporting LGBTQ families, in order for a continuing shared care arrangement to be negotiated and formalised. Serena was offered additional pastoral support at school by a Family Liaison Worker, who also offered individual parenting support sessions to Esther, timed to fit in with her work commitments. Esther and Serena were then provided with Video Interaction Guidance by a Clinical Psychologist and completed four cycles, once initial engagement difficulties were resolved by the provision of flexible sessions and focus being given to establishing a therapeutic relationship. Overall, the intervention period lasted for 12 months. Subsequent to this, Esther and Serena enjoyed a closer and happier relationship and reported spending more time together doing shared activities. Serena was observed to be more settled at school. Esther and Marilyn had agreed on a new shared care schedule that provided Serena with a predictable routine and led to fewer conflicts. Esther's mental health had also improved significantly.

Conclusion

There is significant diversity and complexity in families' presenting needs at the edge of care. The identification and accessibility of evidence-oriented interventions therefore presents challenges for front-line practice and service development. However, an emerging evidence base points to a range of promising approaches. Clinical skills in case formulation, care planning, working within a network and building effective therapeutic relationships are key to maximising their impact. Taken together, these may usefully inform the delivery of direct clinical work with children and families, as well as strategic service planning and decision-making. Given the significance of service user engagement in this area of practice, it would be helpful for the further development of interventions to be closely guided by children and families' input and feedback. Likewise, there is a need for further research undertaken in real-life clinical settings and focused on gaining an enhanced understanding of therapeutic processes.

References

Aggett, P., Swainson, M., & Tapsell, D. (2015). "Seeking permission": An interviewing stance for finding connection with hard to reach families. *Journal of Family Therapy, 37*(2), 190–209.

Alexander, J., & Robbins, M. (2010). Functional family therapy: A phase-based and multi-component approach to change. In R. Murrihy, A. Kidman, & T. Ollendick (Eds.), *Clinical handbook of assessing and treating conduct problems in youth*. New York: Springer.

Alexander, J. F., Barton, C., Schiavo, R., & Parsons, B. (1976). Behavioural intervention with families of delinquents: Therapist characteristics and outcome. *Journal of Consulting and Clinical Psychology, 44*(4), 656–664.

Bambrough, S., Shaw, M., & Kershaw, S. (2013). The family drug and alcohol service in London: A new way of doing care proceedings. *Journal of Social Work Practice, 28*(3), 357–370.

Barlow, J., Bennett, C., Midgley, N., Larkin, S. K., & Wei, Y. (2015). Parent-infant psychotherapy for improving parental and infant mental health. *Cochrane Database of Systematic Reviews*, (1). Art. No.: CD010534. doi:10.1002/14651858.CD010534.pub2.

Barlow, J., & Schrader McMillan, A. (2010). *Safeguarding children from emotional maltreatment: What works?* London: Jessica Kingsley.

Barlow, J., & Scott, J. (2010). *Safeguarding in the 21st century—Where to now?* Dartington: Research in Practice.

Barton, C., Alexander, J. F., Waldron, H., Turner, C. W., & Warburton, J. (1985). Generalising treatment effects of Functional Family Therapy: Three replications. *Journal of Marriage and Family Therapy, 13*, 16–26.

Biehal, N., Dixon, J., Parry, E., Sinclair, I., Green, J., Roberts, C., et al. (2012). *The care placements evaluation (CaPE) evaluation of multidimensional treatment foster care for adolescents (MTFC-A)*. Universities of York and Manchester. London: UK Department for Education.

Biehal, N., Ellison, S., & Sinclair, I. (2011). Intensive fostering: an independent evaluation of MTFC in an English setting. *Children and Youth Services Review, 33*, 2043–2049.

Boston, M., Lush, D., & Grainger, E. (2009). Evaluation of psychoanalytic psychotherapy with fostered, adopted and "in care" children. In N. Midgley, J. Andersen, E. Grainger, T. Nesic-Vuckovic, & C. Urwin (Eds.), *Child psychotherapy and research: New approaches, emerging findings*. London: Routledge.

Brunk, M., Henggeler, S. W., & Whelan, J. (1987). A comparison of multi-systemic therapy and parent training in the brief treatment of child abuse and neglect. *Journal of Consulting and Clinical Psychology, 55*, 311–318.

Carr, A. (2009a). Evidence-based practice in family therapy and systemic consultation I: Child-focused problems. *Journal of Family Therapy, 22*, 29–60.

Carr, A. (2000). Child sexual abuse: A comprehensive family based approach to treatment. *Journal of Child Centred Practice, 6*(2), 45–74.

Chamberlain, P., & Moore, K. (1998). A clinical model for parenting Juvenile offenders: A comparison of group care vs family care. *Clinical Child Psychology and Psychiatry, 3*, 375–386.

Cleaver, H., Unell, I., & Aldgate, J. (2011). *Children's needs: Parenting capacity* (2nd ed.). London: TSO.

Cohen, N., Muir, E., Lojkasek, M., Muir, R., Parker, C. J., Barwick, M., et al. (1999). Watch, wait and wonder: Testing the effectiveness of a new approach to mother-infant psychotherapy. *Infant Mental Health Journal, 20*(4), 429–451.

Cooper, J., & Vetere, A. (2005). *Domestic violence and family safety: A systemic approach to working with violence in families.* London: Whurr/Wiley.

Crittenden, P., Dallos, R., Landini, A., & Koxlowska, K. (2014). *Attachment and family therapy.* Maidenhead: OUP.

Cross, J., & Kennedy, H. (2011). How and why does VIG work? In H. Kennedy, M. Landor, & L. Todd (Eds.), *Video interaction guidance: A relationship-based intervention to promote attunement, empathy and wellbeing.* London: Jessica Kingsley Publishers.

Dallos, R., & Draper, R. (Eds.). (2015). *An introduction to family therapy: Systemic theory and practice.* Maidenhead: OUP.

Dallos, R., & Vetere, A. (2009). *Systemic therapy and attachment narratives.* Hove: Routledge.

Daum, M., & McLean, D. (2015). Emotional neglect, system failure and the early years parenting unit. In M. Diggins (Ed.), *Parental mental health and child welfare work Vol. 1.* Hove: Pavilion Publishers.

Davies, C., & Ward, H. (2012). *Safeguarding children across services.* London: Jessica Kingsley Publishers.

Dekovic, M., Asscher, J., Manders, W., Prins, P., & van der Laan, P. (2012). Within-intervention change: Mediators of intervention effects during multi-systemic therapy. *Journal of Consulting and Clinical Psychology, 80*(4), 574–587.

Elliot, R., Bohart, A., Watson, J., & Greenberg, L. (2011). Empathy. *Psychotherapy, 48*(1), 43–49.

Eyberg, S. M., & Bussing, R. (2010). Parent-child interaction therapy for preschool children with conduct problems. In R. C. Murphy et al. (Eds.), *Clinical handbook of assessing and treating conduct problems in youth.* New York: Springer.

Eyberg, S. M., Nelson, M. M., & Boggs, S. R. (2008). Evidence-based treatments for child and adolescent disruptive behaviour disorders. *Journal of Clinical Child and Adolescent Psychology, 37,* 213–235.

Farmer, E., & Lutman, E. (2012). *Effective working with neglected children and their families.* London: Jessica Kingsley Publications.

Fauth, R., Jelicic, H., Hart, D., & Burton, S. (2010). *Effective practice to protect children living in highly resistant families.* London: C4EO.

Ferguson, H. (2011). *Child protection practice.* Basingstoke: Palgrave Macmillan.

Fisher, P., & Kim, H. (2007). Intervention effects on foster preschoolers' attachment-related behaviours from a randomised trial. *Preventative Science, 8*(2), 161–170.

Fisher, P. A., & Chamberlain, P. (2000). Multi-dimensional treatment foster care: A program for intensive parent training, family support and skill building. *Journal of Emotional and Behaviour Disorder, 8,* 155–164.

Fonagy, P., Gergely, G., Jurist, E., & Target, M. (2004). *Affect regulation, mentalisation and the development of the self.* London: Karnac.

Forrester, D., & Harwin, J. (2006). Parental substance misuse and child care social work: findings from the first stage of a study of 100 families. *Child and Family Social Work, 11*(4), 325–335.

Forrester, D., Holland, S., Williams, A., & Copello, A. (2012). *An evaluation of the option 2 intensive family preservation service.* Final Research Report for Alcohol Research UK: Retrieved from http://alcoholresearchuk.org/downloads/finalReports/FinalReport_0095.pdf

Fraiberg, S., Adelson, E., & Shapiro, V. (1975). Ghosts in the nursery: A psychoanalytic approach to the problems of impaired infant-mother relationships. *Journal of the American Academy of Child Psychiatry, 14*(3), 387–421.

Fraser, J., Lloyd, S., Murphy, R., Crowson, M., Casanueva, C., Zolotor, A., et al. (Eds.). (2013). Child exposure to Trauma: Comparative effectiveness of interventions addressing maltreatment. *Journal of Behavioural and Developmental Paediatrics, 34*(5), 358–368.

Fraser, M., Walton, E., Lewis, R., Pecora, P., & Walton, W. (1996). An experiment in family reunification: Correlates of outcomes at one-year follow-up. *Children and Youth Services Review, 18*(4/5), 335–361.

Fukkink, R., Kennedy, H., & Todd, L. (2012). Video interaction guidance: Does it work? In H. Kennedy, M. Landor, & L. Todd (Eds.), *Video interaction guidance: A relationship-based intervention to promote attunement, empathy and well-being*. London: Jessica Kingsley Publishers.

Fukkink, R. G. (2008). Video feedback in the widescreen: A meta-analysis of family programs. *Clinical Psychology Review, 28*(6), 904–916.

Furniss, T. (1991). *The multi-professional handbook of child sexual abuse: Integrated management, therapy and legal intervention*. London: Routledge.

Graham, C., Carr, A., Rooney, B., Sexton, T., & Satterfield, L. (2014). Evaluation of functional family therapy in an Irish context. *Journal of Family Therapy, 36*(1), 20–38.

Green, J., Biehal, N., Roberts, C., Dixon, J., Kay, C., Parry, E., et al. (2014). Authors' reply to Harold and DeGarmo. *British Journal of Psychiatry, 205*(6), 498–499.

Harold, G., & DeGarmo, D. (2014). Concerns regarding an evaluation of MTFC-A for adolescents in English care. *British Journal of Psychiatry, 205*(6), 498.

Harwin, J., Alrouh, B., Ryan, M., & Tunnard, J. (2014). *Changing lifestyles, keeping children safe: An evaluation of the first family drug and alcohol court (FDAC) in care proceedings*. London: Brunel University.

Heede, T., Runge, H., Storebo, O. J., Rowley, E., & Hansen, K. G. (2009). Psychodynamic milieu-therapy and changes in personality—What is the connection? *Journal of Child Psychotherapy, 35*(3), 276–289.

Henggeler, S. (2012). Multi-systemic therapy: Clinical foundations and research outcomes. *Psychosocial Intervention, 21*(2), 181–193.

Henggeler, S., Schoenwald, S., et al. (2009). *Multi-systemic therapy for antisocial behaviour in children and adolescents* (2nd ed.). New York: Guilford.

Huey, S., Henggeler, S., Brondino, M., & Pickrel, S. (2000). Mechanisms of change in multi-systemic therapy: Reducing delinquent behaviour through therapist adherence and improved family and peer functioning. *Journal of Consulting and Clinical Psychology, 68*, 451–467.

Jenkins, A. (2009). *Becoming ethical. A parallel, political journey with men who have abused*. Lyme Regis: Russell House Publishing.

Jenner, S. (1997). Assessment of parenting in the context of child protection using the parent child game. *Child Psychology and Psychiatry Review, 2*(20), 58–62.

Jenner, S. (1999). *The parent child game: The proven key to a happier family*. London: Bloomsbury.

Keaveny, E., Midgley, N., Asen, E., Bevington, D., Fearon, P., Fonagy, P., et al. (2012). Minding the family mind: The development and initial evaluation of mentalisation-based treatment for families. In N. Midgley & I. Vrouvra (Eds.), *Minding the child: Mentalisation-based interventions with children, young people and their families.* London: Routledge.

Kennedy, E., & Midgley, N. (2007). *Process and outcome research in child, adolescent and parent-infant psychotherapy.* London: North Central Strategic Health Authority.

Kennedy, H., Landor, M., & Todd, L. (2010). Video interaction guidance as a method to promote secure attachment. *Educational and Child Psychology, 27*(3), 59–72.

Kinney, J., Haapala, D., & Booth, C. (2004). *Keeping families together: The Homebuilder® model.* New Jersey: Aldine Transaction.

Klein Velderman, M. (2005). *The leiden VIPP and VIPP-R Study. Evaluation of a short-term preventive attachment-based intervention in infancy.* Leiden: Mostert and Van Onderen.

Kolko, D. J. (1996a). Individual cognitive-behavioural treatment and family therapy for physically abused children and their offending parents: A comparison of clinical outcomes. *Child Maltreatment: Journal of the American Professional Society on the Abuse of Children, 1*, 322–342.

Kolko, D. J. (1996b). Clinical monitoring of treatment course in child physical abuse: Psychometric characteristics and treatment comparisons. *Child Abuse & Neglect, 20*(1), 23–43.

Kolko, D. J., & Kolko, R. P. (2009). Psychological impact and treatment of child physical abuse of children. In C. Jenny (Ed.), *Child abuse and neglect: Diagnosis, treatment and evidence.* Philadelphia: Saunder/Elsevier.

Kolko, D. J., & Swenson, C. C. (2002). *Assessing and treating physically abused children and their families: A cognitive behavioural approach.* Thousand Oaks: Sage Publications.

Kolko, D. J., Iselin, A. M., & Gully, K. (2011). Evaluation of the sustainability and clinical outcome of alternatives for families: A cognitive-behavioral therapy (AF-CBT) in a child protection center. *Child Abuse and Neglect, 35*(2), 105–116.

Korbin, J. (2007). Issues of culture. In K. Wilson & A. James (Eds.), *The child protection handbook: The practitioner's guide to safeguarding children* (3rd ed.). London: Elsevier.

Larrieu, J., & Zeanah, C. H. (1998). Intensive intervention for maltreated infants and toddlers in foster care. *Child and Adolescent Psychiatric Clinics of North America, 7*, 357–371.

Luckock, B., Barlow, J., & Brown, C. (2015). Developing innovative models of practice at the interface between the NHS and child and family social work where children living at home are at risk of abuse and neglect: A scoping review. *Child and Family Social Work.* doi: 10.1111/cfs.12228.

McMahon, R. J., & Forehand, R. L. (2003). *Helping the noncompliant child second edition: Family-based treatment for oppositional behaviour.* New York: Guilford.

McMahon, R. J., Long, N., & Forehand, R. L. (2010). Parent training for the treatment of oppositional behaviour in young children: Helping the non-compliant child. In R. C. Murphy et al. (Eds.), *Clinical handbook of assessing and treating conduct problems in youth.* New York: Springer.

Midgley, N., & Kennedy, E. (2011). Psychodynamic psychotherapy for children and adolescents: A critical review of the evidence base. *Journal of Child Psychotherapy, 37*(3), 232–260.

Milburn, N., Lynch, A., & Jackson, J. (2008). Early identification of mental health needs for children in care: A therapeutic assessment programme for statutory clients of child protection. *Journal of Child Psychology and Psychiatry, 13*(1), 31–47.

Minnis, H., Bryce, G., Phin, L., & Wilson, P. (2010). "The spirit of New Orleans": Translating a model of intervention with maltreated children and their families for the Glasgow context. *Journal of Child Psychology and Psychiatry, 15*(4), 497–509.

Moore, J., Sprengelmeyer, P., & Chamberlain, P. (2001). Community-based treatment for adjudicated delinquents: The Oregon social learning center's "monitor" multi-dimensional treatment foster care programme. In S. Pfeiffer & L. Reddy (Eds.), *Innovative mental health interventions for children: Programmes that work.* New York: Routledge.

Munro, E. (2011). *The Munro review of child protection: Final report. A child-centred system.* London: TSO.

NSPCC. (2014). *Disguised compliance: An NSPCC factsheet.* London: NSPCC Information Service.

Ofsted. (2011). *Edging away from care—How services successfully prevent young people entering care (110082).* London: Ofsted.

Pendry, N. (2012). Systemic practice in a risk management context. In S. Goodman & I. Trowler (Eds.), *Social work reclaimed: Innovative frameworks for child and family social work practice.* London: Jessica Kingsley Publishers.

Pritchett, R., Fitzpatrick, B., Watson, N., Cotmore, R., Wilson, P., Bryce, G., et al. (2013). A feasibility randomised controlled trial of the New Orleans intervention for infant mental health: A study protocol. *The Scientific World Journal, 2013*, 6.

Reder, P., Duncan, S., & Gray, M. (1993). *Beyond blame: Child abuse tragedies revisited*. London: Routledge.

Reder, P., & Fredman, G. (1996). The relationship to help: Interacting beliefs about the treatment process. *Journal of Clinical Child Psychology and Psychiatry, 1*(3), 457–467.

Rist, M. (2011). *Yolo county (California) probation department, report to county commissioners*. Retrieved from fftllc.com.

Rutter, M., Beckett, C., Castle, J., Colvert, E., Kreppner, J., Mehta, M., et al. (2007). Effects of profound early institutional deprivation: An overview of findings from a UK longitudinal study of Romanian adoptees. *European Journal of Developmental Psychology, 4*(3), 332–350.

Schaeffer, C., Swenson, C., Tuerk, E., & Henggeler, S. (2013). Comprehensive treatment for co-occurring child maltreatment and parental substance abuse: Outcomes from a 24-month pilot study of the MST building stronger families program. *Child Abuse and Neglect, 37*(8), 596–607.

Scott, S., & Dadds, R. (2009). Practitioner review: When parent training doesn't work: Theory-driven clinical strategies. *Journal of Child Psychology and Psychiatry, 50*(12), 1441–1450.

Sexton, T. (2011). *Functional family therapy in clinical practice*. New York: Routledge.

Sexton, T. L. (2016). Functional family therapy: Evidence-based and clinically creative. In T. Sexton & J. Lebow (Eds.), *Handbook of family therapy* (2nd ed.). New York: Routledge.

Shemmings, D., Shemmings, Y., & Cook, A. (2012). Gaining the trust of "highly resistant" families: Insights from attachment theory and research. *Child and Family Social Work, 17*, 130–137.

Silver, M., Golding, K., & Roberts, C. (2015). Delivering psychological services for children, young people and families with complex social care needs. *Child and Family Clinical Psychology Review, 3*, 119–129.

Smith, G. (2013). *Working with trauma: Systemic approaches*. London: Palgrave Macmillan.

Stambaugh, L., Mustillo, S., Burns, B., Stephens, R., Baxter, B., Edwards, D., & DeKraai, M. (2007). Outcomes from wraparound and multisystemic therapy in a center for mental health services system-of-care demonstration site. *Journal of Emotional and Behavioural Disorders, 15*(3), 143–155.

Sutton, C. (2001). Resurgence of attachment (behaviours) within a cognitive behavioural intervention: Evidence from research. *Behavioural and Cognitive Psychotherapy, 29*, 357–366.

Swenson, C., Schaeffer, C., Henggeler, S., Faldowski, R., & Mayhew, A. (2010). Multi-systemic therapy for child abuse and neglect: A randomised effectiveness trial. *Journal of Family Psychology, 24*(4), 497–507.

Thorgersen, D. (2012) *Implementation of FFT in Norway.* Presented at the Annual Blueprints for Violence Prevention Conference. San Antonio, TX.

Tighe, A., Pistrang, N., Casdagli, L., Baruch, G., & Butler, S. (2012). Multi-systemic therapy for young offenders: Families' experiences of therapeutic processes and outcomes. *Journal of Family Psychology, 26*, 187–197.

Toth, S., Rogosch, F., Manly, J., & Cicchetti, D. (2006). The efficacy of toddler-parent psychotherapy to reorganise attachment in the young offspring of mothers with major depressive disorder: A randomised preventive trial. *Journal of Consulting and Clinical Psychology, 74*(6), 1006–1016.

Trevarthen, C., & Aitken, K. J. (2001). Infant intersubjectivity: Research, theory, and clinical applications. *Journal of Child Psychology and Psychiatry, 42*(1), 3–48.

Trowell, J., Kolvin, I., Weeramanthri, T., Sadowski, H., Berelowitz, M., Glasser, D., & Leitch, I. (2002). Psychotherapy for sexually abused girls: Psychopathological outcome findings and patterns of change. *British Journal of Psychiatry, 180*, 234–247.

Turner, W., & Macdonald, G. (2011). Treatment foster care for improving outcomes in children and young people: A systematic review. *Research on Social Work Practice, 21*(5), 501–527.

UK Children Act. (1989). London: HMSO.

UK Human Rights Act. (1998). London: HMSO.

United States Department of Health. (2001). *Evaluation of family preservation and reunification programs.* Retrieved from http://aspe.os.dhhs.gov.hsp/fampres94

Urquiza, A., & Runyon, M. (2010). Interventions for physically abusive parents and abused children. In J. E. B. Myers (Ed.), *The APSAC handbook on child maltreatment* (3rd ed.). Thousand Oaks: Sage Publications.

Van der Stouwe, T., Asscher, J., Stams, G., Deković, M., & Van der Laan, P. (2014). The effectiveness of Multi-systemic Therapy (MST): a meta-analysis. *Clinical Psychology Review, 34*(6), 468–481.

Vetere, A., & Cooper, J. (2001). Working systemically with family violence. *Journal of Family Therapy, 23*(4), 378–396.

Vetere, A., & Cooper, J. (2003). Setting up a domestic violence service. *Child and Adolescent Mental Health, 8*, 61–67.

Walton, E. (1998). In-home family focused reunification: A six-year follow-up of a successful experiment. *Social Work Research, 22*(4), 205–214.

Ward, H., Brown, R., & Hyde-Dryden, G. (2014). *Assessing parental capacity to change when children are on the edge of care: An overview of current research evidence.* Loughborough University: UK Department of Health.

Weisz, J., & Bearman, S. K. (2008). Psychological treatments: Overview and critical issues for the field. In M. Rutter, D. Bishop, D. Pine, S. Scott, J. S. Stevenson, J. Taylor, & A. Thapar (Eds.), *Rutter's child and adolescent psychiatry* (5th ed.). Oxford: Blackwell.

Westermark, P., Hansson, K., & Olsson, M. (2011). Multi-dimensional treatment foster care: Results from an independent replication. *Journal of Family Therapy, 33*(1), 20–41.

Wood, S., Barton, K., & Schroeder, C. (1988). In-home treatment of abusive families: Cost and placement at one year. *Psychotherapy, 25*(3), 409–414.

Worcel, S., Furrer, C.J., Green, B.L, Burrus, S.W. and Finigan, F.W. (2008) Effects of family treatment drug courts on substance abuse and child welfare outcomes. *Child Abuse Review, 17*(6) 427-443.

Zeanah, C., Larrieu, J., Heller, S., Valliere, J., Hinshaw-Fuselier, S., Aoki, Y., & Drilling, M. (2001). Evaluation of a preventive intervention for maltreated infants and toddlers in foster care. *Journal of the American Academy of Child and Adolescent Psychiatry, 40*(2), 214–221.

5

Attending to Infant Mental Health

Abel Fagin

Introduction

Infancy warrants special consideration in discussion of edge-of-care practice, as it holds the potential for both significant positive change and the highest risk of harm. Infants are entirely dependent on their caregiving environment for safety and nurturance; and their experiences here are key to their developmental trajectory and longer-term outcomes. Where these are negative or harmful, the consequences can be severe. In England, nearly half of serious case reviews relate to infants under one year old, whilst infants are over eight times more likely to die as a result of abuse and neglect than older children in England and Wales (NSPCC 2011).

It is now well-evidenced that the perinatal and postnatal period is a critical stage that influences life-long development (Grossmann et al. 2005). Therefore, planned and targeted interventions with families at

A. Fagin (✉)
London, UK

© The Author(s) 2016
L. Smith (ed.), *Clinical Practice at the Edge of Care*,
DOI 10.1007/978-3-319-43570-1_5

risk should begin as early as possible. Campaigns to promote early intervention such as The 1001 Critical Days (http://www.1001criticaldays.co.uk) show acknowledgement and vision to encourage better outcomes for infants. However, these have not yet been well integrated into public policy or reflected in service provision. Moreover, there is an uneven distribution of specialist services, resulting in a shortage of access to appropriately equipped and skilled practice to assist the most vulnerable infants, who are at risk of or experiencing significant harm.

It is also possible for infants to "fall through the gaps" when there are narrow remits around what services are able to provide. For example, where there are perinatal services available, interventions may seek to improve parental mental health but not necessarily focus on the quality of parent-infant relationship. Similarly, at-risk infants rarely meet the threshold for child mental health services, and it is often beyond a CAMHS remit to focus on parental functioning.

The context of working with families on the edge of care creates a distinct environment where traditional psychotherapeutic approaches do not wholly apply. This changes the nature of relationships with families and may challenge notions of what is considered to be therapeutic. Families are less likely to be actively seeking help, may actively resist offers of support and are often highly sensitive to conditions which reinforce mistrust, harm and unreliability.

This chapter will therefore highlight the need for early intervention with infants at the edge of care, what this may usefully look like, and will consider systemic factors that influence opportunities for change. The overall premise for approaches discussed is that trust, safety and understanding are the foundation for effective intervention, not only to facilitate change in the immediate family but in the quality of relationship networks around them.

At-Risk Infants

The psychological and developmental needs of infants who are being abused or neglected—or who are considered to be at risk of harm—are key considerations. It is well established that abuse and neglect have a range of significant negative effects, including those related to infants' development of secure attachment relationships, internal representations of relationships, their ability to manage stress, their ability to recognise emotions in others and their behaviour (Crittenden 1988, 1992; Pollak et al. 2000).

Primary caregivers play a significant role in emotionally and physically regulating infants, and this is associated with parents' own capacity for self-regulation (Tronick 2007). Disturbances in this area are associated with poorer developmental outcomes across a range of domains including attachment status, emotional wellbeing, social-cognitive functioning, behavioural adjustment, peer relations and educational achievement (Sroufe et al. 2005). Risk is heightened when there are communication errors, hostility/intrusiveness and discordant responses from the parent. For example, responding to distress by withdrawing or dissociating, with frightening or threatening behaviour, surprise, teasing, smiling or laughter, has been associated with poor infant outcomes (Lyons-Ruth et al. 2013; Beebe and Lachmann 2014). Disturbances in the infant's behaviour and relationship with a parent can be observed and are predictive of attachment from as early as 4 months old. Low levels (withdrawal) and high levels (hypervigilance) of self and interactive contingency between parent and infant are more likely to lead to insecurity. A mid range of contingency has been found to develop secure attachments and facilitates the infant to develop "feeling sensed and known" (Beebe and Lachmann 2014).

A parent's capacity for mind-mindedness or reflective function in relation to their infant (being able to accurately interpret what a child might be thinking and feeling) is linked with the quality of parental behaviour and is also an important factor for developmental outcomes (Fonagy et al. 1991; Meins et al. 2012; Slade et al. 2005). These become compromised when there is an absence of this capacity—often linked to parental risk factors. It is understood that parents who have experienced trauma, abuse and neglect may not have developed an organised system to manage stress when traumatic experiences are not resolved. This can lead parents to respond in an atypical fashion to their infant (Main and Hesse 1990). For example, parents may feel persecuted and threatened by their infant's distress and respond with punitive behaviour, whether this is motivated by a projection of their own feelings or is a means of asserting control in response to feelings of helplessness.

Contingent and attuned parental responses are not only more likely to predict secure attachment relationships but also "epistemic trust" (Fonagy and Allison 2014). Within a secure attachment relationship, these responses trigger learning in the infant as the communication is socially and personally relevant. "Epistemic trust" facilitates confidence in one's own experience and judgement. It is suggested that psychopathology is more likely to develop when there is a disruption in the process of attaining information from the social world. In these circumstances, new information may be dismissed or misunderstood as potentially harmful, especially when it creates a sense of vulnerability because the information triggers becoming emotionally overwhelmed. This may influence the degree to which individuals become more rigid in their thinking and have a lower tolerance for ambiguity.

There are a range of individual, relational and environment factors which may impinge on parental function. Examples of some of these factors are listed in Box 5.1.

Box 5.1 Factors affecting the parenting of infants

Individual Level
Infant prematurity, intrauterine trauma and drug exposure, disability, illness and congenital factors
Physical and mental parental illness
Intellectual disability
Parental substance misuse
Impact of intergenerational abuse and trauma
Stressful life events including birth trauma
Personality factors and adjustment difficulties
Adolescent parents
Relational Level
Domestic violence
Community violence
Societal and organisational abuse
Lack of personal and social support
Marginalisation and racism
Environmental Level
Poverty
Poor housing
Isolation and cultural dislocation

Intervening on parental issues separately is unlikely to be sufficient to reduce the risks surrounding the infant, but mitigating them may offer increased possibilities for positive change in the parent-infant relationship. Each should be understood in the specific context of the parent-infant relationship and the parents' capacity to protect and moderate its impact upon the child. It is unlikely that there can be a causal relationship between a particular risk factor and a specific outcome in the infant. Therefore, risks to infant development should best be understood in terms of how they influence and amplify each other. For these reasons, compared to traditional psychotherapeutic interventions, the primary goal with infants on the edge of care is to mitigate the risks to enable an environment that is safe enough, rather than focusing solely on the parent-infant relationship.

Organisational and Family Contexts

A decisive factor in edge-of-care work with infants and their families is addressing high levels of mistrust and fear of potential harm that can arise between families and professionals. The family's capacity to engage and collaborate on addressing risks can be significantly impeded by their previous experiences. They may have been misunderstood, abused and let down by important adults in their lives, who may have failed to protect them from harm. Individuals who have not developed secure attachment relationships are less likely to see others as benevolent and consequently may be suspicious of other's communication and intent. As stated, epistemic mistrust generates risks for the infant in caregiving relationships, but this also influences how families are likely to engage with professionals and the organisational system. At-risk families are more likely to be vigilant about professionals' intent to help and protect them, and this is likely to continue whilst they remain in contexts and systems that reinforce the view that the world is not safe and trustworthy. Mistrust may be further intensified by pressure or obligation for families to engage in organisational systems that hold considerable power and influence.

Creating an environment where families can explore new ways of relating demands more than a shift in their immediate interpersonal environments.

There also needs to be sufficient felt safety, understanding and emotional availability from the system around the family (e.g. extended family and social network, community, professional organisations). Without this facilitating environment, it is more likely that positioning will remain rigid and less amenable to address the presenting concerns, especially if this is a consequence of adaptive responses to experiences to date. Hence the suggestion that "it is a given (often ignored) that any programme that aims to improve the relationship between parent and baby can only deliver if it is embedded within a 'relationship-based organisation' where the quality of the relationships within the team match the quality of the relationships they aim to foster within the families being supported" (Balbernie 2014).

Working in an edge-of-care context often limits professional capacity to build the quality of relationships needed with a parent, despite best intentions. Clinical work with families and infants at risk is often highly emotionally demanding and intensive, as it involves identifying with the infant's vulnerability and helplessness. In organisational environments where there are limited available resources, the impact of work with high levels of risk, trauma and abuse is heightened. Common repercussions of secondary trauma/vicarious traumatisation include a tendency towards denial, avoidance, disconnectedness and lack of integrated thinking (Henry 1974; Britton 1981; Emanuel 2002; Wakelyn 2011). There may also be a tendency for professionals to re-enact family dysfunction, as well as protecting and avoiding recognition of extreme suffering. This may prevent organisational systems from effective engagement with families and being able to keep the infant in mind, particularly when there is a need to substantiate emotionally harmful interaction. For example, doubts can emerge about whether the predicament of the infant is severe enough, or interventions focusing on parents' own needs for care may be prioritised.

In these contexts, clinicians can play a vital role in co-ordinating networks and assisting decision-making with an infant mental health focus. There may be considerable variance in how individuals in the professional system identify and align themselves to the family, which may create conflict. There is often competition between the high needs and vulnerability of each family member for care and intervention. Some agencies may have different priorities for the focus of their intervention, or other services may overlap, creating role confusion and overwhelming the family with the number of people they are expected to engage with.

Regular reflective supervision with an infant mental health focus can be key to enabling practitioners to remain emotionally available and effective with families. Offering a dedicated space to reflect in a safe and trusting environment is essential, to conceptualise and understand the work and recognise the significance of one's own emotional responses to parents and infants.

Clinical Practice

Parent-infant assessments and interventions need to take into account the circumstances of the family and the resources, risk and pressures guiding decision-making. Utmost effort should be made to facilitate "good enough" parenting in as timely way as possible. Particular consideration is given to the infant's developmental stage for intervention and how this may impact upon future outcomes.

Parental capacity assessments focusing on the parent-infant relationship must therefore keep in mind factors which will facilitate optimal current functioning of the parent-infant dyad and the infant's future developmental trajectory. Assessment without intervention can be offered in exceptional circumstances, such as when an immediate risk is posed to the infant. Whilst this is sometimes necessary, it is less likely to offer an accurate representation of the family and may limit opportunities for future engagement and assessing capacity to change. The associated decision-making process needs thorough consideration and analysis, not only of the family circumstances but also whether the organisational system has (inadvertently) hindered the provision of a facilitating environment.

It becomes increasingly difficult when parents lack awareness around factors which may be causing harm to their infant and feel criticised when these are highlighted by others. Confronting the individual, social and environmental contexts that perpetuate risk can be highly challenging, and there may not be a "quick fix" solution. Professionals should be mindful that infants cannot be relied upon to be a force for change for the parent and that babies cannot wait in situations of risk due to their developmental timescales. It is common that parents wish to protect their infants from the harm that they experienced as a child. Whilst this may be a motivating factor, it is rarely enough in itself to shift behaviours and patterns of relationships (Ward et al. 2014).

The selected areas of intervention and assessment discussed below can be co-ordinated with wider casework in an edge-of-care context. Although intervention and assessments are discussed separately, in practice there is likely to be considerable overlap. Broadly, the degree to which these are drawn upon should find a balance between:

- Addressing risk, deciding on the immediacy of action and what should be prioritised
- Considering how to help the family and deciding what can assist them in the short and long term (without overwhelming them and impeding the infant being kept in mind)
- Factors that limit engagement and increase levels of mistrust.

Assessment Stages

Formal infant mental health assessments in edge-of-care contexts might be organised around the following stages:

First Stage

The initial stages of the assessment process may usefully follow a common clinical route (e.g. consultation, mapping social and professional networks, information gathering, constructing hypotheses and proposing focal points of assessment and possible intervention). Importantly, this should include an agreement on how and when information will be shared with the family and professional systems and when there will be opportunities for feedback. Thought should be given to the nature of introductions to the family by the link professional, commonly the child's social worker. It is conventional for the clinician to explore areas that the family wish to receive help with, to listen to their difficulties in a culturally sensitive manner and to empathically explore their understanding of the professional concerns and the impact these have had on them. With an infant-led focus, the clinician also begins engagement by communicating the value of the primary caregiving relationship with the infant. They may also relate directly to the infant, imbuing a sense of interest, sensitivity and curiosity about them. The clinician infers what the subjective experience might be like for the baby and imagines what it may be like for them in their relationship with their parent. This may rally parental investment in the child and may also start to give an indication of how much the parent is aware of the infant as a sensitive and responsive being. At this stage, it is important for the clinician to note what feelings are evoked in themselves and those involved with the family, as they might provide significant clues to the emotional life of the child.

It is important to liaise with the professional network and the family, to co-ordinate how the plans for clinical work will be sit alongside other parts of the assessment and intervention process. This helps to foster an environment of transparency, avoids overlap and develops a sense of reliability and safety.

Second Stage

Initial interviews with a baby's primary caregiver(s) are a central component of the assessment process. They provide an opportunity to explore their narrative of family life, background history and focal points for the assessment. Through an infant mental health lens, they may consider the circumstances of the conception and birth of the child, how the family have adjusted, how relationships may have changed between a parental couple and what the impact has been on siblings. The quality of the co-parenting relationship and its capacity to share warmth, co-operate, address difficulties and demonstrate a degree of child-centredness can provide indications to how the infant may develop within the context of this triangular relationship (Fivaz-Depeursinge and Philipp 2014). The clinician may explore how the impact of parental conflict, separation and loss influences the caregiving environment, which can be more demanding when one parent is considered to be the main source of risk—for example, due to mental health or substance misuse concerns.

Although it is recommended that a formal assessment of parental reflective functioning is completed, throughout the interview process, the clinician can gain insights into how the parent is mentalising about themselves, their infant and importantly how the risks impact upon their infant. If parents are presenting in a dysregulated or hostile manner, it may be necessary to consider how to reduce levels of stress or, if this is not possible, to be aware of the risks this presents to the infant.

The clinician should allow flexibility around whether the infant is present. For example, it may be wise to arrange alternative care for the infant when discussing sensitive or highly emotive topics, such as previous losses, trauma and abuse. If other children have been removed from the parent's care, there should be consideration of how this has been reflected upon, whether past risk factors are acknowledged with congruent affect and how their circumstances may have changed (Reder et al. 2003). Further assessment may need to take place if parents continue to have contact with these children. Whether this is the case or not, it remains a significant loss. Feelings about these relationships are likely to impact upon the developing relationship with a new baby, particularly if the losses significantly limit the parent seeing them as an individual in their own right.

A formal assessment of parental reflective functioning can provide an indication of the developing attachment relationship, and the findings can be usefully be triangulated with other assessment components. The Adult Attachment Interview (AAI) (George et al. 1985) and Parent Development Interview (PDI) (Slade et al. 2004) are commonly used. The AAI benefits from examining how parents are mentalising in the face of trauma, which is particularly relevant for this client group. Unresolved trauma and an absence of trauma-specific mentalisation in mothers with a history of child maltreatment have been found to significantly influence attachment disorganisation (Berthelot et al. 2015). The PDI benefits from a focus on the specific relationship with a child and has been evidenced to indicate attachment quality (Kelly et al. 2005). The strength of a parent's mentalising capacity can indicate the way in which therapeutic interventions can be tailored to need and whether more reflective or behavioural components should be emphasised.

Infant observation offers a reflective space which can allow the clinician to identify and resonate with the emotional and psychological life of the baby. It can be an opportunity to observe detailed sequences of behaviour and interaction in relationships and to consider their emotional and interpersonal meanings. This space can facilitate further reflection on the clinician's own feelings, perceptions, assumptions and hypotheses (Bick 1964). Observing may also enable the clinician to take an outside perspective with respect to how the parent-infant relationship is positioned in the wider systemic matrix (Briggs 1999). Traditionally, infant observation is non-participatory, although effort is made to instil the process with a sense of warmth, curiosity and interest. It can be helpful to offer a number of sessions if possible. Notes are not generally written concurrently, in order to immerse oneself in the role and reduce parental anxiety. However, the process of completing detailed notes after an observation can aid reflection and open up opportunities for in-depth analysis.

Videoing the parent-infant relationship enables a microanalysis of sequences of interaction which can be difficult to observe in natural settings. There are a number of tools which can be used to code interaction, indicating the level of risk and quality of the parent-infant relationship more generally. These include the following:

- CARE Index (Crittenden 1984)
- Parent-Infant Relational Assessment Tool (Broughton 2014)
- Atypical Maternal Behaviour Instrument for Assessment and Classification (Lyons-Ruth et al. 1999)
- Emotional Availability Scale (Biringen et al. 2000)
- Coding Interactive Behaviour (Feldman 1998)

Videos also provide an opportunity to offer a brief video feedback intervention during assessment.

The Strange Situation experiment is considered to be the most robust way of assessing attachment security if a formal assessment is required, although this can only be carried out when the child is between 9 and 18 months old (Ainsworth et al. 1978). In situations where the infant has been affected by prematurity, illness or other disorders, a neurodevelopmental and development assessment (such as the NBAS (Brazleton and Nugent 2011) and Bayley (Bayley 2006) respectively) can identify delays in the infant's development, capacity to self-regulate and attain physiological stability. The manner in which parents adjust and respond to their infant's condition, as well as utilise support and advice that is offered, is likely to influence the parent-infant relationship and future developmental outcomes.

Third Stage

The final stages of the assessment process are likely to have parts in common with standard procedures. These may include:

- An analysis of the available information to aid the construction a formulation and risk analysis of parental and infant need
- Realistic and attainable recommendations for intervention in the short and long term, and to indicate whether there are available resources to provide them
- Proposals on how the recommendations can be implemented, tracked and evaluated. Ongoing evaluation of parents' attributions about their infant, their capacity to mentalise and empathise with their infant's experience of harm and the degree of satisfaction and pleasure in the parent-infant relationship are important indicators of change
- A framework for how feedback and progress will be recorded and guide ongoing assessment of family's needs.

What is often specific to clinical assessments of parents and infants in edge-of-care contexts is making projective assumptions of an infant's developmental trajectory in their caregiving context. The reliability of these predictions may be disputed. Dilemmas frequently arise in balancing the infant's rapid need for changes in the caregiving context with a parent's need for longer-term intervention.

Interventions

A review of the range of parent-infant interventions is beyond the scope of this chapter. Whilst there are identified interventions for at-risk families, there is limited evidence of the effectiveness of interventions with infants on the edge of care, and the evidence of parent-infant interventions with high-risk groups has smaller effect sizes (Berlin et al. 2008; Toth et al. 2013; Balbernie 2014).

The success of edge-of-care interventions for this population is likely to rely on well-resourced specialist practice being situated within an engaged multi-agency professional network. Interventions should include a relational focus and be guided by changes which influence the quality of parent-infant attachment and the development of the infant's healthy self-regulation (Stronach et al. 2013). Creating accessible "ports of entry" can help families access vehicles of change (Stern 1995). The most effective interventions are likely to be multi-modal (Maldonado 2002) and supported within a professional network to match the complexity of need. For example, the New Orleans model (Larrieu and Zeanah 2004) seeks to offer a single access point to a multidisciplinary team and offers comprehensive assessment and treatment to infants, foster carers and biological parents. This team is embedded within legal, child welfare, mental health services, health and education services and assumes responsibility for co-ordinating care.

Separate interventions to address parental needs (as listed above) and family functioning (e.g. individual, couple, family and group therapy) should be co-ordinated to aid the success of direct work on the parent-infant relationship. These should aim to:

- Promote sensitive and contingent parent-infant interaction.
- Enhance the capacity to mentalise, particularly in the context of trauma.
- Address parents' internal mental representations of themselves and their infant.
- Develop epistemic trust in significant relationships.

Parent-infant interventions for high-risk families tend to be offered to single dyadic/triadic relationships, although are also offered in groups (Baradon 2016b) and parenting unit settings (Daum and McLean 2015). Considering intervention for both parents, even if separated, can enable possibilities for amicable discussions between parents to focus on their child's needs, which can have an important bearing on the child's sense of security and trust in adults.

Commonly, interventions that focus primarily on improving sensitivity have an observational and behavioural component. For example, video feedback interventions seek to reinforce successful moments of parental sensitivity and attunement with their child (Fukkink 2008). Other interventions seek to address change at a representational level and are guided by the assumption that unconscious processes and procedural memories influence caregiving behaviour (Fraiberg et al. 1975; Lieberman et al. 2006; Baradon 2016a).

Interventions which have both a behavioural and representational component will likely share an emphasis on improving a parents' mentalising capacity, by assisting them to understand communications, meanings and intentions that guide behaviour and interactive sequences. Some interventions, such as parent-infant psychotherapy, are more distinctive in their efforts to address communication errors and impingements in the caregiving relationship. Parents are helped to see their child as a unique individual rather than perception being clouded by figures from the parent's past and/or parts of the self that are split off and projected onto them. It also underlines the importance of addressing the impact of trauma on a parent's mentalising capacity. Interventions that involve exploring the links between the parent's and infant's subjective experiences, and how these influence their relationship, require that the parent has some desire to discuss and process difficult experiences and can tolerate associated negative affect, without placing the child at further risk. Parents who have a lower mentalising capacity, are less emotionally available, and/or are cognitively limited are more likely to benefit from strengths-based interventions that have an observational and behavioural component. However, this is not a clear-cut "rule of thumb", particularly when families require longer engagement periods that inevitably demand a psychotherapeutic focus.

One would expect that therapeutic gains would only begin when there is a sufficient sense of safety in the working relationship, and the immediate threats or risks to the family have been mitigated. A clinician's desire to understand, capacity to empathise and openness to the possibility of change can facilitate this, as well as easing up epistemic mistrust. Throughout the intervention process, the network should work to establish and protect the therapeutic frame. Communicating to the family that there is an appreciation of their strengths can enable more opportunities to discuss risks about the care of their infant in a genuine way. It has been highlighted that intensive efforts to engage families in edge-of-care contexts are imperative (Larrieu and Zeanah 2004; Osofsky et al. 2007). Broadening trusting relationships within a group context can also aid engagement in the therapeutic process. For example, the "New Beginnings in the community" intervention offers families involved with Children's Social Care the opportunity to work together and draw on peer support (Baradon 2016b).

Box 5.2: Case example: Charice Background

Charice (20) and Adam (2 months) were referred for clinical support by the Local Authority who had removed her previous son, David. He had been adopted when she was 17 years old, in response to concerns of physical and emotional neglect. Adam was subsequently conceived following a brief encounter with a man with whom Charice no longer had contact. There were concerns about Charice's "lack of bonding" with Adam and emotional neglect.

Charice's own history was of neglect and physical abuse in her birth family. This had led to her coming into care as a teenager. She maintained contact with her birth family and described them as being largely unsupportive and critical of her.

Initial clinical consultation with Adam's social worker offered an opportunity to analyse the historical information and create hypotheses on possible ways to engage with Charice and manage and mitigate the risks to Adam. The social worker shared that Charice was minimising and denying difficulties surrounding the circumstances of David's removal and believed herself to be the victim of poor social work practice. Charice did not disclose that she had previously had a child removed when screened by the midwife during her pregnancy with Adam.

In light of these circumstances, proceeding within the Public Law Outline (PLO) was considered by the Local Authority. It was agreed the Charice be given a window of opportunity to engage with interventions offered; however, this was closely monitored and reviewed within a short time frame.

Assessment

The clinician was introduced to the family by the social worker. Initially, Charice said that she did not want any intervention, although at the same time indirectly communicated a sense of her vulnerability and need for care. She shared intense feelings of loss and anger, particularly related to how she felt let down by her family and feeling persecuted and deceived by Social Services.

Adam was a small baby for his age and looked vulnerable and pale. He seemed floppy and sleepy and made only limited attempts to make contact. The clinician felt an immediate sense of concern about how Adam was exposed to the intensity of his mother's feelings and how he might be over-shadowed by grief surrounding David's absence. The clinician empathised with Charice's loss and anger and offered an understanding of how professional involvement had felt like an unwanted pressure. The clinician also communicated an interest in Adam's experience by commenting on his occasional bids to relate. Charice joined the discussion of how an interventive assessment could help her with managing David's loss, support her relationship with Adam and work together to represent an accurate picture of her family.

A reflective functioning assessment was completed. Charice made few references to mental states with regard to herself or Adam. Upon deciding on an overall rating, a category of low reflective functioning was considered to be the most appropriate.

Charice was not in agreement to be videoed, and this prevented a formal analysis of the parent-infant relationship and consideration of a video feedback intervention. A parent-infant observation was completed and used the PIRAT (Broughton 2014) framework to assist consideration of different dimensions of the parent-infant relationship.

Adam had occasional moments where he sought contact with his mother through eye gaze, vocalisations and making physical contact. He was perhaps somewhat self-sufficient and withdrawn. However he could communicate his wish to interact and have his distress attended to, although his discomfort often seemed to linger. There were brief moments when Charice and Adam shared warmth with one another, such as during a feed. These interactions were short lived and were followed by interactions which seemed less close and more self-sufficient. Occasionally, Adam seemed to avoid eye contact and zone out, and these behaviours may have been indicative of times where he felt overwhelmed and disconnected. However, these moments were only brief and were often followed by interactions which appeared more tolerable. Charice initiated and allowed body contact but with a degree of tension. She held Adam tenderly and often positioned him to make eye contact with her. Adam responded in a mixed way to these interactions, sometimes shifting his body away and disengaging or at other times being curious about his mother's face.

It was not clear that Charice's emotional communication and behaviour could easily be anticipated by Adam in the context of their interaction. Her emotional responses to him were mostly nonverbal, whereby she did not regularly articulate her own or his emotional states. She did mismatch his affect at times, particularly seeming that she was becoming more irritable with him when he was in a fussy state. There were times when her anger was unmodulated and Adam was exposed to this, however, she was able to direct this towards others rather than it clearly manifesting in her behaviour with him. When Charice presented as being dysregulated, the clinician began talking from Adam's point of view, making suggestions about how there were "such strong feelings from mummy's past that might be hard to make sense of". These interventions seemed effective in bringing Charice back to the present and rallied her wishes to be protective of Adam. She was able to move to more positive feelings and mutually satisfying interactions.

During feedback, the clinician offered an understanding of Charice's experiences of loss, rejection and lack of care. It was indicated how these feelings were still present for her and impacting upon Adam and relationships. Charice seemed willing to explore opportunities for help with the impact of these past experiences on her and Adam, and a formulation was developed with her and presented to the wider professional network. Charice's openness to receive help was seen as a positive step by the social work team. The clinician played a significant role in assisting other professionals to understand Charice's anger about being let down and deceived and shared the hypothesis that splits in the professional system might arise in response to this.

Intervention

In light of her intense feelings of mistrust of others, a New Beginnings group intervention was suggested, as this offered the opportunity to invite Charice into a different relational context where she might feel less criticised and persecuted, as well as reducing her social isolation by enabling her to form relationships with other mothers. The model's transparent framework for feedback was also felt likely to be a good fit for Charice. Progress during the intervention was compiled into a report which was completed collaboratively with Charice, including her views and those of the group facilitators. Ongoing social work input and family support work occurred alongside and helped facilitate Charice's attendance at group sessions.

In the first few sessions, Charice presented with an air of hostility and tended to not speak unless she was directly asked. Her narrative involved descriptions of past losses, told as if they were happening in the present and indicated a traumatised and unresolved state of mind (Main and Hesse 1990). The facilitators were highly concerned about Adam. He spent much of the sessions sleeping and appeared unresponsive. He was described by one of the group facilitators as "looking as if he was dead". Despite Charice's air of hostility and defensiveness, she opened up to the group and became very upset and tearful when talking about David. Charice seemed to yearn for the facilitators' focused attention on her and Adam. It seemed relevant that she would often pile her plate with food during the group mealtime and only start eating when it was time to leave, thereby delaying her departure.

The facilitators' interest in Adam, communicated with a sense of appreciation and emotional warmth, seemed to encourage Charice to initiate her own positive interactions with him. This in turn appeared to stimulate Adam. He became more vocal, curious and responsive. He seemed to more readily communicate a sense of enjoyment in his interactions with his mother and those around him.

As the group progressed, the unpredictable nature of Charice's hostile feelings was able to become an area of discussion. Charice acknowledged that these feelings might make Adam confused or upset and talked about how she tried to protect him from them. Charice said the group had helped her to think more about how Adam might be feeling. She felt her bond was becoming closer with him. Her anger and hostility subsided, although she continued to voice her beliefs about the untrustworthiness of social workers. There were no longer concerns about Adam's tendency to disconnect in a defensive way. He readily enjoyed contact with others and was adept in communicating his feelings and intentions. It was clear that his mother was the primary source of his affection, and he looked to her for comfort and support.

By the end of the group programme, Charice had developed meaningful relationships with other mothers and facilitators. She suggested that, like a snail, she was "still in my shell, but poking my head out to see the world". The social work team incorporated the feedback into their continued work, and it was agreed that the risk of significant harm had lessened. Professional relationships improved, but Charice was keen to be discharged and continued to report feelings of harassment. However, she accepted the offer of parent-infant psychotherapy. This provided an opportunity to consolidate therapeutic gains over a longer-term period and further reinforce flexibility in trusting others.

Alternate Care

It may be the case that there is no available option but to consider removal of an infant from their parent's care. Even though this may be in their best interests, infants are biologically primed to seek out a relationship with their primary caregiver and will therefore experience the separation as dysregulating. In the context of short-term alternate care arrangements, it should be noted that extended and prolonged periods of instability can compound developmental risk in infants who have already experienced significant adversity. Infants are also hindered by experiencing multiple caregivers who have differing degrees of nurturing care and investment in the child (Dozier et al. 2001). It is too often the case that infants face long delays within organisational and legal systems whilst decisions about future placements are made (Brown and Ward 2013).

Multiple infant-caregiver relationships therefore need to become the focus of assessment and intervention where alternative care is in place (temporarily or with a view to permanency), in order to ensure that a safe, stable and nurturing environment is provided as soon as possible. This may involve a myriad of complex systems, where the individual needs of biological parents, relatives, foster carers or adoptive parents are considered, as well as how the child is positioned.

Infants who have experienced poor caregiving and abuse are less likely to be able to elicit nurturing care from subsequent caregivers and may "lead the dance" in future bids for care (Stovall-McClough and Dozier 2004). For example, an infant's avoidant behaviour may evoke a rejecting response from the caregiver. Interventions have been developed for new caregivers in these contexts to help their infant to regulate their emotions, respond to their infant's distress and help understand the meanings of the child's behaviour (Dozier et al. 2005).

Whilst a period of separation may allow birth parents to focus on addressing risks that they and their situation pose to the child and may motivate them to seek reunification, the impact of the loss requires sensitive management. Reunification becomes more troublesome after separation if the parent is unable to manage strong negative feelings during contact. Lengthy periods of separation may also compromise parents' and infants' capacity to repair the rupture in their relationship, where increased feelings of unfamiliarity and lack of connection can be highly unsettling. Therefore, contact arrangements and the contact environment need to be psychologically informed and/or supported clinically.

When legal decisions are being made, the clinician may also play a significant role in sharing expertise about the infant's developmental trajectory and recommended interventions, indicating whether sufficient change is possible within their developmental time frame (Reder 1995).

Conclusion

Infants at the edge of care require specialist and intensive intervention that is co-ordinated within complex systems and tailored to individual need. This necessitates a collaborative, relationship-based approach by practitioners and the organisational and professional system, in order to influence change in the parent-infant relationship.

References

Ainsworth, M. D., Blehar, M., Waters, E., & Wall, S. (1978). *Patterns of attachment: A psychological study of the strange situation.* Hillsdale, NJ: Lawrence Erlbaum.

Balbernie, R. (2014). An infant mental health service—The importance of the early years and evidence-based practice. Retrieved from http://www.understandingchildhood.net/posts/an-infant-mental-health-service-the-importance-of-the-early-years-and-evidence-based-practice/

Baradon, T. (2016a). *The practice of psychoanalytic parent-infant psychotherapy.* Hove: Routledge.

Baradon, T., Sleed, M., Atkins, R., Campbell, C., Fagin, A., Van Schaick, R., et al. (2016b). New Beginnings in the community: A time-limited group intervention for high-risk infants. In H. Steele & M. Steele (Eds.), *Handbook of attachment-based interventions.* New York: Guilford.

Bayley, N. (2006). *Bayley scales of infant and toddler development administration manual.* San Antonio: Harcourt Assessment.

Beebe, B., & Lachmann, F. M. (2014). *The origins of attachment: Infant research and adult treatment.* New York: Routledge.

Berlin, L., Zeanah, C. H., & Lieberman, A. F. (2008). Prevention and intervention programs for supporting early attachment security. In J. Cassidy & P. Shaver (Eds.), *Handbook of attachment: Theory, research, and clinical applications* (2nd ed.). New York: Guilford.

Berthelot, N., Ensink, K., Bernazzani, O., Normandin, L., Luyten, P., & Fonagy, P. (2015). Intergenerational transmission of attachment in abused and neglected mothers: The role of trauma-specific reflective functioning. *Infant Mental Health Journal, 36*(2), 200–212.

Bick, E. (1964). Notes on infant observation in psychoanalytic training. *International Journal of Psychoanalysis, 45*, 558–566.

Biringen, Z., Robinson, J. L., & Emde, R. N. (2000). Emotional availability scales (3rd edition). *Attachment and Human Development, 2*, 257–270.

Brazleton, T. B., & Nugent, J. K. (2011). *The neonatal behavioural assessment scale.* Cambridge: Mac Keith Press.

Briggs, S. (1999). Links between infant observation and reflective social work practice. *Journal of Social Work Practice, 13*(2), 147–156.

Britton, R. (1981). Re-enactment as an unwitting professional response to family dynamics. In S. Box, B. Copley, J. Magana, & E. Moustaki (Eds.), *Psychotherapy with families: An analytic approach.* London: Routledge and Kegan Paul.

Broughton, C. (2014). Measuring parent–infant interaction: The parent–infant relational assessment tool (PIRAT). *Journal of Child Psychotherapy, 40*(3), 254–270.

Brown, R., & Ward, H. (2013). *Decision-making within a child's timeframe.* Loughborough: Loughborough University Centre for Child and Family Research.

Crittenden, P. M. (1984). *CARE-Index: Coding Manual.* Unpublished manuscript, Miami, FL. Available from the author.

Crittenden, P. M. (1988). Distorted patterns of relationship in maltreating families: The role of internal representational models. *Journal of Reproductive and Infant Psychology, 6*, 183–199.

Crittenden, P. M. (1992). Children's strategies for coping with adverse home environments. *International Journal of Child Abuse and Neglect, 16*, 329–343.

Daum, M., & McLean, D. (2015). Emotional neglect, system failure and the early years parenting unit. In M. Diggins (Ed.), *Parental mental health and child welfare work* (Vol. 1). Hove: Pavilion Publishers.

Dozier, M., Lindhiem, O., & Ackerman, J. P. (2005). Attachment and biobe-havioral catch-up: An intervention targeting empirically identified needs of foster infants. In L. J. Berlin, Y. Ziv, L. Amaya-Jackson, & M. T. Greenberg (Eds.), *Enhancing early attachments: Theory, research, intervention, and policy.* New York: Guilford.

Dozier, M., Stovall, C., Albus, K., & Bates, B. (2001). Attachment for infants in foster care: The role of caregiver state of mind. *Child Development, 72,* 1467–1477.

Emanuel, L. (2002). Deprivation x 3. *Journal of Child Psychotherapy, 28*(2), 163–179.

Feldman, R. (1998). *Coding interactive behaviour manual.* Unpublished manu-script. Ramat Gan, Israel: Bar-llan University.

Fivaz-Depeursinge, E., & Philipp, D. A. (2014). *The baby and the couple. Understanding and treating young families.* London: Routledge.

Fonagy, P. and Allison, E. (2014). The role of mentalising and epistemic trust in the therapeutic relationship. *Psychotherapy, 51*(3), 372–380.

Fonagy, P., Steele, M., Moran, G., Steele, H., & Higgitt, A. (1991). The capacity for understanding mental states: The reflective self in parent and child and its significance for security of attachment. *Infant Mental Health Journal, 13,* 200–216.

Fukkink, R. (2008). Video feedback in widescreen: A meta-analysis of family programs. *Clinical Psychology Review, 28*(6), 904–916.

George, C., Kaplan, N., & Main, M. (1985). *The adult attachment interview.* Unpublished manuscript. Berkeley, CA: University of California at Berkeley.

Grossmann, K., Grossmann, K., & Waters, E. (2005). *Attachment from infancy to adulthood.* New York: Guilford Press.

Henry, G. (1974). Doubly deprived. *Journal of Child Psychotherapy, 3*(4), 15–28.

Kelly, K., Slade, A., & Grienenberger, J. (2005). Maternal reflective function-ing, mother–infant affective communication, and infant attachment: Exploring the link between mental states and observed caregiving behaviour in the intergenerational transmission of attachment. *Attachment and Human Development, 7*(3), 299–311.

Larrieu, J., & Zeanah, C. (2004). Treating parent-infant relationships in the context of maltreatment: An integrated systems approach. In A. Sameroff, S. C. McDonough, & K. L. Rosenblum (Eds.), *Treating parent-infant rela-tionship problems: Strategies for intervention.* New York: Guilford Press.

Lieberman, A. F., Van Horn, P., & Ghosh Ippen, C. (2006). Child-parent psy-chotherapy: 6-month follow-up of a randomised control trial. *Journal of the American Academy of Child and Adolescent Psychiatry, 45*(8), 913–918.

Lyons-Ruth, K., Bronfman, E., & Parsons, E. (1999). Maternal frightened, frightening, or atypical behaviour and disorganised infant attachment patterns. *Monographs of the Society for the Research in Child Development, 64*, 67–69.

Lyons-Ruth, K., Bureau, J.-F., Easterbrooks, M. A., Obsuth, I., & Hennighausen, K. (2013). Parsing the construct of maternal insensitivity: Distinct longitudinal pathways associated with early maternal withdrawal. *Attachment and Human Development, 15*(5–6), 562–582.

Main, M., & Hesse, E. (1990). Parent's unresolved traumatic experiences are related to infant disorganized attachment status: Is frightened and/or frightening parental behavior the linking mechanism? In M. T. Greenberg, D. Cicchetti, & E. D. Cummings (Eds.), *Attachment in the preschool years: Theory, research, and intervention*. Chicago: University of Chicago Press.

Maldonado Durán, J.M., & Lartigue, T. (2002). Multimodal parent infant psychotherapy. In Maldonado Durán, J.M. (Ed.), *Infant and toddler mental health. Models of clinical intervention with infants and their families*. Washington, DC: American Psychiatric Press.

Meins, E., Fernyhough, C., de Rosnay, M., Arnott, B., Leekam, S. R., & Turner, M. (2012). Mind-mindedness as a multidimensional construct: Appropriate and nonattuned mind-related comments independently predict infant–mother attachment in a socially diverse sample. *Infancy, 17*(4), 393–415.

NSPCC (National Society for the Prevention of Cruelty to Children). (2011). *All Babies Count*. Retrieved from https://www.nspcc.org.uk/services-and-resources/research-and-resources/pre-2013/all-babies-count/

Osofsky, J., Kronenberg, M., Hammer, J., Lederman, J., Katz, L., Adams, S., et al. (2007). The development and evaluation of the intervention model for the Florida infant mental health pilot program. *Infant Mental Health Journal, 28*(3), 259–280.

Pollak, S. D., Cicchetti, D., Hornung, K., & Reed, A. (2000). Recognising emotion in faces: Developmental effects of child abuse and neglect. *Developmental Psychology, 36*(5), 679–688.

Reder, P. (1995). *Assessment of parenting: Psychiatric and psychological contributions*. Oxford: Routledge.

Reder, P., Duncan, S., & Lucey, C. (2003). *Studies in the assessment of parenting*. Hove: Brunner-Routledge.

Slade, A. (2005). Parental reflective functioning: An introduction. *Attachment and Human Development, 7*, 269–281.

Slade, A., Aber, J. L., Bresgi, I., Berger, B., & Kaplan. (2004). *The Parent Development Interview, revised*. Unpublished protocol. The City University of New York.

Slade, A., Grienenberger, J., Bernbach, E., Levy, D., & Locker, A. (2005). Maternal reflective functioning and attachment: Considering the transmission gap. *Attachment and Human Development, 7*, 283–292.

Sroufe, L. A., Egeland, B., Carlson, E., & Collins, W. A. (2005). *The development of the person: The Minnesota study of risk and adaptation from birth to adulthood*. New York: Guilford.

Stern, D. N. (1995). *The motherhood constellation: A unified view of parent-infant psychotherapy*. New York: Basic Books.

Stovall-McClough, K. C., & Dozier, M. (2004). Forming attachments in foster care: Infant attachment behaviours during the first 2 months of placement. *Development and Psychopathology, 16*, 253–271.

Stronach, E., Toth, S., Rogosch, F., & Cicchetti, D. (2013). Preventive interventions and sustained attachment security in maltreated children. *Development and Psychopathology, 25*(4pt1), 919–930.

Toth, S., Gravener-Davis, J., Guild, D., & Cicchetti, D. (2013). Relational interventions for child maltreatment: Past, present, and future perspectives. *Development and Psychopathology, 25*(4pt.2), 1601–1617.

Tronick, E. Z. (2007). *The neurobehavioral and social-emotional development of infants and children*. New York: Norton.

Wakelyn, J. (2011). Therapeutic observation of an infant in foster care. *Journal of Child Psychotherapy, 37*(3), 280–310.

6

Safeguarding Children with Disabilities

Pamela Parker

Context

Families of children with disabilities often face practical, emotional and financial challenges, above and beyond those of families with typically developing children. Parents may experience demands and pressures such as lack of sleep, attending frequent medical appointments, coping with challenging behaviour, interacting with a wide professional network and advocating for essential services. In spite of this, the majority of children with disabilities are well supported and well cared for. There is increasing attention paid in the literature to positive perceptions and experiences in families where a child is disabled. It is proposed that positive coping and adaptation are common processes in families of children with disabilities, whose experiences draw on and develop strengths and resilience (Hastings and Taunt 2002). Likewise, Greer et al. (2006) investigated

P. Parker (✉)
Cambridge, UK

© The Author(s) 2016
L. Smith (ed.), *Clinical Practice at the Edge of Care*,
DOI 10.1007/978-3-319-43570-1_6

the perceptions of Irish mothers of children with intellectual disabilities. They reported that the majority of women in their study saw their children as a source of happiness or fulfilment, strength and family closeness, personal growth and maturity.

The purpose of this chapter is to focus on clinical practice with families where there are less positive experiences, leading to safeguarding concerns for their child or children with disabilities. It is beyond its scope to do justice to the complexity of which terms should be used to describe people with disabilities. Sinason (2010) provides an account of how society has struggled with this. She refers to it as a process of euphemism, as words are brought in to replace others when terms begin to feel too raw. She also talks about the importance of remembering that abuse lies in the relationships between people rather than terms used. For the purpose of this chapter, the broad term children/young people with disabilities will be used. The children and young people in mind are those whose needs are beyond those of a non-disabled child of the same age and whose disabilities mean that they are likely to require lifelong support.

Two significant overview reports have informed the context for this chapter and will therefore be discussed in some detail. In 2014, the National Society for Prevention of Cruelty to Children (NSPCC) produced a report titled, "We have the right to be safe": Protecting disabled children from abuse (Miller and Brown 2014). This comprehensive review of the literature, covering prevalence rates of abuse in relation to disabled children, concluded that they are at significantly greater risk of physical, sexual and emotional abuse and neglect than non-disabled children. Included in the review were two key studies. Sullivan and Knutson (2000) undertook a population-based epidemiological study to establish the prevalence rate of maltreatment amongst children with disabilities in the USA. They concluded that children with disabilities are nearly four times more likely to be maltreated than non-disabled peers. They also report that children with behavioural and neurological problems are significantly more likely to experience abuse than non-disabled peers. The NSPCC report also draws on a systematic review and meta-analysis of observational studies to explore the risk of violence towards children with disabilities (Jones et al. 2012). The authors of this study conclude that children with disabilities are more likely to be victims of violence than their peers who are not disabled.

Whilst there are significant challenges with interpreting and synthesising some of the research in this field, these studies offer compelling evidence to support the view that children with disabilities are at greater risk of harm. The NSPCC highlights the importance of developing research in this area, giving more explicit consideration to the complexity of the subject, rather than treating disability as a dichotomous variable. They go on to identify key factors that increase risk and reduce the effectiveness of protection services. These include professionals' attitudes and beliefs about children with disabilities. The authors suggest that people struggle to believe that children with disabilities are vulnerable to abuse and that they are not afforded the same rights as non-disabled peers. Their signals of distress can be misattributed to their disability so that signs of abuse or neglect go unrecognised. The impact of abuse on children with disabilities can be minimised when professionals hold the mistaken and harmful belief that a disabled child is somehow less affected by domestic violence, neglect or emotional abuse than their peers. Children with disabilities are also more reliant on adults, giving increased opportunities for abuse to take place. They are less likely to be able to communicate what happens to them, understand what is abusive and know what their rights are. The NSPCC report also outlines potential issues with child protection services. It suggests there may be barriers to the identification of concerns and to delivering an effective child protection response, such as lack of holistic child-focused assessments and a reluctance to challenge parents/carers and professional colleagues.

These concerns should be considered in the context of a second key report in this area. In 2012, OFSTED produced a report titled, "Protecting disabled children: A thematic inspection". This concurred that disabled children are more at risk. The authors concluded that low-level risks were generally managed effectively through timely multi-agency early intervention. They reported a range of good practice across services for disabled children, resulting in marked improvements in outcomes for those children who were made subject to Child Protection Plans. However, it found that children with disabilities were also less likely to be safeguarded via Child Protection Plans. In addition, concerns were also highlighted in keeping with those identified by the NSPCC. For example, in child protection cases where the main risk was neglect, there were delays in recognising that statutory thresholds had been met. There was a lack of focus on parenting and what was good enough, and the child's voice and experience was often lost.

There is extensive UK guidance available through the Department for Education and Local Safeguarding Children Boards around how to overcome some of the challenges outlined above. However, very little has been written about the specific contribution of clinical practice to the safeguarding process, where children with disabilities are at risk of harm and on the edge of care. This chapter will therefore seek to outline possibilities for effective clinical contributions, drawing on relevant theory and practice examples.

Assessment and Formulation

The process of undertaking clinical assessments with families where one or more children have disabilities is highly complex. Multiple professionals from a variety of backgrounds are generally involved. Depending on the complexity of the child's health needs, more than one medical team may be involved, as well as allied health professionals, family support and special education services. Professionals may hold opposing views about what is in the child's best interest and what is the highest priority for intervention—with quality of life considerations sometimes being weighed against longevity. Parents may also have professionals involved due to their own needs.

Families have often been asked to tell and retell their story in order to gain access to services. It can be difficult to take a curious and challenging position in this context, whilst still holding a compassionate approach, keeping in mind the family's experience. Children's stories are often complicated by physical health needs, diagnoses and medical interventions. Whilst it may be reasonable to invite parents to take an expert position in relation to this, it is not reasonable to assume that all parents can or will give a thorough and accurate account of this history. Creative and sensitive approaches are therefore required to help families tolerate and benefit from the assessment process, whilst still ensuring that it is robust and thorough. As with all clinical assessments, making time to consider contexts of social difference will help to identify which aspects of the assessment are more or less comfortable for the worker to undertake with a family, so that important issues are not overlooked or avoided (Burnham 2011).

Finding a balance between considering biological, psychological and social factors in assessment can also be challenging, as families and professionals privilege different factors at different times. For example, the question of behavioural phenotypes has drawn controversy in the past, with critics suggesting that the field minimises the impact of psychosocial processes for children and adults with disabilities. There are well documented issues with attributing changes in personality, presentation or behaviour to learning disability, resulting in missed opportunities for intervention from a safeguarding, mental and physical health point of view (Michael and Richardson 2008; Senior 2009). This issue is frequently referred to as diagnostic overshadowing. In a safeguarding context, it can mean that indicators of abuse or neglect are left unchallenged or unrecognised, as professionals consider difficulties to be solely biological in nature.

However, caution must be balanced against the usefulness of accurate information about a child's diagnosis and possible phenotypic behaviour. Barnard and Turk (2009) propose that this has an important contribution to make when assessing children's presenting needs. In a safeguarding context, clinicians are well placed to bring extended knowledge of typical and atypical child development and to challenge inaccurate attributions of behaviour or distress to specific phenotypes or developmental processes. It is therefore useful to retain a respectful curiosity when information about diagnosis and phenotypic behaviour is presented as a fact, sometimes without clarity as to where and when a diagnosis was made. There is always a risk that inaccuracies can arise when children's narratives are being constructed between family members and professionals. This should be held in mind, particularly when the documented story is partial. It is also important to be mindful that documentation may be the only account of a person's childhood experience that is available later in adulthood, if their communication and learning disabilities are more severe.

The challenges of interrupting intergenerational cycles of abuse and neglect are well documented (Brown and Ward 2014; Appleton and Sidebotham 2015; Stalker and McArthur 2012). Evidencing neglect when children have a disability can be even more difficult. For example, practitioners working in a safeguarding context can get caught up in debates about whether the child's developmental delay is caused by organic factors or results from inappropriate or insufficient care. In many cases, it is not possible to know with any certainty how pre-birth and early experiences have impacted on the child's development, even when a clear medical and social history is available. However, this can provide extremely helpful information about the pattern of care and the child's development over time. If historical information is not available, it may be useful for clinicians to support the process of thoroughly assessing a child's development in the here-and-now over a period of time, being clear about what would be required of parents/carers to promote this and undertaking regular reviews to ascertain whether required actions are being undertaken. Contracts with parents are recommended to support this process (Brown and Ward 2014). These may include expectations around attending health appointments, accessing and using appropriate equipment, organising modifications to the home environment and providing appropriate stimulation. Psychologically trained clinicians can contribute to this through their knowledge of child psychosocial, emotional and cognitive development, as well as checking out what beliefs and assumptions are guiding practitioners' thinking in relation to risk and safeguarding actions. A multi-disciplinary approach is often useful, as this brings access to expertise in different areas of child development. Practitioners may also usefully comment on the implications for the child's social, emotional and behavioural development if changes identified in their circumstances are not addressed, for example, drawing on the growing body of literature linking neglect to a range of poorer outcomes for children (Bentovim 2009).

There is a small but growing body of literature to support the process of differentiating between the developmental impact of child maltreatment and underlying neuro-developmental disorders. Autism and Reactive Attachment Disorder (RAD) have received considerable attention in recent years (Davidson et al. 2015; Sadiq et al. 2012) due to the considerable overlap in core features between both disorders (Moran

2010). This issue has particular relevance in a safeguarding context. The *Diagnostic and Statistical Manual of Mental Disorders* (4th ed.) (*DSM-IV; American Psychiatric Association* 2000) and International Classification of Disease (*ICD 10*) state that a diagnosis of RAD should only be made where there is evidence of serious early neglect and maltreatment. Making a diagnosis therefore has implications for child protection services when a child has remained with the parents/carers responsible for their early care. Even when a child has been placed elsewhere, the diagnosis may have significant implications for their identity development and family relationships. Conversely, however, parents may experience blame or criticism for children's behavioural difficulties or developmental delay if issues are misattributed to attachment problems when a neuro-developmental problem has been overlooked.

The Coventry Grid (Moran 2010) was devised by CAMHS clinicians to systematically describe the qualitative differences observed in their work with children with autistic spectrum conditions (ASC) and those with attachment difficulties. Whilst this is not a validated, standardised assessment tool, it offers a useful framework when working clinically with children who present with social communication difficulties. Davidson et al. (2015) looked specifically at the issue of differentiating between RAD and autism using standardised measures. They observed a difference in the quality of social interaction between children diagnosed with RAD and autism, which was in keeping with the conclusions from the Coventry Grid. Structured observation was most effective in differentiating between RAD and ASC for children in this study, although there were a minority of children for whom this was not the case. Deficits were observed in this study between verbal and performance IQ in the ASC group, not present for the children with RAD, suggesting that cognitive profiles could also be helpful when considering differential diagnoses, although the authors caution that further research is needed. In a safeguarding context, this study has implications for clinicians working in this complex field and highlights the importance of thorough multi-disciplinary assessments drawing on structured observation, an accurate developmental history and standardised measures.

The process of getting to know young people as part of the assessment is crucial if we are to correctly and accurately identify indicators of risk, distress and possible abuse. There is a growing body of literature and guidance for psychiatrists and mental health professionals to support the process of identifying and diagnosing mental health problems amongst people with intellectual disabilities (Carlisle et al. 2012), such as the *Diagnostic Manual—Intellectual Disability* (DM-ID) (Fletcher et al. 2007). Although it is not necessarily our task in a safeguarding context to make diagnoses, this framework can be very useful in thinking about how to make sense of a young person's presentation and come to a wider formulation. Carlisle et al. (2012) also recommend that clinicians consider how a particular symptom or pattern of behaviour relates to what could be expected of a person of a given developmental stage, as well as thinking about how subjective feeling states might be communicated in the context of that person's skills and abilities.

The issue of recognising and acknowledging trauma symptoms in people with intellectual disability is particularly challenging and complex. The DM-ID has included adapted Post Traumatic Stress Disorder (PTSD) criteria based on clinical consensus. PTSD symptoms are increasingly well defined in pre-school age children and are included as a separate category in the *Diagnostic and Statistical Manual of Mental Disorders* (5th ed.; *DSM-V*) (American Psychiatric Association 2013). These descriptions of presenting symptoms may be more helpful in working with children with intellectual disability than traditional criteria. For example, it is recognised that intrusive thoughts may not necessarily appear distressing and may be re-enacted through play or behaviour. Avoidance may present as non-compliance. Dreams may be distressing and present but without recognisable content, and fear may be communicated through disorganised or agitated behaviour.

As for any individual, the experience of trauma is highly subjective. Therefore, clinicians must keep in mind how a child may have understood and processed events given their developmental level, strengths and protective factors. It is also important to hold in mind the impact of cumulative life events on psychopathology amongst children with disabilities, as the evidence suggests a clear association between social disadvantage, the number of adverse events they experience and mental health outcomes (Emerson and Hatton 2007). Research investigating PTSD amongst children diagnosed with mild to borderline learning disabilities indicates that symptoms correspond with those of people without learning disabilities (Mevissen et al. 2014).

There is a risk amidst this complexity that the child's day to day experience, personality, likes and dislikes are to an extent lost or diminished. Children can be playfully and thoughtfully included in the assessment process, using basic clinical skills and drawing on the expertise of colleagues—such as teaching assistants and speech and language therapists—to learn how each child can be most helpfully engaged. Observations of children in different settings can be very helpful, but there is a risk of assessments being done "to" children with disabilities rather than with them, if we are too reluctant to challenge ourselves to learn how to engage with this client group directly.

The task of collecting and integrating assessment information into a helpful formulation is a complex but crucial part of developing a plan to assess and understand risk. There are a range of frameworks used in social care to analyse and assess risk (Barlow et al. 2012), which integrate information from a variety of professionals. From a clinical perspective, social ecological approaches have frequently been used to understand families with disabilities in context (Seligman and Darling 2009). The Three Column Formulation model also offers a helpful framework for integrating developmental and medical information with understanding the processes involved in maintaining risk for children, such as family beliefs and coping styles (Carr 1990). The British Psychological Society Division of Clinical Psychology (DCP 2011) raises a number of ethical issues in relation to the use of formulation with disadvantaged groups such as children with disabilities. In particular, they highlight the need for formulation to be accessible to children and families, undertaken collaboratively and openly, and adapted to maximise their capacity to engage with the process where needed. This is a particular skill in a safeguarding context, when concerns about risk are to be shared openly with parents and carers, linked to interventions to increase safety. A sensitive and compassionate formulation, developed as part of an interventive assessment, can support parents and young people to engage meaningfully with services.

Family Life Cycle Stressors and Increased Risk

Carter and McGoldrick's Family Life Cycle Model (Carter and McGoldrick 1998) has been modified and adapted to consider the experience of families of children with disabilities across the lifespan (Seligman and Darling 2009; Turnbull et al. 1984). When considering the question of why a family has reached crisis at a particular point in time, this can be a helpful framework for exploring the horizontal and vertical stressors impacting on family life and possibly contributing to the presenting risk.

Seligman and Darling (2009) provide a thorough account of the potential impact of caring for a child with disabilities at each stage of the family life cycle. Each of these stages will therefore be considered in turn as a frame for discussion of associated issues. At the "Childbearing Stage", they identify getting an accurate diagnosis, making emotional adjustments and informing other family members as key tasks for a family when a child is born with disabilities. The majority of parents navigate this potentially very painful period in a way that still enables the formation of a secure attachment. However, from a safeguarding point of view, it is important to consider how this challenge can impact on the parent/child relationship. The period of time when a parent develops awareness of their child's difference or diagnosis can be traumatic and stressful, so that parents of infants most in need of sensitive attuned parenting may struggle to provide this. The experience of learning that a child has been born with a disability is often compared with the process of grief and loss (Blacher 1984; Foley 2006; Howe 2006). At each transition point in the family life cycle, parents may experience again those feelings which had begun to resolve, as the contrast between their child and non-disabled peers is highlighted (Goldberg et al. 1995).

The extent to which parents can resolve their feelings about their child's diagnosis has been shown to predict parental sensitivity and responsiveness (Feniger-Schaal and Oppenheim 2013). If parents respond to their disabled child as though they were the child they had hoped for pre-birth, the child may struggle to ever meet their expectations or experience unconditional love and acceptance. Similarly, if parents can only respond to their child through the lens of their diagnosis, the child's experience of themselves is restricted, their identity formation will be constrained and the reciprocity of the relationship may be significantly compromised. This in no way suggests a linear relationship between having a child with a disability and insecure attachment (Howe 2006). However, it does highlight the importance of ensuring that timely, well co-ordinated and sensitive support is available for parents during this period, offering clear information about diagnosis, support with communication and practical help to reduce stress.

Howe (2006) provides an overview of the literature regarding disability, attachment and maltreatment. This review concludes that, when parents experience unresolved states of mind with regard to attachment, this can be considered a risk factor for maltreatment for children with particular forms of disability. For some families, there is an immediate awareness of the child's disabilities, although there may still be a high degree of uncertainty about their prognosis and future development. For others, there is a period of uncertainty during which they may gradually question their child's development and responses to them as parents. At a time when they may already feel very vulnerable, parents may question their ability to connect with their child and struggle to make sense of the relationship they find themselves in. Infants with developmental delay may signal their needs differently to non-disabled infants, impacting in a reciprocal and circular way on parental response (Barrera and Vella 1987). If parents can respond to their children in non-defensive, mind-minded ways, this may be overcome. For parents who are already vulnerable, perhaps as a consequence of their own experiences of being parented, this can be extremely challenging.

For clinicians contributing to safeguarding processes for children with disabilities, this kind of dynamic and transactional model of attachment can provide a helpful framework for both considering parenting capacity and offering relationally focused interventions to address identified barriers.

The third task identified at the "Childbearing Stage" is informing other family members of the child's condition. Family and cultural scripts about disability play an important role in this process. For clinicians working in safeguarding contexts, it will be important to think with parents about the affordances and constraints of those scripts and how they might contribute to risk. For example, disability may be seen as a punishment from God or something that could be "cured" (NSPCC 2016). Parents may experience shame, distress and guilt as a result, which limits the extent to which they can access support and also impacts on their relationship with their child. This can also place an additional burden on the child to meet expectations and achieve what is expected of non-disabled peers.

At the "School Age" stage of the family life cycle, parents may be required to make decisions about inclusion as opposed to specialist, separate education provision. This is followed by "Adolescence", which is very often a time of challenge for families in general. For children with disabilities and their families, this may be a time of growing awareness about the extent and chronicity of their difficulties (Seligman and Darling 2009). Typically, the key developmental tasks in adolescence include separating from parents and connecting with peers, taking risks and exploring sexual identity. This may conflict with parents needing to provide personal care and supervision for teenagers with disabilities, resulting in both intrapsychic and interpersonal tensions. These may result in over- or underprotection, as parents struggle to find a safe balance. The resulting anxiety may lead some parents to resort to attempted solutions which are then seen as abusive and indeed may be harmful for their children.

The struggle to find a balance when protecting teenagers with disabilities is also shared by professionals and services. There is growing recognition of the increased vulnerability of teenagers with disabilities to child sexual exploitation (CSE) and the barriers to protecting them (Franklin et al. 2015). These also mirror barriers to successful adaptation within families such as infantilisation, lack of appropriate resources to educate young people or false perceptions about disability and sexuality.

The "Launching" stage, which refers to transition to adulthood, presents further challenges to the family system. The potential for stress and anxiety as a consequence of navigating and accessing services at this stage cannot be overstated. Parents may be trying to relinquish the day to day care of their chronologically adult "child", when many of their care needs haven't changed, in the context of limited service and community resources. Safeguarding concerns can arise at this stage when it is no longer possible for the young person's needs to be met at home, but parents find the task of separating difficult. In this context, the young person's wellbeing may be compromised despite parents' best intentions. Professionals may experience the parent as obstructive, critical or impossible to please. The parent's sense of guilt, failure and trauma may be projected onto professionals as they try to work on a transition plan which is consciously/ostensibly accepted by parents but unconsciously/privately rejected as intolerable.

Working with the Professional Network

Statutory guidance is very clear on the importance of inter-agency working to safeguard children (Department for Education 2015); yet barriers continue to arise in effectively sharing information and working collaboratively (NSPCC 2016). Whilst each professional is accountable for their own practice in this context, clinicians are often well-placed to take a meta-position and draw on systemic and psychological models to make sense of how organisational defences, contexts of social difference and beliefs about disability are impacting on the network's capacity to identify and manage risk.

The work of Isabel Menzies-Lyth on organisational defences is highly applicable when thinking about services for children with disabilities (Menzies-Lyth 1960). This important work describes how individuals and organisations can experience overwhelming and intolerable anxiety associated with the task of caring for distressed and ill people on a daily basis. In order to cope with this, defensive processes arise to make the task bearable. These ideas have been applied specifically in work with children with disabilities. Obholzer (1994) provides an account of working psychodynamically with a staff team in a special school for children with physical disabilities. He identified a number of personal and organisational defensive processes, such as splitting and denial, which served a function for the teams but created difficulty in delivering a well-integrated service for the children. Obholzer writes about the importance of being aware of the personal and organisational anxieties impacting on our work, so that functional, containing processes can also be put in place to manage anxiety and the defences do not become contrary to service delivery. In a safeguarding context, this approach offers a potentially helpful way of thinking about dilemmas such as why professionals who appear highly anxious about a child may nevertheless fail to attend key meetings; why different professionals involved with the same family have polarised views about risk; why discussions about the emotional life of young people with disabilities can feel trite and infantilised; and why it is that professionals become critical and attacking of each other's skills and competence, laying the "blame" for problems on one part of the system. These issues can arise for a multitude of reasons. Looking beyond the surface to question what function they serve for individuals and networks can be an important step towards resolution, so that the important work of the group can be carried out effectively.

Social workers and others in case management roles are often highly skilled at pulling together a network of people and managing meetings, so that the focus remains on the needs of the child and the plan to meet those needs. Clinicians taking a complementary, consultative position can support this process by attending to how the child is being held in mind, for example, by addressing non-mentalising or pseudo-mentalising (Allen et al. 2008), when these are impacting on the effectiveness of the plan for the child. Process comments can draw awareness to unhelpful defences and support people to keep focused on the task, reframing potential conflicts as shared challenges and dilemmas. Basic systemic interventions can also be very effective in helping the network to think about what beliefs are organising their actions at any given time. For example, it can be helpful to ask questions about what a child would tell us if they could clearly articulate their thoughts and feelings; what we imagine they would tell us if they were listening to our conversations; what conversation we would be having with a family if we were not talking about a child's disability and what possibilities would that offer for change; what if anything would be challenging about that conversation; whether the current arrangements for a child be acceptable for a non-disabled child and, if not, what needs to change; and who do we imagine the child would nominate from the network to speak for them and why. As unhelpful and inaccurate beliefs about disability are one of the barriers to effective safeguarding, these simple interventions have the potential to make significant differences.

Interventions and Ethical Considerations

In writing this, there is a dilemma as to whether it is right to present clinical interventions for safeguarding children with disabilities separately from discussion of interventions with non-disabled children. Clearly, children and families with disabilities have a right to the same range of evidence-based clinical interventions as any other child and family. The considerations here are therefore intended to augment existing approaches and highlight some specific approaches relevant to edge-of-care work, rather than proposing different models.

Families are entitled to the provision of additional support and resources to address the social and economic challenges of caring for a child with disabilities, based on assessed need. Incorporating social models of disability into safeguarding assessments is ethically very important, so that families are not further disadvantaged by clinical judgements about their capacity to parent, made in the context of discrimination and under-resourcing. Howe (2006) calls for the sensitising of health and social care services to potential risks and vulnerabilities so that appropriate preventative support can be provided for all families.

Positive Behaviour Support (PBS) is the evidence-based approach most commonly recommended for working with families to address challenging behaviour (National Institute for Health and Care Excellence 2015). Guidance has been produced on the provision of PBS for families of children with disabilities, also making reference to the emotional and financial cost of unaddressed challenging behaviour; which is a particular risk factor in edge-of-care contexts, as it can potentially lead to children being placed away from their families where associated risks cannot be managed at home. The Challenging Behaviour Foundation (CBF 2014) presents compelling evidence about the moral and financial imperatives to improve services for children with challenging behaviour at risk of family breakdown. Dilemmas can arise for practitioners working with families who appear unwilling or unable to engage with evidence-based approaches being offered to manage challenging behaviour. Specialist services may experience pressure to close these cases, the result being that the children most in need are not accessing the appropriate service. This lack of engagement may constitute a safeguarding issue where the child's quality of life and development is compromised.

How then should we respond as a professional network to reduce this risk? The clinical contribution to this dilemma may be to develop hypotheses regarding the barriers for families in accessing services, and to work within an interventive assessment framework to test these out and address them. Clinicians may consider the family's relationship to help and how this supports or constrains their ability to work collaboratively with professionals (Reder and Fredman 1996). For example, when parents believe that their children's disabilities are the consequence of medical neglect, whether this is in fact the case or not, this can impact significantly on their capacity to trust professional advice, whether medical or psychological. In these kinds of situations, clinicians may advise colleagues on how to approach working with the family. This is likely to involve making the dilemma explicit and thinking with the family about how to make those relationships tolerable for them, given their feelings of anger and loss. This requires a considerable level of skill and relational reflexivity on the part of the worker. A "team around the worker" approach may be required to support those who are directly engaged with the family to manage the transference and countertransference invoked. It can be particularly difficult to challenge parents in this context. Therefore, workers may also need support to think about how to clearly and sensitively state concerns for the child and possible consequences, if parents cannot engage with the services recommended.

When unresolved loss or trauma about the child's disability is identified as a key barrier to engagement, direct clinical work with parents can be very effective in helping them to process those feelings. Foley (2006) describes a process of reframing the inner representation of the child through finding some of the hoped-for child in the real child, separating from the significant lost dream, building attachment to and reinvestment in the real child, and recalibrating expectations. In a safeguarding context, Compassion Focused-Cognitive Behavioural Therapy offers a clear and helpful framework for connecting parental beliefs about their child, or their disability, with problematic behaviours such as avoiding clinic appointments or distancing their child from family life. It also offers a sensitive approach to challenging self-blame, shame and intrusive thoughts, which, for some parents, impact significantly on their own wellbeing and that of their family. In edge-of-care practice, this approach has the benefit of clearly linking the risk to the child with the intervention offered. It can also be quite readily woven into behavioural or family therapy approaches as required. Although there is very little attention to this area of clinical practice in the literature relating to families of children with disabilities, clinical experience suggests that this work has the potential to impact significantly on quality of life, whilst also reducing the financial cost of placing children with disabilities elsewhere, including use of specialist residential provisions.

Where relational issues are identified as the key concern, then interventions such as Theraplay (Lindaman and Booth 2010), Video Interactive Guidance (Kennedy et al. 2011) and Circle of Security (Powell et al. 2013) may be indicated and often require only minimal adaptations, if any, when working with children with disabilities. Interventions with particular applicability in safeguarding children with disabilities are discussed further below in more detail.

Theraplay

Theraplay is a play-based, relational intervention for building and enhancing secure attachment (Booth and Jernberg 2010). There is a growing evidence base to suggest that Theraplay can be helpful specifically for families of children with autism and pervasive developmental disorders (Lindaman and Booth 2009). A Marschak Interaction Method (MIM) assessment may be undertaken at the outset of this work, to guide practitioners and parents regarding which dimensions of parenting should be privileged in sessions. Formal Theraplay then consists of approximately 20 sessions involving the child, parent and qualified Theraplay therapist. A structured approach is not always required. For some parents, having an opportunity to use Theraplay activities, with the support of a compassionate, trusted professional, can be enough to help them experience their child differently and talk open about the struggles they have in relating to them. Parents often speak about the difficulty of relating to children who express themselves differently or appear cut off from their attempts at interaction. The therapist may also choose to engage in Theraplay sessions with the parent, if the assessment information suggests that the parent will not be able to connect with the child in a playful way without some additional support. Through these means, Theraplay can act as a bridge to further engagement of the parent with professional concerns and wider care plans to manage risk. It is important to bear in mind contra-indications for this work, particularly in a safeguarding context. These include concerns about ongoing physical abuse, recent sexual abuse, dangerous acting out behaviour, or parents unable to respond to their child's initiatives, even with support (Booth 2010). Practitioners must also be clear that the aim of Theraplay is to enhance and build secure attachments, which may reduce some difficulties associated with the child's condition, but it is not a treatment for disabilities or for specific mental health difficulties.

Systemic Family Work

Baum and Lynggaard (2006) have written about the application of systemic ideas when working with people with intellectual disabilities. In relation to family therapy, they highlight the usefulness of this approach for intervening with families who are re-experiencing grief and loss, navigating transitions and struggling with relationships with professionals. Family therapy may also be indicated when siblings are affected by the family's response to the child with disability or individuals are at different stages in adapting to the child's condition and require support with this. It is beyond the scope of this chapter to do justice to the literature on supporting siblings of children with disabilities (Emerson and Giallo 2014; Hartling et al. 2014; Tudor and Lerner 2015). However, it is important to note that the consideration of siblings is a recommendation from Serious Case Reviews involving children with disabilities. Opportunities to see the whole family together are therefore very important and helpful for keeping siblings in mind.

It can be understandably very difficult for families to think beyond the child's condition, or limited resources allocated to support them, when they have been struggling with the same difficulties over a long period of time; which is most often the case by the time safeguarding concerns are identified and the child is deemed at risk of coming into the care. Systemic approaches can support the family to widen their perspective on problems, taking a both/and position in relation to these. For example, parents may initially arrive for therapy with the view that the child's behaviour has deteriorated as a consequence of puberty and he/she is no longer safely able to live at home. They may report that they have tried all behaviour modification approaches possible and nothing has worked. Tracking the development of the problem over time, exploring different perspectives and inviting family members to speak from the position of the child can highlight other hypotheses and avenues for change. Similarly, parents may have opposing beliefs about how behavioural approaches should be implemented, leading to confusion and a lack of fidelity to the plan. Scripts about gender and adolescence may be impacting on parent's ability to connect with the child and relate to them as they used to. Parents or other systems' expectations of the child may have overtaken what is manageable for them, resulting in unnecessary and intolerable stress. There may be cultural pressures for the child to conform to particular roles which are not possible for the child, leading to excessive stress and tension. The child may be struggling to find ways to separate from their parents in the same way that typically developing adolescents might, due to being more dependent on their parents than their peers. Challenging behaviour may become a way of creating distance in the relationship. Including children with disabilities in family work, regardless of the nature or extent of their difficulties, thus offers hugely important information about communication, patterns and processes. Where possible, clinicians will need to work flexibly and creatively by meeting the family at home, school or wherever they can be seen together.

Box 6.1 Key points and recommendations for practice

The majority of children with disabilities are well cared for under difficult circumstances and there is increasing recognition of the positive impact of those children on their families.

Parents are entitled to an assessment of support to ameliorate the challenges of caring for a child with disabilities.

Timely, accurate diagnosis, followed by sensitive early intervention to support parents with adjusting to their child's condition, is critical for parents, particularly those who may be more vulnerable.

Children with disabilities are more vulnerable to all forms of abuse than non-disabled peers.

Professional networks are complex and may be vulnerable to adopting unhelpful defence mechanisms in order to manage the distress associated with thinking about the abuse of children with disabilities.

Professionals should be aware of the identified barriers to safeguarding children with disabilities and reflect on their own practice.

Children and families with disabilities are entitled to the same range of evidence-based interventions as any other family, linked to the assessment and formulation of risk.

Individual children should be at the centre of all thinking and planning and not overshadowed by their diagnosis.

Conclusion

Working clinically to safeguard children with disabilities requires a capacity to think psychologically and systemically about children, families and professional networks. Children with disabilities and their families may need support from education, medical, allied health and social work professionals to enable their children to live safely at home. There is an ethical and financial imperative to improve safeguarding and edge-of-care services for children with disabilities who are more vulnerable to abuse, more likely to become Looked After and more likely to be placed in residential provision than non-disabled peers. Clinical approaches have a key role to play in identifying and clarifying underlying issues of concern, what would need to change for a family to continue safely caring for their child at home, contributing to a plan to achieve that where possible, and supporting professional network processes to keep the child at the centre of decision-making.

References

Allen, J. G., Fonagy, P., & Bateman, A. W. (2008). *Mentalising in clinical practice*. Arlington: American Psychiatric Publishing.

American Psychiatric Association. (2000). *Diagnostic and statistical manual of mental disorders: DSM-IV-TR*. Washington, DC: American Psychiatric Association.

American Psychiatric Association. (2013). *Diagnostic and statistical manual of mental disorders* (5th ed.). Washington, DC: American Psychiatric Association.

Appleton, J. V., & Sidebotham, P. (2015). The child at the centre of care. *Child Abuse Review, 24*(2), 77–81.

Barlow, J., Fisher, J. D., & Jones, D. (2012). *Systematic review of models of analysing significant harm*. London: Department for Education.

Barnard, S., & Turk, J. (2009). *Developing mental health services for children and adolescents with learning disabilities*. London: The Royal College of Psychiatrists.

Barrera, M. E., & Vella, D. M. (1987). Disabled and non-disabled infants' interactions with their mothers. *American Journal of Occupational Therapy, 41*(3), 168–172.

Baum, S., & Lynggaard, H. (Eds.). (2006). *Intellectual disabilities: A systemic approach*. London: Karnac.

Bentovim, A. (2009). *Safeguarding children living with trauma and family violence: Evidence-based assessment, analysis and planning interventions*. London: Jessica Kingsley Publishers.

Blacher, J. (1984). Sequential stages of parental adjustment to the birth of a child with handicaps: Fact or artifact? *Mental Retardation, 22*(2), 55.

Booth, P. B., & Jernberg, A. M. (2010). *Theraplay: Helping parents and children build better relationships through attachment-based play* (3rd ed.). San Francisco, CA: Jossey-Bass.

Brown, R., & Ward, H. (2014). Cumulative jeopardy: How professional responses to evidence of abuse and neglect further jeopardise children's life chances by being out of kilter with timeframes for early childhood development. *Children and Youth Services Review, 47*, 260–267.

Burnham, J. (2011). Developments in Social GRRRAAACCEEESSS: Visible-invisible and voiced-unvoiced. In I. B. Krause (Ed.), *Culture and reflexivity in systemic psychotherapy: Mutual perspectives*. London: Karnac.

Carlisle, L. L., King, B. H., & Maerlender, A. (2012). *Intellectual disability (Mental retardation)*. In W. M. Klykylo & J. Kay (Eds.), *Clinical child psychiatry* (3rd ed.). Chichester: John Wiley and Sons.

Carr, A. (1990). A formulation model for use in family therapy. *Australian and New Zealand Journal of Family Therapy, 11*(2), 85–92.

Carter, B., & McGoldrick, M. (1998). *The expanded family life cycle: Individual, family, and social perspectives.* Boston, MA: Allyn and Bacon.

Challenging Behaviour Foundation. (2014). *Paving the way. How to develop effective service for children with learning disabilities whose behaviour challenges.* Retrieved from http://www.challengingbehaviour.org.uk/learning-disability-files/Paving-the-Way.pdf

Davidson, C., O'Hare, A., Mactaggart, F., Green, J., Young, D., Gillberg, C., et al. (2015). Social relationship difficulties in autism and reactive attachment disorder: Improving diagnostic validity through structured assessment. *Research in Developmental Disabilities, 40,* 63–72.

Department for Education. (2015). *Working together to safeguard children: A guide to inter-agency working to safeguard and promote the welfare of children.* Retrieved from https://www.gov.uk/government/uploads/system/uploads/attachment_data/file/419595/Working_Together_to_Safeguard_Children.pdf

Division of Clinical Psychology. (2011). *Good practice guidelines on the use of psychological formulation.* Leicester: British Psychological Society Division of Clinical Psychology.

Emerson, E., & Hatton, C. (2007). Mental health of children and adolescents with intellectual disabilities in Britain. *The British Journal of Psychiatry, 191*(6), 493–499.

Emerson, E., & Giallo, R. (2014). The wellbeing of siblings of children with disabilities. *Research in Developmental Disabilities, 35*(9), 2085–2092.

Feniger-Schaal, R., & Oppenheim, D. (2013). Resolution of the diagnosis and maternal sensitivity among mothers of children with Intellectual Disability. *Research in Developmental Disabilities, 34*(1), 306–313.

Fletcher, R., Loschen, E., Stavrakaki, C., & First, M. (2007). *Diagnostic manual intellectual disability.* Kingston: NADD and APA.

Foley, G. M. (2006). The loss-grief cycle: Coming to terms with the birth of a child with a disability. In G. M. Foley & J. D. Hochman (Eds.), *Mental health in early intervention: Achieving unity in principles and practice.* Baltimore, MD: Brookes Publishing.

Franklin, A., Raws, P., & Smeaton, E. (2015). *Unprotected, overprotected.* Retrieved from http://socialwelfare.bl.uk/subject-areas/services-client-groups/children-mental-health/barnardos/176121cse_learning_and_disability_policy_briefing_paper_england.pdf

Giallo, R., Roberts, R., Emerson, E., Wood, C., & Gavidia-Payne, S. (2014). The emotional and behavioural functioning of siblings of children with special health care needs across childhood. *Research in Developmental Disabilities, 35*(4), 814–825.

Goldberg, D., Magrill, L., Hale, J., Damaskinidou, K., Paul, J., & Tham, S. (1995). Protection and loss: Working with learning-disabled adults and their families. *Journal of Family Therapy, 17*(3), 263–280.

Greer, F. A., Grey, I. M., & McClean, B. (2006). Coping and positive perceptions in Irish mothers of children with intellectual disabilities. *Journal of Intellectual Disabilities, 10*(3), 231–248.

Hartling, L., Milne, A., Tjosvold, L., Wrightson, D., Gallivan, J., & Newton, A. S. (2014). A systematic review of interventions to support siblings of children with chronic illness or disability. *Journal of Paediatrics and Child Health, 50*(10), E26–E38.

Hastings, R. P., & Taunt, H. M. (2002). Positive perceptions in families of children with developmental disabilities. *American Journal on Mental Retardation, 107*(2), 116–127.

Howe, D. (2006). Disabled children, parent–Child interaction and attachment. *Child and Family Social Work, 11*(2), 95–106.

Jones, L., Bellis, M. A., Wood, S., Hughes, K., McCoy, E., Eckley, L., et al. (2012). Prevalence and risk of violence against children with disabilities: A systematic review and meta-analysis of observational studies. *The Lancet, 380*(9845), 899–907.

Kennedy, H., Landor, M., & Todd, L. (2011). *Video interaction guidance: A relationship-based intervention to promote attunement, empathy, and wellbeing.* London: Jessica Kingsley Publishers.

Lindaman, S., & Booth, P. B. (2010). Theraplay for children with autism spectrum disorders. In P. B. Booth & A. M. Jernberg (Eds.), *Theraplay: Helping parents and children build better relationships through attachment-based play, Third Edition.* San Francisco, CA: Jossey-Bass.

Menzies Lyth, I. (1960). Social systems as a defence against anxiety: An empirical study of the nursing system of a general hospital. *The Social Engagement of Social Science: A Tavistock Anthology, 1*, 1–625.

Mevissen, L., Barnhoorn, E., Didden, R., Korzilius, H. P. L. M., & De Jongh, A. (2014). Clinical assessment of PTSD in children with mild to borderline intellectual disabilities: A pilot study. *Developmental Neurorehabilitation, 17*(1), 16–23.

Michael, J., & Richardson, A. (2008). Healthcare for all: The independent inquiry into access to healthcare for people with learning disabilities. *Tizard Learning Disability Review, 13*(4), 28–34.

Miller, D., & Brown, J. (2014). *"We have the right to be safe": Protecting disabled children from abuse: Main report.* Retrieved from https://www.nspcc.org.uk/globalassets/documents/research-reports/right-safe-disabled-children-abuse--summary.pdf

Moran, H. (2010). Clinical observations of the differences between children on the autism spectrum and those with attachment problems: The Coventry Grid. *Good Autism Practice (GAP), 11*(2), 46–59.

National Institute for Health and Care Excellence. (2015). *Challenging behaviour and learning disabilities: Prevention and interventions for people with learning disabilities whose behaviour challenges.* Retrieved from https://www.nice.org.uk/guidance/ng11

NSPCC. (2016). *Deaf and disabled children: Learning from case reviews. Summary of risk factors and learning for improved practice when working with deaf and disabled children.* Retrieved from https://www.nspcc.org.uk/preventing-abuse/child-protection-system/case-reviews/learning/

Obholzer, A. (1994). Fragmentation and integration in a school for physically handicapped children. In A. Obholzer & V. Z. Roberts (Eds.), *The unconscious at work. Individual and organisational stress in the human sciences.* London: Routledge.

OFSTED. (2012). *Protecting disabled children: A thematic inspection.* Retrieved from https://www.gov.uk/government/publications/protecting-disabled-children-thematic-inspection

Powell, B., Cooper, G., Hoffman, K., & Marvin, B. (2013). *The circle of security intervention: Enhancing attachment in early parent-child relationships.* New York: Guilford.

Reder, P., & Fredman, G. (1996). The relationship to help: Interacting beliefs about the treatment process. *Clinical Child Psychology and Psychiatry, 1*(3), 457–467.

Sadiq, F. A., Slator, L., Skuse, D., Law, J., Gillberg, C., & Minnis, H. (2012). Social use of language in children with reactive attachment disorder and autism spectrum disorders. *European Child and Adolescent Psychiatry, 21*(5), 267–276.

Seligman, M., & Darling, R. B. (2009). *Ordinary families, special children: A systems approach to childhood disability.* New York: Guilford.

Senior, K. (2009). Greater needs, limited access. *Bulletin of the World Health Organisation, 87,* 252–253.

Sinason, V. (2010). *Mental handicap and the human condition: An analytical approach to intellectual disability.* London: Free Association Books.

Stalker, K., & McArthur, K. (2012). Child abuse, child protection and disabled children: A review of recent research. *Child Abuse Review, 21*(1), 24–40.

Sullivan, P. M., & Knutson, J. F. (2000). Maltreatment and disabilities: A population-based epidemiological study. *Child Abuse and Neglect, 24*(10), 1257–1273.

Tudor, M. E., & Lerner, M. D. (2015). Intervention and support for siblings of youth with developmental disabilities: A systematic review. *Clinical Child and Family Psychology Review, 18*(1), 1–23.

Turnbull, A. P., Summers, J. A., & Brotherson, M. J. (1984). *Working with families with disabled members: A family systems approach.* Lawrence, KS: Research and Training Center on Independent Living, University of Kansas.

World Health Organisation. (1992). *The ICD-10 classification of mental and behavioural disorders: Clinical descriptions and diagnostic guidelines.* Geneva: World Health Organisation.

7

Late Entries into Care

Stella Christofides

Introduction

Children who enter care in adolescence have consistently been found to have worse outcomes than those who become Looked After at a younger age. Whilst there are many young people who go on to have positive outcomes, disparities compared to younger children include a more disrupted experience of care, poorer educational achievement and more difficulties when leaving care subsequently. Therefore, the needs of this group, and clinical perspectives on these, bear specific consideration.

The proportion of older children entering care is significant. UK Department for Education figures (Department for Education 2015a) indicate that around 30 % of children entering care are currently aged 10–15 years old, and another 16 % are aged 16 or over. These young people's circumstances can be more complex than those of younger children.

S. Christofides (✉)
London, UK

© The Author(s) 2016
L. Smith (ed.), *Clinical Practice at the Edge of Care*,
DOI 10.1007/978-3-319-43570-1_7

Often more risks are present, including parental, peer, and individual factors. Difficulties may have been present for longer and there is often a substantial history of experiencing abuse and neglect, which may present in different ways over time. For example, parental neglect of adolescents can present differently to neglect of younger children, including a lack of supervision and extending to pressure on the young person to leave home. Several other risk issues are also disproportionally present for this age group, including child sexual exploitation, offending behaviours, and homelessness. By the age of 14 years, common factors precipitating entry into care therefore include a mixture of acute family stress, family dysfunction, and socially unacceptable behaviour. Characteristics of adolescent development including impulsivity, emotional highs and lows, and sensitivity to peer influence, may also play a part. These can contribute to risks such as self-harm, gang involvement, violence, and exploitation (Hanson and Holmes 2014). A cumulative effect of exposure to adversity and predisposing risk factors, and increased opportunities for risk-taking, arguably makes some young people more vulnerable to further harm. Hence, diverse risk factors for individual adolescents mean that clusters of triggers may contribute to imminent risk requiring potential accommodation away from home.

As a result, it is important to consider both the opportunities and rationale for interventions at this relatively late stage of a child's development. Adolescence can be a time of opportunity and agency in a young person's life (Hanson and Holmes 2014). Current edge-of-care systems do not always meet the needs of this group, but there are promising examples of good practice emerging, including intensive family and residential interventions. Indeed, there is an increasing movement towards considering the specific needs of adolescents, including a number of reviews from both statutory services (Department for Education 2014; Ofsted 2011) and charities (Action for Children 2015). UK Local Authority provision of distinct services for adolescents at the edge of care has also emerged, supported partly by the recent introduction of the Department for Education Innovation Fund (Department for Education 2014).

Whilst these services tend to aim to prevent young people entering care, in other countries—such as Germany, Denmark, and France—this boundary is less clearly demarcated, as placement away from home or shared care for adolescents is conceptualised as a more positive choice amongst options for intervention with a child and family (Bowyer and Wilkinson 2013). Whilst professionals and systems aim to prevent young people entering care where possible, the act of going into care may sometimes be psychologically protective or necessary. Recent initiatives have found that periods of respite, or a residential stay, can be a helpful means of provoking change and act as interventions in themselves, if planned and implemented effectively (Dixon et al. 2015). Conversely, delaying entry into the care system for some children may be extremely costly, both in terms of increasing damage to the child's emotional and social development, increasing difficulty in meeting their needs, delaying permanence, and leading to increased cost of placements (National Children's Bureau 2013).

Due to the diversity of need in adolescents, there is therefore an argument that the focus for clinical intervention should be on developing care pathways that best meet the needs of each young person and their longer term wellbeing, rather than shifting between prevention or permanency approaches (Hannon et al. 2010).

Towards a Clinical Perspective

In this context, a clinical perspective can help to make sense of complex situations, using individualised case formulation as a tool for making evidence-based theory-to-practice links. This understanding can then be used to target support and interventions most effectively, in what are often anxious and exhausted systems. If interventions do not accurately target the relevant factors which led to crisis points, then it is unlikely that positive changes will be effective or sustained. It is therefore useful to consider key clinical risk factors associated with late entries into care and how to prioritise, target, and deliver interventions to address these in a coordinated and considered manner. There are also ways in which clinical roles can be more effective when working with multi-agency partners and contexts, as well as in direct work with young people and their families.

Clinical understandings can be particularly useful in shedding light on complex family systems or to make sense of a young person's behaviour, particularly when this is difficult to sanction. For example, a clinical formulation using a bio-psycho-social approach might assist by making psychologically informed connections between early experiences (such as witnessing domestic violence) and current behaviour (such as sexually harmful behaviour or risk-taking). A clinical perspective can then guide effective intervention and support the system to provide more appropriate and targeted responses to need.

Priorities set at a strategic level, such as reducing financial cost or managing a shortage of suitable foster placements, can understandably distract from holding young people's psychological and developmental experiences at the centre of decision-making and practice development. Day-to-day pressures on frontline workers responsible for risk management can also mean that the emotional wellbeing of young people can be de-prioritised as a focus for action. This is despite the fact that, on entering care, young people have described feeling sad, upset, worried, anxious, scared, surprised, confused, rejected, abandoned, angry, and relieved. Once in care, some described additional feelings of happiness or excitement, whilst others also felt lonely. Many reported anxiety at the prospect of returning home (Farmer et al. 2015). Applying psychological concepts including adjustment to loss, and the function of attachment-related behaviours, can assist in providing the right kind of support at the right time and avoiding "knee-jerk" responses to a young person's emotional state or behaviour that can be better understood as part of their journey of coping and adjustment.

Developmental Influences

Children with developmental, emotional, and behavioural difficulties are over-represented in the care system (Jones et al. 2011). Additional difficulties in accessing appropriate specialist support both cause and result from unstable placement journeys (Hannon et al. 2010). Children who have experienced trauma such as abuse and neglect are at increased risk of a range of mental health difficulties including depression, post-traumatic stress disorder, and borderline personality disorder in adulthood (Kendall-Tackett 2002; Howe 2005).

The psychological impact of chronic abuse and neglect may underlie some of the acute triggers for concern common in adolescence, such as family conflict and behavioural difficulties, and this may increase iteratively over time (Institute of Public Care 2015). Contrary to the assumption that children become more resilient as they mature, it is proposed that maltreatment in adolescence is no less harmful than at a younger age. Evidence highlights the cumulative developmental and psychological harm of risks such as exposure to domestic violence and neglect (Hanson and Holmes 2014). Older children are also open to a wider range of risks; at age 14 they are most at risk of "poly-victimisation" (having multiple experiences of different kinds of abuse), especially those in dangerous and disrupted community and family contexts (Finkelhor et al. 2009).

For adolescents on the edge of care, understanding behaviours which place the young person or others at risk is essential in establishing safety and working towards stabilisation. When faced with young people who have experienced difficult early relational experiences, an attachment framework can help to provide an alternative explanation for problematic behaviour. High-risk behaviour tends to activate the attachment system of caregivers and others, triggering care-enhancing or care-reduction behaviours (Rogers and Budd 2015). From this perspective, the child may have developed high-risk behaviours as an adaptive response in order to elicit care from a parent or have become hyper-vigilant to increase safety in a chaotic environment. Whilst this may have been functional in early life, in other contexts or as the child develops physically into adolescence, the behaviour is no longer adaptive and is viewed as challenging or aggressive. Identifying the need behind the behaviour is important to ensure that the young person receives the care needed, whilst also avoiding inadvertent reinforcement of the problematic behaviour.

It is also the case that young people with emotional, behavioural, physical, and learning disabilities are at greater risk of late entries into care (Institute of Public Care 2015). This includes those on the autistic spectrum or with a diagnosis of attention deficit hyperactivity disorder (ADHD). Many have been previously adequately cared for by their families prior to difficulties developing during adolescence. Those with parents who have mental health problems are at particular risk of late accommodation, possibly as these make caregiving roles more challenging as children's needs become more complex (Asmussen et al. 2012). Some children's needs may become heightened during adolescence when demands of the school or social environment increase, alongside cognitive and pubertal changes. For example, the transition to secondary school can be particularly unsettling for children with additional needs and can be associated with school refusal or an increase in behavioural problems. In addition, changes during the family life cycle may not follow the expected path, for example, with issues emerging around separation and independence placing strain on family relationships.

The issue of undiagnosed neuro-developmental and cognitive difficulties, and their impact on young people on the edge of care, is also an issue in clinical practice. Some parents may have sought help previously from the young person's school or GP, but children's difficulties have been attributed solely to an unstable family environment or poor parenting. In such circumstances, parents can feel blamed and not listened to, leading to distrust and fear of services (Farmer et al. 2015). Parents may also have taken forward an understanding that their child is intentionally "naughty", particularly when difficulties have an impact in school, leading to increasingly punitive rather than caring responses.

Educational progress is often impacted by family, emotional, and behavioural circumstances. However, education and qualifications can serve as a protective factor, for example, in helping young people lead law-abiding lives and so reducing the likelihood of contact with the criminal justice system (Taylor 2016).

The impact of harm in early childhood can also manifest in different ways in adolescence. Children exposed to domestic violence may become hyper-vigilant to perceived danger as a survival strategy and so later may be at increased risk of gang involvement due to the perceived protective benefits (Pitts 2013). Young people may form and remain in abusive relationships in an attempt to meet an earlier unmet need to be loved or noticed (Hanson and Holmes 2014). Adolescents may be at greater risk of self-harm and substance use as available coping responses to life stressors than younger children, adding to concern. Taking the time to try to understand these often unspoken drivers to problematic "choices" can help with identifying healthier or safer ways for young people's needs to be met.

Family Factors

A key transitional process for a family with an adolescent child may be conceptualised systemically as involving a shift in family boundaries (Carter and McGoldrick 2005). This requires the adjustment of parent-child relationships, to enable adolescents to move in and out of the relational system more flexibly. Parenting responses also need to adapt in order to meet adolescents' changing characteristics (Dixon et al. 2015) and attachment-related needs (Byng-Hall 1995). A clinical lens can help to consider how a young person and their wider family may have come to feel stuck or powerless to change. For example, this may involve looking at the family history, patterns of interaction, and for exceptions to difficulties, including relationships and experiences that enable ambition, confidence, and change (Selekman 2005).

Family adjustment may be problematic when parent-child relationships are rigid or complex, including patterns of enmeshment and conflict, parentification, and co-dependency, issues that may have their origins in earlier family or parenting difficulties as well as those evident currently. These may in turn contribute to presenting difficulties such as school refusal, self-harm and suicidality, and somatic difficulties (amongst other mental health concerns). Sibling relationships may also be complex and when problematic can be characterised by rivalry, conflict, aggression, and dominance (Lord and Borthwick 2014).

There may also be concerns raised when societal expectations are not met, for example, if a child continues to sleep in the parent's bedroom. Such behaviours may not be viewed as problematic for the family, or serve a psychological function, which may be usefully understood in order to inform interventions. Likewise, a young person's aggressive or difficult behaviour can often be understood as psychological sequelae of high levels of mistrust, criticism, fear, and rejection within family relationships (Farmer et al. 2015).

Intergenerational conflict related to expectations around roles and responsibilities may also manifest in adolescence, including the influence of transcultural contexts (Singh and Clarke 2006). Dilemmas can occur when there is conflict between parental authority and the adolescent's refusal to take part in a cultural practice, a professional belief that the practice would harm the child, and differing parent-child relational norms. For example, a child's behaviour may be labelled as "parentified" when they take a nurturing role towards their mother, which may be permitted or valued in some cultures (Maitra 2000).

Often, exploration of a parent's own history of being parented, of relationships, or their experiences at school, can lead to a better understanding of how a parent may be trying to compensate. Parents who have been able to notice and understand how their experiences have affected them are less likely to perpetuate unhelpful trans-generational patterns of responding to difficulties (Howe 2005).

In edge-of-care practice, there is a particular dilemma when working with families where parenting is sub-optimal and difficult to change over a long period of time, but fluctuating around or below the threshold for children's removal into care. In these cases, building on a young person's resilience may be one way to minimise associated harm. Interventions to support adolescents' resilience can build on their developing skills in self-reflection and conscious decision-making, differentiation of their own identity from that of the family, and building supportive relationships with peers and others. This is most likely to be effective when it also addresses risks inherent in the community and peer group such as substance use or gang-related behaviours (Orbke and Smith 2013). A focus on resilience may feel uncomfortable as an intervention path when significant concerns about family functioning are ongoing. In these circumstances, a clinical voice and analysis can help to ensure that potential harm, especially emotional harm such as internalising symptoms, continues to be considered by the system as part of ongoing risk assessment.

Community Factors

During adolescence, peer relationships become more influential and young people tend to have greater independence and mobility in their community. As noted, there has been an increase in the recognition of associated risks, including child sexual exploitation, going missing from home, and exposure to violence (Hanson and Holmes 2014) both in the home and in couple relationships (Barter et al. 2009). Young people may also start to come into contact with the criminal justice system, which significantly increases the risk that a young person may become Looked After in secure residential settings (Rogers and Budd 2015).

Parenting can assist young people to navigate community level risks. Whilst a flexible parenting style may be seen as preferable in safer communities, firm rules and a detailed awareness of children's whereabouts can be protective in high-risk environments (Hill et al. 2001). Factors associated with protecting young people from involvement in crime and substance use in high-risk areas include parental affection, involvement, and pro-education values. Conversely, parents who feel disempowered or are preoccupied by their own difficulties can provide less of a buffer to external pressures.

In an American study, girls who were involved in gangs were more likely to have been sexually abused, to experience family conflict, and to run away from home, compared to girls who were able to resist pressure to join (De La Rue and Espelage 2014). Those with family members who were gang-involved were also more likely to be part of a gang themselves. The associated impact of early trauma, including sexual abuse, highlights a need to understand the multiple influences on a young person's behaviour and therefore to seek to address trauma from a therapeutic angle, as well as to consider safety planning in the here and now.

Children known to services due to child sexual exploitation (CSE) also have high levels of contact with the Youth Justice system, with almost half of boys and more than a quarter of girls having criminal records (Cockbain et al. 2014). A recent enquiry concluded that adult perpetrators were aware of and taking advantage of children's vulnerability, alongside a failure of agencies to act on disclosures made by young people effectively (Jay 2014). Key risk factors associated with children who were exploited were missing episodes, alcohol or substance abuse, and mental health difficulties (which were exacerbated or caused by the abuse). Difficulties for young people in accessing appropriate mental health services were also evident (Jay 2014). Over a third of young people affected were previously known to children's services due to abuse or neglect, with high levels of domestic violence, parental substance use, and mental health problems. However, Fox (2016) draws attention to the diversity of children who may be at risk of sexual exploitation, including boys, those identifying as lesbian, gay, bisexual, trans, queer, or questioning (LGBTQ), young people with disabilities, and those from a range of ethnic minorities.

There is also a blurring of victim and perpetrator roles where CSE is a risk factor. Young people can become involved in recruiting or exploiting others, sometimes as part of a pattern of violent offending, and young people can be coerced into performing acts as part of a group or gang. The need for a contextualised approach is therefore key to addressing peer-on-peer harmful sexual behaviours. Firmin (2015) highlights the development of harmful norms in the context of the home, peer group, school and neighbourhood, including sexual harassment and peer recruitment taking place in schools and community settings frequented by young people.

Young people who are involved in criminal behaviour share many risk factors with children in care, namely, living in poverty and family dysfunction including abuse and neglect (Darker 2008). Those who face both issues risk a future pathway of social exclusion and unemployment due to difficulties in education and family or placement stability (Jonson-Reid and Barth 2000). For young people at the edge of care, pathways into offending are complex. Looking to the literature on survivors of abuse and neglect, factors which may place a young person at higher risk of offending are varied. These include higher rates of drug taking and associated risks (Kendall-Tackett 2002), increased reliance on peers who may be involved in antisocial behaviour (Orbke and Smith 2013) and emotional dysregulation difficulties associated with emerging personality difficulties (Howe 2005), which can contribute to aggressive or violent incidents. Young people with existing vulnerabilities are also at more risk of becoming victims of crime, for example, through risk of gang association or through a proneness to experience more violent relationships (Howe 2005; Waddell et al. 2015).

Psychological characteristics developed in a social or familial context may also contribute to offending behaviours, including emotional recognition errors and lower levels of benign attribution bias (Schofield et al. 2015). These are thought to impact on young people's ability to form positive relationships with peers and adults, as well as influencing offending behaviour directly. One implication is that clinical interventions focusing on building trusting relationships and sensitive caregiving could increase young people's capacity for recognising and understanding emotions in others. This gives further weight to the argument for improving mentalisation skills in parents and carers. Cognitive behavioural approaches can also be incorporated into wider frameworks of support to help understand and develop young people's problem-solving and coping skills in the community (Fox and Ashmore 2014; Rogers and Budd 2015).

Clinical Approaches in Practice

Engagement and Assessment

There are particular considerations applicable to beginning direct work with adolescents in edge-of-care contexts. Firstly, as young people are developing their autonomy, careful consideration needs to be given to how to manage the tension between confidentiality and communication within the family and professional system. In addition, young people may value the involvement of their peers or partners, which validates their relationships and shows a willingness to engage with the people who are important to them. Genograms and ecomaps can be a starting point for exploring the relational networks that hold meaning, including wider family, friends, and other supportive adults. These can also give an insight into contextual risks. The growing importance of peers in young people's lives means that often issues of concern—such as substance use, problematic sexual behaviour, and criminal activity—are embedded in the context of school and community-based peer networks. Therefore these networks need to be understood as much as, or more than, issues for the individual young person and their family (Firmin 2015).

A thorough developmental assessment can be helpful, both in helping to engage parents and in gaining a broader formulation of the range of factors contributing to a young person's difficulties. Young people may have anxieties about formal assessment. To support engagement, it can therefore be helpful to consider how the assessment could benefit the young person and to offer reassurance about potential outcomes and the meaning of diagnostic labels. Assessments can also be used to recognise areas of strength and skill, balanced with difficulties, and can be an opportunity to increase self-esteem or value difference. Specific assessment tools may helpfully cover potential difficulties and strengths in cognition and executive functioning, global and specific learning difficulties, social communication, attention, and hyperactivity. In contexts where there is a high risk of harm to the young person, flexibility may be needed in order to provide assessments on an outreach basis and to sidestep long waiting lists.

Making definitive diagnoses can be challenging when there are complexities such as missed schooling, adverse early experiences, and difficulty in accessing a full developmental history from a caregiver. A clinically effective approach usually involves triangulating information through gathering reports from a range of sources and records, observing how difficulties present across different settings, the use of well-validated assessment tools, and referring to best practice guidelines. A functional formulation can be helpful to ensure that, whether or not a diagnosis is appropriate, the assessment process leads to practical strategies and recommendations.

Strong mentalisation skills in professionals can assist in the formation of a sensitive and attuned relationship with young people and their families and help to build trust, whilst supporting the negotiation of barriers to engagement. Dialectical behaviour therapy (DBT), an intervention applied for young people who can be described as showing signs of emerging personality difficulties (such as emotional dysregulation and suicidal behaviour), emphasises the therapeutic relationship and utilises strategies that may appeal to adolescents, including irreverence (Miller et al. 2007). Another team framework which is designed for working with young people with complex difficulties is the AMBIT model (Bevington et al. 2013). AMBIT supports work with "hard to reach" young people through applying a mentalisation-based approach, to support different levels of intervention with a young person's system and particularly in the relationship between the young person and their key worker. Research into this approach is promising: a team designed to work with families at risk of breakdown using an AMBIT-informed approach reduced the number of children entering care to 26 % from an expected 86 % (Brodie et al. 2009).

Formulation

Formulation is the integration of knowledge about a situation with psychological theory to form hypotheses (Johnstone and Dallos 2006), with the aim of helping to bring together the information gathered during the assessment process, make sense of the current situation based on the known history, and guide a targeted intervention plan. Without a formulation, interventions can lack direction or measurable goals (Butler 1998). The needs of a young person/family can feel overwhelming, and anxiety and lack of structure can result in an approach which is too risk focused or pathologising, or conversely may ignore or minimise important information. A formulation can help to understand professionals' countertransference (emotional responses) to a young person and family, which can sometimes impact on effective practice and provide a key to understanding replicated relational patterns (Leiper 2006).

Due to the complexity and diversity of adolescents' presentations, there is a need for a broad framework for making sense of current difficulties, often drawing from more than one theoretical model and focusing on more than one presenting problem, which can then be narrowed down to focus on specific goals and therapeutic or system level interventions. This could take various forms, with the most useful being perceived as accessible and flexible and developed collaboratively with young people, their families, and wider systems, with the clinician taking a facilitative role (Christofides et al. 2012).

As a formulation is a working hypothesis, it needs to be able to hold conflicting perspectives, including the views of the family and support network. A formulation may focus on current maintaining factors or may place more emphasis on a young person's early experiences, depending on what is considered to be most helpful. For adolescents who may continue to reside at home, care needs to be taken to ensure that a formulation is communicated in a way which is not blaming or pathologising of parents and instead helps to understand and empathise with those involved and incorporates views of the young person and family. A formulation developed collaboratively in individual therapy may look different to one used to guide a system's planning, as the main aim is for the formulation to be useful for its intended purpose.

Considerations for Intervention

Whilst various intervention packages for adolescents at the edge of care are gaining an evidence base, no single model can provide for all young people at risk. However, research has found a consistent set of attributes which contribute to successful outcomes of interventions for adolescents on the edge of care, including:

- The consistency and quality of the relationship between the young person/family and their main worker (Ofsted 2011; Mason 2012; Hanson and Holmes 2014)
- SMART Goals for the intervention targeted at addressing risk factors and triggers which led to the current difficulties (Farmer et al. 2015)
- Involvement of the birth family (Department for Education 2014)
- A focus on resiliency models and the unique opportunities of adolescence (Hannon et al. 2010; Hanson and Holmes 2014)
- Ensuring mental health support is provided to young people, including through staff training to those working directly with adolescents (Hannon et al. 2010)
- Transparent and consistent referral pathways, including forward planning for case closure and sustainability (Ofsted 2011) and to work with young people for as long as needed (Department for Education 2014)

- Clearly stated models and methods of intervention, including preventative interventions alongside assessment (Ofsted 2011)
- Strategic level planning including understanding the needs of the cohort, investment in services, and strong multi-agency working (Ofsted 2011)
- Focus on addressing peer and education-related difficulties (Fox and Ashmore 2014; Firmin 2015).

There are therefore a number of key considerations needed when designing and implementing interventions with adolescents. The intervention plan could start with prioritising the young person and family's motivations and goals, considering the goals of the professional network and how to incorporate these collaboratively, increasing motivation and hope through engagement and stabilisation work, and managing and addressing immediate risks (e.g. through use of risk management to address self-harm or sexually harmful behaviour). Timing and priorities also need to be established if there are a number of issues to address, taking into account the evidence base, timescales for change, and planning around life events such as key school exams or length of Youth Rehabilitation Orders. The location of the intervention is also important; it may be possible to work on an outreach basis to improve generalisability. Local provision of specialist interventions also influences what can be offered, or there may be opportunities to commission services based on individual need.

There is an emerging evidence base for specialist models of intervention with this client group. These tend to take a whole systems approach and often start with an intensive phase. Whilst describing interventions in detail is beyond the scope of this chapter, key players include Multi-systemic Family Therapy and Functional Family Therapy (for overviews see Fox and Ashmore 2014; Henggeler et al. 2009; Sexton 2010). These approaches have also been used to address the risk of a young person coming into care due to offending (Rogers and Budd 2015). Residential interventions for adolescents also bear consideration, as a means of providing respite but also proactive intervention to assist rehabilitation home when appropriate. Families using residential and foster care as respite tend to have a high level of need, entrenched family difficulties, contact with a number of support agencies, and previous care episodes (Dixon and Biehal 2007). Therefore, there is a strong case for providing intervention alongside. Whilst involving families collaboratively is recognised as important, this can be difficult to achieve in practice and requires practitioners, foster carers and residential care workers to buy into the rationale for empowering parents, as well as consideration of barriers such as the distance to the placement (Geurts et al. 2012). Specialist interventions which are problem specific are also valuable. For example, for young people displaying sexually harmful behaviour, the AIM2 assessment and associated Good Lives intervention model integrates formulation-based risk management and strengths-based intervention (Willis and Ward 2013).

Some service models draw on a theme of sequencing or combining interventions in a planned and thought through manner, such as Action for Children's Step Change model (Dixon et al. 2015). Set up as a single pathway incorporating Multi-systemic Therapy, Functional Family Therapy, and Treatment Foster Care, one dedicated worker supports the adolescent and family throughout their journey to support them to access whichever intervention best suits their needs. Arguably, combining interventions in a systematic manner is theoretically congruent with the wider evidence base for edge-of-care practice, whilst reflecting the complexity of adolescents' needs in this context. However, as noted by Dixon et al. (2015), the impact of combining interventions for this population is as yet unknown, and there can be challenges when models are not directly compatible. For example, Multi-systemic Therapy is designed to take place in the home or a long-term placement and may not be transferable to a short-term residential stay, due to its focus on working via the young person's primary caregiver.

Box 7.1 Case example: Ibrahim

Ibrahim was a 16-year-old boy, living with his mother and 12-year-old brother. His father had not had regular contact for a number of years and was thought to be working abroad. Ibrahim was at risk of entry into care due to conflict with his mother, which escalated into verbal aggression and physical altercations, sometimes with Ibrahim going missing for a number of hours afterwards. These incidents had become more difficult to contain

Box 7.1 (continued)

over time and had resulted in the police being called. Ibrahim also had behavioural problems in school and had been excluded from mainstream education on a number of occasions. However, he continued to attend supplementary school sessions at a local madrassa, where fewer difficulties were reported. Ibrahim struggled to maintain peer relationships, although he did have one friend whom he had known since primary school.

Initial engagement with clinical support led to a recognition of the impact of the current difficulties on the family, including Ibrahim's younger brother, and acknowledgement of the strengths and resources that had enabled them to live together until this point. Ibrahim's mother had sought help in managing his behaviour as a toddler (via a local Muslim Community Centre), and there had been one previous contact with Children's Social Care, due to concerns about domestic violence. A written risk management agreement was put in place early on. The family were struggling financially and housing was overcrowded, but Ibrahim's mother had a close network of friends who could offer practical and emotional support. She had experienced domestic abuse, which Ibrahim had witnessed in his early years, as well as a period of depression. Due to exploration of triggers to his school difficulties, a cognitive assessment was conducted, which revealed that Ibrahim had moderate verbal comprehension and expression difficulties that contributed to his frustration and trouble in following instructions when these were presented in less structured ways. The way that teaching was delivered at the madrassa was generally very structured and didactic, which he appeared to find easier to manage. It also emerged that there were strong negative family narratives linking masculinity and aggression and that Ibrahim's mother feared the antisocial or violent route that both boys might take as they approached adulthood. Formulation took into account the contextual pressures on the family, religious and cultural context, Ibrahim's early unpredictable and frightening experiences and his language difficulties, to help understand the pattern of altercations and reduce blame between family members. New strategies for communication and problem-solving were tried out to help de-escalate disagreements and there was a focus on developing the family's shared hopes for day-to-day life together. During this process, a trusted family friend's house was identified as a place that Ibrahim could visit without forward planning if relations at home became too heated. Ibrahim was offered the opportunity for therapeutic support to help process his early experiences and help to regulate his emotions, alongside a mentoring role with younger children at the madrassa to promote his sense of positive identity and self-efficacy. His school encouraged him and his brother to try a lunchtime martial arts club that they had been considering joining. Ongoing clinical input involved liaison with education and supporting Ibrahim's mother to access a support group for survivors of domestic violence.

Multi-agency/Multi-professional Approaches

Adolescents at the edge of care often come into contact with a number of supportive agencies, as well as the usual health care and educational environments. There is often a need for liaison with community groups, school and youth services, and mental health services, in order to share risk management and care planning. Local services may develop care pathways for young people identified as at risk, sometimes focusing on specific risks or behaviours such as gang involvement, child sexual exploitation, or harmful sexual behaviour. Multi-agency Planning meetings, overseen by Safeguarding Children Boards, can be helpful to coordinate and monitor the effectiveness of local arrangements (Department for Education 2015b). Effective practice can include mapping out social connections between young people who are known to be at risk, the use of risk management forums for professional support and review of casework progress, developing evidence-based pathways to meet local need, and robust guidelines for cross agency working (Ofsted 2013). A clinical perspective at a strategic level can also help to evaluate and interpret the evidence base, in order to help shape local services.

One multi-agency aspiration might be that, through sharing of local information and knowledge of the wider evidence base, community level interventions can be targeted to groups of young people most at risk of entering the care system. Through consultation, a clinical perspective can assist here, by helping the network to consider life span developmental factors and understand individual or system level problems, in order to consider how best to address issues through targeted intervention (Rogers and Budd 2015).

Conclusion

Young people who are at risk of entering care during their teenage years are, clinically, a very diverse group. Whilst there may be threads that run through young people's experiences and provide practitioners with the opportunity to learn from experience and the evidence base, there are no quick fixes or "one size fits all" models that answer all the needs of the families we aim to support. Working in this challenging arena requires drawing on a broad theoretical base and employing reflective practice during crisis situations. Often, the ability to clinically assess and formulate can add value and can complement and add to the work of a professional and family network. This chapter has also explored how understanding the meaning and function of challenging behaviour of young people from a psychological perspective can help a system to respond in a compassionate and productive way. Whether living with birth families or in temporary alternate care, clinical skills in direct work and consultation can be applied to assist in effective, evidence-based planning and support of this group of young people. In recent years, there appears to be a growing acknowledgement of the needs of older children and the strengths and resources they have potential to activate. Whilst this had led to a number of innovations, there is still a need to continue to focus on adolescence as a unique life stage and to build on the evidence base for effective interventions.

References

Action for Children. (2015). *Impact Report 2015: Making their lives better: Now, tomorrow and every day.* Retrieved from http://www.actionforchildren.org.uk

Asmussen, K., Doolan, M., & Scott, S. (2012). *Intensive interventions suitable for children on the edge of care: Report and recommendations for social finance.* London: Kings College, National Academy for Parenting Research.

Barter, C., McCarry, M., Berridge, D., & Evans, K. (2009). *Partner exploitation and violence in teenage intimate relationships.* London: NSPCC.

Bevington, D., Fuggle, P., Fonagy, P., Target, M., & Asen, E. (2013). Innovations in practice: Adolescent mentalization-based integrative therapy (AMBIT): A new integrated approach to working with the most hard to reach adolescents with severe complex mental health needs. *Child and Adolescent Mental Health, 18*(1), 46–51.

Bowyer, S., & Wilkinson, J. (2013). *Evidence scope: Models of adolescent care provision.* Dartington: Research in Practice.

Brodie, I., Lanyon, C., & Forrester, D. (2009). *Evaluation of an adolescent multi-agency support service (AMASS) Islington.* Luton, UK: University of Bedfordshire, Child and Family Welfare Unit.

Butler, G. (1998). Clinical formulation. In A. S. Bellack & M. Hersen (Eds.), *Comprehensive clinical psychology*. Oxford: Pergamon.

Byng-Hall, J. (1995). Creating a secure family base: Some implications of attachment theory for family therapy. *Journal of Family Process, 34*, 45–58.

Carter, B., & McGoldrick, M. (2005). *The expanded family life cycle: Individual, family and social perspectives*. Boston: Pearson.

Christofides, S., Johnstone, L., & Musa, M. (2012). "Chipping in": Clinical psychologists' descriptions of their use of formulation in multidisciplinary team working. *Psychology and Psychotherapy: Theory, Research and Practice, 85*, 424–435.

Cockbain, E., Brayley, H., & Ashby, M. (2014). *Not just a girl thing; A large-scale comparison of male and female users of child sexual exploitation services in the UK*. London: University College London.

Darker, I. (2008). An analysis of offending by young people looked after by local authorities. *Youth Justice, 8*(2), 134–148.

De La Rue, L., & Espelage, D. L. (2014). Family and abuse characteristics of gang-involved, pressure to join, and non-gang involved girls. *Psychology of Violence, 3*, 253–265.

Department for Education. (2014). *Rethinking support for adolescents in or on the edge of care*. London: Department for Education Children's Social Care Innovation Programme.

Department for Education. (2015a). *Children looked after in England including adoption: 2014 to 2015*. Office of National Statistics National Statistics SFR 34/2015: 1 October 2015.

Department for Education. (2015b). *Working together to safeguard children: A guide to inter-agency working to safeguard and promote the welfare of children*. London: TSO.

Dixon, J., & Biehal, N. (2007). *Young people on the edge of care: The use of respite placements*. Heslington: University of York, Social Work Research and Development Unit.

Dixon, J., Lee, J., Ellison, S., & Hicks, L. (2015). *Supporting adolescents on the edge of care. The role of short term stays in residential care. An evidence scope*. Action for Children Commissioned Report.

Farmer, E., Sturgess, W., O'Neill, T., & Wijedasa, D. (2015). *Achieving successful returns from care: What makes reunification work?* London: British Association for Adoption and Fostering (BAAF).

Finkelhor, D., Ormrod, R., Turner, H., & Holt, M. (2009). Pathways to poly-victimisation. *Child Maltreatment, 14*(4), 316–329.

Firmin, C. (2015). *Peer on peer abuse: Safeguarding implications of contextualising abuse between young people within social fields*. Professional Doctorate Thesis, University of Bedfordshire.

Fox, C. (2016). *"It's not on the radar": The hidden diversity of children and young people at risk of sexual exploitation in England*. Essex: Barnado's.

Fox, S., & Ashmore, Z. (2014). Multisystemic therapy as an intervention for young people on the edge of care. *British Journal of Social Work, 45*(7), 1968–1984. doi:10.1093/bjsw/bcu054.

Geurts, E., Boddy, J., Noom, M., & Knorth, E. (2012). Family centred residential care: The new reality? *Child and Family Social Work, 17*, 170–179.

Hannon, C., Wood, C., & Bazalgette, L. (2010). *In loco parentis*. London: Demos.

Hanson, E., & Holmes, D. (2014). *Evidence scope: That difficult age: Developing a more effective response to risks in adolescence*. Dartington: Research in Practice/ADCS.

Henggeler, S., Schoenwald, S., Borduin, C. M., Rowland, M. D., & Cunningham, P. (2009). *Multisystemic therapy for antisocial behaviour in children and adolescents* (2nd ed.). New York: Guilford.

Hill, K. G., Lui, C., & Hawkins, J. D. (2001). *Early precursors of gang membership: A study of Seattle Youth*. Washington, DC: Department of Justice, Office of Juvenile and Delinquency Prevention.

Howe, D. (2005). *Child abuse and neglect: Attachment, development and intervention*. London: Palgrave Macmillan.

Institute of Public Care. (2015) *Hampshire County Council: Effective interventions and services for young people at the edge of care, rapid research review*. Oxford Brookes University: IPC. Retrieved from http://ipc.brookes.ac.uk/publications/pdf/Rapid_Research_Review_relating_to_Edge_of_Care_July_2015.pdf

Jay, A. (2014) I*ndependent inquiry into child sexual exploitation in Rotherham (1997–2013)*. Report commissioned by Rotherham Metropolitan Borough Council. Retrieved from http://www.rotherham.gov.uk/downloads/file/1407/independent_inquiry_cse_in_rotherham

Johnstone, L., & Dallos, R. (2006). *Formulation in psychology and psychotherapy: Making sense of people's problems*. Hove: Routledge.

Jones, R., Everson-Hock, E. S., Papaioannou, D., Guillaume, L., Goyder, E., Chilcott, J., et al. (2011). Factors associated with outcomes for looked-after children and young people: a correlates review of the literature. *Child: Care, Health and Development, 37*, 613–622.

Jonson-Reid, M., & Barth, R. P. (2000). From maltreatment report to juvenile incarceration: The role of child welfare services. *Child Abuse and Neglect, 24,* 505–520.

Kendall-Tackett, K. (2002). The health effects of childhood abuse: Four pathways by which abuse can influence health. *Child Abuse and Neglect, 26*(6), 715–729.

Leiper, R. (2006). Psychodynamic formulation. In L. Johnstone & R. Dallos (Eds.), *Formulation in psychology and psychotherapy: Making sense of people's problems.* Hove: Routledge.

Lord, J., & Borthwick, S. (2014). *Together or apart? Assessing siblings for permanent placement.* London: British Association for Adoption and Fostering.

Maitra, B. (2000). Giving due consideration to the family's racial and cultural background. In P. Reder & C. Lucey (Eds.), *Assessment of parenting; Psychiatric and psychological contributions.* London: Routledge.

Mason, C. (2012). Social work and the "art of the relationship": Parents' perspectives on an intensive family support project. *Child and Family Social Work, 17,* 368–377.

Miller, A., Rathus, J. H., & Linehan, M. M. (2007). *Dialectical behaviour therapy with suicidal adolescents.* New York: Guildford Press.

National Children's Bureau. (2013). Children on the edge of care: Topic briefing. Retrieved from http://www.ncb.org.uk/media/967542/corp_parenting2_children_on_the_edge_of_care_topic_briefing.pdf

Ofsted. (2011). *Edging away from care: How services successfully prevent young people entering care.* Retrieved May 14, 2016, from https://www.gov.uk/government/publications/how-services-prevent-young-people-entering-care-edging-away-from-care

Ofsted. (2013). *Multi-agency children and young people's partnership panel supporting youth crime reduction work in Hackney: London borough of hackney. Good practice example: Children and families services.* Retrieved from https://www.gov.uk/government/publications/supporting-youth-crime-reduction-work-in-hackney

Orbke, S., & Smith, H. (2013). A developmental framework for enhancing resiliency in adult survivors of childhood abuse. *International Journal for the Advancement of Counselling, 35*(1), 46–56.

Pitts, J. (2013). Drifting into trouble: Sexual exploitation and gang affiliation. In M. Melrose & J. Pearce (Eds.), *Critical perspectives on child sexual exploitation and related trafficking.* London: Palgrave Macmillan.

Rogers, A., & Budd, M. (2015). Developing safe and strong foundations: The DART framework. In A. Rogers, J. Harvey, & H. Law (Eds.), *Young people in forensic mental health Settings: Psychological thinking and practice.* London: Palgrave Macmillan.

Schofield, G., Biggart, L., Ward, E., & Larsson, B. (2015). Looked after children and offending: An exploration of risk, resilience and the role of social cognition. *Children and Youth Services Review, 51,* 125–133.

Selekman, M. (2005). *Pathways to change; Brief therapies with difficult adolescents.* New York: Guilford Press.

Sexton, T. L. (2010). *Functional family therapy in clinical practice: An evidence-based treatment model for working With troubled adolescents.* Hove: Routledge.

Singh, R., & Clarke, G. (2006). Power and parenting assessments: The intersecting levels of culture, race, class and gender. *Journal of Clinical Child Psychology and Psychiatry, 11*(1), 9–25.

Taylor, C. (2016). *Review of the Youth Justice System: An interim report of emerging findings.* Ministry of Justice. Retrieved from https://www.gov.uk/government/publications/review-of-the-youth-justice-system

Waddell, S., O'Connor, R.M., & Cordis Bright Consulting. (2015). *Preventing gang and youth violence: Spotting signals of risk and supporting children and young people.* Early Intervention Foundation.Retrieved from http://www.eif.org.uk/publication/preventing-gang-and-youth-violence/

Willis, G. M., & Ward, T. (2013). The good lives model. In L. A. Craig, L. Dixon, & T. A. Gannon (Eds.), *What works in offender rehabilitation: An evidence-based approach to assessment and treatment.* Oxford: John Wiley and Sons.

8

Working with Trauma

Andrea Shortland

Introduction

Traumatic experiences are almost universal among families at the edge of care. For these families, there have often been multiple traumas across the lifespan and different generations. Trauma is experienced at a child, parental, family and community level. Common experiences include witnessing or being the victim of domestic violence; parental incarcerations; police entering the home, exposure to distress and disruption due to parental mental illness and drug or alcohol misuse; physical and sexual abuse including witnessing adult sexual activity; neglect; the removal and separation of children from a parent's care; and community violence.

More is known about the prevalence of trauma symptoms for children within a child protection context, whilst relatively little is known with respect to parents. An American study of children referred to child welfare for investigation of abuse or neglect found Post-Traumatic Stress

A. Shortland (✉)
London, UK

© The Author(s) 2016
L. Smith (ed.), *Clinical Practice at the Edge of Care*,
DOI 10.1007/978-3-319-43570-1_8

(PTS) symptoms in over 10 % of the children (Kolko et al. 2010). They identified four factors that contributed to heightened PTS symptoms: younger child age, abuse by a non-biological parent, violence in the home and child depression. Another study of 3–5-year-olds found that more than a quarter of children referred to child welfare agencies exhibited trauma symptomatology. Neglect and domestic violence were found to be strongly predictive of trauma symptoms (Fusco and Cahalane 2013).

Trauma rates in children rise significantly for children in foster care. For example, Dale et al. (1999) found that one in three children entering foster care met the criteria for Post-Traumatic Stress Disorder (PTSD). Dubner and Motta (1999) found that 60 % of sexually abused children in foster care had PTSD, as well as 42 % of those who had been physically abused, compared to 18 % of a group not exposed to either type of abuse.

There are differing reactions to traumatic experiences, with the impact and psychological consequences of trauma extending beyond PTS or PTSD. Trauma presentations are often a highly significant factor in creating and maintaining risk within families on the edge of care. Trauma lies at the root of many of the difficulties that are routinely identified in social work and psychological assessments. However, trauma is rarely directly assessed or treated and is often misunderstood within a social care context.

This chapter will therefore explore understandings and treatment approaches for working with trauma within families at the edge of care and suggest further developments in practice. Both children and parents will be considered.

Defining and Formulating Traumatic Responses

Traumatic experiences and reactions are extremely diverse. This has led to disparate understandings of trauma in research and clinical practice. As highlighted by Blaustein and Kinniburgh (2010), "trauma varies in source, chronicity, and impact; it is experienced at different developmental stages, within different contexts—family, community and in the presence or absence of different internal and external resources and challenges".

Post-Traumatic Stress Disorder

Much has been written and researched about the diagnosis and treatment of PTS and PTSD following the experience of a single incident trauma. Post-Traumatic Stress symptoms include (1) intrusions; (2) avoidance; (3) alterations in arousal including heightened arousal, hyper-vigilance and anger outbursts or very low arousal; and (4) alterations in cognitions and mood, such as low mood and increased perception of threat. For children aged 6 years old and younger, symptoms may present slightly differently. For example, intrusions may be apparent through trauma re-enactments in play and in night terrors. However, not everyone who experienced the same event will go on to suffer PTSD. The psychological impact of an event depends upon several factors and the nature of the event is significant. The risk of traumatisation is increased following sudden, uncontrollable, unpredictable, recurrent and interpersonally violent events that create physical harm or threat to life and those that include attachment loss or betrayal by an attachment figure. An individual's ability to understand, integrate and avoid events of a similar nature—for example, due to being younger at the time of the trauma, having a lack of social support, having a personal or family history of psychological difficulties and avoidance of thinking about the event—also increases the risk of experiencing subsequent trauma symptoms (Van der Hart et al. 2014).

Complex Developmental Trauma

The importance of such contextual factors to how trauma develops and is experienced has led to the clinical conceptualisation of Complex and/or Developmental Trauma. This refers to repeated interpersonal trauma, including physical abuse, sexual abuse, emotional abuse, neglect and domestic violence in early childhood, particularly when experienced in the context of caregiver-child relationships (Van der Kolk et al. 2005; The National Child Traumatic Stress Network 2003). Complex Trauma is considered to result in more serious and extensive symptoms than PTSD with dysregulation across a range of areas. These include emotional, behavioural, interpersonal, psychological and cognitive functioning (Fonagy et al. 2015).

The consequences of Developmental/Complex Trauma are mediated by the impact of the trauma and the quality of caregiving on the developing brain and central nervous system. The human brain is extremely immature at birth, with the majority of neurological development occurring within the first three years of life when the infant is highly dependent upon their primary caregiver for survival. The chances of survival are maximised as the individual develops to accommodate a particular caregiving and physical environment. However, particular systems and areas of the brain that require environmental and caregiver input for healthy development may be adversely affected by traumatic relational experiences. In particular, the pre-frontal cortex and the limbic system are affected leading to disruptions in the stress-response system and the capacity for emotional regulation. Learning, memory and executive functioning may also be compromised (Siegel 2015).

A complex interplay of neurological, psychological and behavioural sequelae may therefore result from Developmental Trauma. For example, the child's arousal and attentional systems may develop to ensure that they are highly vigilant to potential threat and in a constant state of high alert. At a cognitive level, this may lead to difficulties focusing their attention on one thing whilst developing a strong ability to split (e.g., being able to watch television whilst also monitoring adult conversation). At an emotional level, this may create an intolerable situation of high stress, with a limited ability to regulate such intense feelings. These responses serve a function whilst trauma is ongoing, as hyper-vigilance may increase a child's ability to stay safe when a parent is unpredictable and dangerous. However, at the same time, they limit the child's ability to play and learn and restrict the development of more mature and higher level skills (Brown and Ward 2012).

Differential Diagnosis and Co-morbidity

Traumatic reactions in children can often be misdiagnosed or misunderstood as attention-deficit hyperactivity disorder (ADHD), autistic spectrum disorder (ASD) or oppositional defiant disorder (ODD). Ford et al. (2000) considered that tens of thousands of children with disruptive behaviour disorders may have been exposed to traumatic maltreatment and may experience undetected PTSD symptoms.

For example, a hyper-vigilant child who is constantly in an alert state and "looking out" for danger will not be able to concentrate or learn and may present as hyperactive. Similarly, a child that has "cut off" from their feelings and body and has developmental delay due to neglect and attachment-related difficulties may present as though they are on the Autistic Spectrum (Howe 2005; Silver 2013). Of course, it is possible that a child may have both ADHD or ASD and a Complex Trauma presentation. Indeed, the risk of trauma may be increased for a child growing up in a family where several members of the family have ADHD (Adler et al. 2004).

Clinicians have attempted to explore differential diagnosis. For example, the Coventry Grid (Moran 2010) explores the different presentations of a child with ASD compared to attachment difficulties and early adversity. However, often it may be necessary to treat trauma symptoms prior to being able to confidently give an ASD, ADHD or ODD diagnosis.

Trauma symptoms may also underlie other psychological presentations. For example, Greeson et al. (2011) found that young people with traumatic histories were at increased risk for internalising behaviour problems and having at least one clinical diagnosis other than PTSD. In parents, responses to trauma may underlie or link difficulties such as Borderline Personality Disorder, substance misuse and domestic violence. For example, Gratz et al. (2008) found higher rates of Borderline Personality Disorder in substance misusers.

Dissociation is also a common trauma presentation that may be misinterpreted or misunderstood. This can vary widely in presentation and can present as disconnection from emotional reactions and/or physical sensations such as pain, absences where the person seems blank or vacant, dissociative seizures and, rarely, dissociative identity disorder. In edge-of-care work with families, dissociative responses may be responsible for parents appearing disengaged or lacking in emotional warmth, not appearing to take in professional concerns, and demonstrating incongruent or contradictory ways of relating (e.g., appearing suddenly very sleepy in the middle of a conversation). For children, there may be concerns about concentration, limited awareness of pain or emotions, sudden rages or periods of regressed behaviour, memory lapses and confusion.

Formulating Trauma with Families at the Edge of Care

It is important to consider the impact of trauma at a family level and across generations. There are interactions between trauma experienced by parents and their children's psychological wellbeing. Extended interpersonal trauma of a violent nature, in particular experienced within a community or family context, has been found to mediate the impact of parental PTSD on child psychological distress (Lambert et al. 2014).

Families in edge-of-care contexts are often suffering with the most serious and Complex Trauma reactions. Their trauma experiences are often repeated, inescapable, happened at a young age and were perpetrated by their caregivers, within the context of poor social support and additional psychological and family difficulties. Trauma becomes trans-generational as traumatised parents may be more likely to expose their children to trauma and less able to contain their child's negative emotions. They are also more likely to avoid their child's proximity/safety seeking behaviours and may be less able to act protectively towards their children. Banyard et al. (2003) found that higher rates of trauma exposure in parents are related to decreased parenting satisfaction, reports of child neglect, use of physical punishment and a history of protective service reports—especially when a mediating factor is maternal depression (Banyard et al. 2003). Likewise, Lyons-Ruth and Block (1996) found that abused women with PTSD were less involved with their infants. This type of maternal withdrawal has been found to be one of the biggest predictors of an array of psychopathology for children in the transition to adulthood, particularly suicidality, dissociation and borderline and antisocial personality disorder presentations (Lyons-Ruth et al. 2013).

In understanding and formulating trauma responses with families, it is helpful to consider that trauma symptoms reflect a survival instinct—being attempts to understand and integrate experiences and avoid experiencing a similar danger again. For example, as noted above, hyper-arousal and hyper-vigilance may develop as a way of monitoring and managing potential threat. Resultant associated symptoms may include anger, irritability and difficulties in responding congruently to non-threatening interactions. Substance misuse may function to help manage arousal and distress. Children exposed to parental trauma may also present clinically in ways that indicate attempts to adaptively respond, in order to get their needs met. For example, infants of mothers with PTSD may activate their approach-seeking and caregiving behaviours and deactivate their "flight or fight" responses in order to maximise caregiving from their withdrawn and hyper-vigilant mother (Lyons-Ruth et al. 2013).

Assessment Considerations and Methods

When assessing the individual and family impact of Developmental and Complex Trauma, several different areas of psychological and interpersonal functioning may usefully be considered. These may be addressed in the context of clinical interviews, case file reviews and the engagement of the child and parents' networks. Areas affected, associated trauma symptoms and suggested assessment tools and strategies that may be used are outlined in Table 8.1.

Table 8.1 Assessment of different areas affected by trauma

Areas affected by trauma	Examples of trauma symptoms	Means of assessment
Neuropsychological: Executive functioning Memory Attentional difficulties Language	Poor organisation Difficulty focusing on tasks such as reading or school work Speech and language problems/difficulties	Psychometric testing
Emotional literacy and regulation difficulties	Hyper- or hypo-arousal Uncontrollable anger Dissociation Self-harm Substance misuse	Assessment of triggers for anger, self-harm, substance misuse Dissociative Experiences Scale (DES) or Child Dissociative Checklist (CDS) Difficulties in Emotional Regulation Scale
Internal working models of relationships	Perception of others and world as dangerous Sense of self as bad or vulnerable	Story stem assessment methods for young children Child Attachment Interview (CAI) for middle aged children Adult Attachment Interview (AAI) for Adults
Re-experiencing and avoidance	Avoidance of situations or thoughts that trigger memories or feelings evoked by the trauma, e.g., avoiding feeling powerless Nightmares, flashbacks (visual, auditory or body feelings), behavioural re-enactments, traumatic play	Impact of Events Scale-Revised (IES-R) or Child Impact of Events Scale-Revised (CRIES) Play based assessments or observations of children

Table 8.1 (continued)

Areas affected by trauma	Examples of trauma symptoms	Means of assessment
Mood and mental state	Depression Anxiety	PHQ-9 for adults Generalised Anxiety Disorder Scale (GAD-7) for adults Beck scales or moods and feelings questionnaire for children
Parent-child interaction	Parenting stress and finding parenting unrewarding Low parental reflective functioning Parental withdrawal/lack of initiating interaction, comfort or speech	Parenting Stress Index (PSI) Parent Development Interview (PDI) CARE index, Marschak Interaction Method (MIM)

Trauma-Focused Interventions

Key Principals and Considerations

Currently, there is an established evidence base for the treatment of single incident-related PTSD (NICE Guideline 2005). However, the evidence base and guidance for working with Developmental/Complex Trauma is potentially more useful and applicable to clinical practice with families at the edge of care. These suggest that several over-arching elements or issues should be considered. Firstly, interventions should be multi-modal, integrating a variety of approaches and working across a range of areas and domains of functioning. Therefore, treatment may include behavioural training, exposure, psycho-education, anger management, anxiety management, substance misuse work, techniques to support learning, social skills development and family work. Within these strands of the work, it is important to apply concepts and treatment models flexibly and sensitively according to cultural, religious or family belief systems (Lab et al. 2008).

Secondly, as discussed above, trauma is often trans-generational and impacts upon all members of the family. Therapeutic work should therefore address the impact of the trauma within the family system and across family members. When several members of a family have experienced multiple traumas, it is often difficult to decide who and which trauma reactions to prioritise. This can only be decided on a case-by-case basis, but factors such as risk and accessibility of change should be considered in line with the overall priorities for working in edge-of-care contexts. Often, it is appropriate to treat adult trauma before treating child trauma in order to ensure that caregivers are able to provide the safety needed by the child to undertake trauma-focused work.

In addition, due to the pervasive nature of Developmental/Complex Trauma, successful intervention approaches need to include work across the parent or child and family's systems of influence. It is therefore crucial that there is consistent goal-setting and feedback across systems, to both maximise and create a context that can tolerate and create enough safety for trauma-focused work to be completed. Family, education/employment, social care, mental health and peer group systems should be considered. For example, it is usually helpful for all members of the family or key people within the system (such as teachers, family support workers or youth workers) to have psycho-education around the impact of trauma for the particular child, parent or family. This needs to be undertaken sensitively with respect to confidentiality and safety issues. Collaboratively written therapeutic letters or clinically facilitated network meetings may provide useful ways forward. Likewise, safety planning and skills building will often need to be completed at a family level and across systems. This is especially necessary when trauma-focused interventions are ongoing, as these may involve the (re)emergence of painful feelings and responses to these, especially when avoidance has been a significant coping strategy previously. Trauma-processing work is typically done at an individual level, although it can be done with a family together in order to increase support around the process and maximise its impact. An example of a programme that addresses trauma in this way is Multi-systemic Therapy—Child Abuse and Neglect (MST-CAN) (Swenson et al. 2009).

In addition, it is crucial to consider when it is "safe enough" to begin trauma-focused work with families at the edge of care. This often requires the child, parent or family to give up old survival or coping strategies and to risk the increase of symptoms and feelings of distress. This can feel (and indeed become) very unsafe for the parent or child if their surrounding circumstances are risky and unsupportive. Professionals need to consider and manage risks of significant harm to children as a priority. It may be that it is sufficient to provide assessment and formulation from a trauma perspective, together with safety and stabilisation work, in order to improve functioning within the family. It may not be considered to be safe enough for the family to progress to the trauma-processing phase of the work during a particular time or context. That said, there is an increasing recognition that trauma work is often avoided unnecessarily by clinicians and can be safely managed with high-risk populations if there is sufficient preparation.

It may be helpful to consider the following questions when deciding if it is safe enough to proceed with trauma-focused interventions:

- Does the parent or child, family and system have the necessary skills and processes in place to safely manage an increase in distress?
- Can the parent or child safely make changes to their belief system or functioning without risks to family functioning?
- Is the treating professional sufficiently supported and able to access specialist expertise in Developmental/Complex Trauma?

Finally, when working with families at the edge of care, it is important to maximise engagement through considering relevant trauma-related issues. For example, both children and parents suffering with trauma are likely to be hyper-sensitive to threat, which can be easily triggered by interactions with professional and legal systems. People suffering with trauma presentations often have a very small "window of tolerance" or space within which they can think logically. Fear and anxiety can be triggered very easily by either internal factors (e.g., a thought, body sensation or memory) or external factors (tone of voice, place, word or phrase). When triggered, flight, fight or freeze responses limit parents' and children's ability to think logically or learn. Given the interpersonal nature of Complex Trauma, triggers can often be interpersonal experiences, such as feeling out of control, criticism and changing expectations. In general, it is likely to be helpful to keep interactions as predictable and routine-based as possible, to be very explicit and consistent with expectations, to contract how and when to give feedback and to be strengths-focused. It may also be helpful to have one person co-coordinating care plans who can act as a contact point for the family. Approaches such as the Family Partnership Model can help to work to manage threat triggered by professional relationships (Davis and Day 2010).

Box 8.1 Case example: Marlene

Marlene was a single mother of three children, all of whom were made subject to Child Protection Plans. Social Workers had concerns about the children's mental health (all were open to Child and Adolescent Mental Health Services due to anxiety, self-harm and ADHD), exposure to domestic violence, sexual abuse and neglect.

Marlene experienced Complex/Developmental Trauma. She experienced repetitive sexual abuse from a very early age by family members whom she trusted and also witnessed unpredictable violence in the family home. Marlene's mother was very depressed and withdrawn and did not help Marlene to learn to regulate her emotions. She often felt rejected and worthless and needed the comfort and kindness she got through her abusive relationships and occasionally from her mother. Marlene therefore learnt to be very compliant in her interactions. However, she was often frightened and suffered frequent pain and humiliation as part of her sexual abuse. Marlene therefore learnt to dissociate by cutting off from her body and her feelings to enable her to cope.

In adulthood, Marlene continued to replicate her early abusive experiences and sought comfort in sexual relationships with abusive men. Becoming a parent triggered a lot of painful memories and feelings for her, particularly as her children developed and became challenging in their behaviour. Marlene continued to use a lot of dissociation to cope but also resorted to drug and alcohol use in an attempt to manage distress. Marlene was co-operative with professionals but her dissociation and trauma reactions meant that, despite engaging in several parenting courses, she had not been able to implement her learning.

Marlene did not experience typical flashbacks, but as her brain tried to process her traumatic experiences, she experienced a lot of psychosomatic pain and dreams of being suffocated. Marlene's biggest difficulty, both in terms of parenting and maintaining her psychological and functional difficulties, was her high levels of anxiety and dissociation. This was often triggered by her children's fighting and challenging behaviour as they vied for her attention and struggled to regulate their own feelings of distress.

Box 8.1 (continued)

Marlene would completely withdraw psychologically when triggered and was unable to meet her children's needs or protect them from harm. Marlene's relationships with abusive men also meant that they were exposed to domestic violence.

Intervention was very much focused on creating safety, stabilisation and skills building. The children's Social Worker worked closely with Adult Mental Health professionals to create an understanding of Marlene's functioning and her family, which reduced feelings of shame. Creating safety both for Marlene and her children was also paramount. Initially the family was supported by family support workers for most of the waking day, but Marlene found the experience of different people coming in and out of her home too difficult to manage—her dissociation and alcohol use increased. An experienced foster carer and a family member then agreed to provide consistent support to Marlene to help ensure a high level of routine, safety and appropriate childcare within the family home and Marlene was able to manage this. CAMHS also continued to provide support to Marlene's older children around emotional regulation skills. A mental health clinician provided Marlene with psycho-education and support to begin to understand and regulate her emotions, understand and reduce periods of dissociation and increase safety within her day-to-day life. Marlene was also supported to identify relationship patterns and form more healthy adult relationships. Finally, Marlene was given a lot of support to implement changes to her parenting and increase her ability to understand and respond more sensitively to her children's needs without dissociating. This was very challenging and continued to be an area of difficulty for Marlene. Marlene decided to put off trauma-processing work until her youngest child was settled in school and her eldest child was less distressed, in order to ensure she had the space to cope with this work.

Phased Approaches

There is a clinical consensus favouring a phased or sequenced approach as the first line treatment for Complex Trauma (Cloitre et al. 2011). The International Society for Traumatic Stress Studies (ISTSS) has produced Expert Consensus Treatment Guidelines for Complex PTSD in Adults. These outline three phases of intervention (Cloitre et al. 2012). Models or methods of intervention for Complex Trauma in children also fit broadly within these three phases, although there is an increased focus on the first phase of intervention and more attention is given to working with caregiving and professional systems: This is the case in Struik's

Sleeping Dogs Method (Struik 2014), in The National Child Traumatic Stress Network's Child Welfare Trauma Training Toolkit (Child Welfare Committee 2008) and in Blaustein and Kinniburgh's ARC Treatment Model (Blaustein and Kinniburgh 2010). The three phases are detailed below. During treatment, it is necessary to move interactively and flexibly through the phases as required by the client.

Phase 1: Safety, Stabilisation and Skills Strengthening

This phase of treatment is very focused upon symptom relief and functional improvement. It is generally considered that a period of around six months is required for this phase in adults. For children, it may be shorter depending upon their needs and environment. Struik's Sleeping Dogs Method (Struik 2014) and Blaustein and Kinniburgh's ARC Treatment Model (Blaustein and Kinniburgh 2010) provide detailed approaches to assessing and working within this particular phase in children. Components of this phase include:

- *Psycho-education* around trauma symptoms and the impact upon the individual's functioning and life. This is particularly important as traumatised individuals often feel that they are going "mad" and blame themselves for their experiences and difficulties. The associated shame for the traumatised parent is often a significant factor in maintaining risky behaviours, whilst for children it leads to an escalation in problematic behaviours. Compassion Focused Therapy for Trauma (Lee 2012) provides a particularly useful and accessible framework for addressing shame and providing psycho-education about trauma whilst encouraging the person to take responsibility for their behaviour and choices. Struik's Sleeping Dogs and Blaustein and Kinniburgh's ARC model provide additional useful ideas for undertaking this work in relation to traumatised children.
- *Safety and stability* within daily life, the environment and caregiving relationships are addressed. Safety is crucial if the traumatised individual is to be expected to let go of some of their symptoms, which may function to protect them in some way. Attention is paid to ensuring physical safety and addressing any issues which create chaos in daily life. Work is also undertaken to reduce or increase control over risky or distressing

symptoms such as flashbacks, aggression, self-injurious behaviours and drug and alcohol abuse. A focus on stabilisation and safety does not have to be limited to psychological work, but rather should include creating these in the system and families' day-to-day lives. For example, as trauma can lead to difficulties with memory and executive functioning, the parent may repeatedly forget appointments and the child may often misplace their school jumper or sports bag and forget about homework. It can be helpful to provide diaries and organisation strategies to ensure that essential daily tasks are completed. Wider support strategies could include the provision of parenting support, additional childcare or extra classroom support for children. This might also involve a safety plan for children should parents' symptoms increase, regular GP or Psychiatry appointments to manage medication and a pause in any legal proceedings whilst trauma work is ongoing.

- *Emotional regulation*, capacity to tolerate and moderate strong affect, stress management and problem solving skills may be taught to both children and adults. Dialectical Behaviour Therapy (DBT) is one approach that may be helpful for adults and adolescents in this phase of the work (Linehan 1993). With children with Complex Trauma, it is recommended that prior to developing self-regulation skills, the child's affect should be co-regulated and managed through attuned and sensitive caregiving (e.g., Blaustein and Kinniburgh 2010; Silver et al. 2015). The following approaches are examples of programmes available to assist caregivers in their ability to attune to and co-regulate children:

  - Dyadic Development Psychotherapy/DDP (Hughes 2004)
  - The Connect Programme for Adolescents and their carers (e.g., Moretti and Obsuth 2009)
  - Nurturing Attachments Programme for Adoptive, Foster or Kinship Carers (Golding 2013)
  - Theraplay (Booth and Jernberg 2010)

- *Relational/social skills* are taught to adults and children. With children, it is recommended that attachment-related work, as outlined above, is completed in order to ensure that carers are able to be emotionally available to the child and that the child is able to make use of the caregiving relationship when distressed. For adults, social skills work and help in managing relationships is provided.

Phase 2: Trauma Processing

The ISTSS suggest that this phase of the work should be approximately 3–6 months in duration for adults (Cloitre et al. 2012). Again, it is likely to be shorter for children. Struik (2014) recommends between 4–8 sessions for trauma processing with children. The focus in this phase is on helping the individual to face up to, re-experience and fully process traumatic events that have been previously held in a "raw"/highly emotive state. At a cognitive level, new information is introduced, old beliefs challenged and alternative understandings facilitated to help create new meanings and learning around the traumatic events. At an emotional level, powerful and overwhelming negative emotions such as fear, disgust, anger and shame are processed creating a different "felt sense" of the experiences. At a behavioural level, avoidance is addressed and new situations and responses mastered. Traumatic experiences and new behaviours and responses are integrated to create a more compassionate, adaptive and coherent life story and sense of self.

Trauma-Focused Cognitive Behavioral Therapy (TF-CBT) and Eye Movement Desensitisation Reprocessing (EMDR) are the current NICE recommended therapies for this phase of the work (NICE Guidelines 2005). Both EMDR and TF-CBT have particular approaches aimed at working with more Complex Trauma, such as Attachment Focused EMDR (Parnell 2013). In addition, Narrative Exposure Therapy/KidNet for children is an additional and very useful approach for working with families at the edge of care, as it is particularly strong in dealing with multiple traumas, helping to contextualise and integrate events within an overall life story and addressing human rights and advocacy as part of the work (Robjant and Frazel 2010).

It may be that parents or children do not feel ready to undertake trauma-processing work, and they should never be forced or coerced. A parent may fear their symptoms increasing and be worried about the implications for risk and their children. A child may fear the implications of changing trauma-related beliefs upon their relationship with their parent. It may be more adaptive at that particular time for a child to believe that a traumatic incident was their fault, rather than experiencing anger towards a parent or experience a sense of helplessness. Where possible, work should be completed within the family to address these fears and make room for change. However, it is possible that risk can be sufficiently reduced and stabilisation sufficiently achieved through Phase 1 interventions. Difficulties may re-emerge at another time following another traumatic event or developmental stage and the individual may choose to undertake trauma-processing work at that time.

Box 8.2 Case example: Toby

Toby is a 14-year-old boy who lives at home with his mother and younger sister. Toby has a diagnosis of ADHD and ODD. Professionals were extremely concerned about Toby because he often went missing for several nights at a time, had admitted to multidrug use and could be very violent. Toby witnessed a lot of domestic violence between his parents in his formative years and his mother was quite depressed and emotionally unavailable when he was young because of the domestic violence. Toby's parents separated and Toby went to live with his father when he was 8 years old. However, Toby was physically assaulted several times by his father and returned to his mother's care a few years later.

Toby presented with flashbacks and nightmares relating to the physical assaults. Toby had never developed good emotional regulation skills and wanted to avoid the horrible feeling of fear and vulnerability that was triggered so easily for him. Toby spent a lot of time drinking alcohol and abusing substances that made him feel carefree and strong. Toby also got involved in criminal activity with a group of older boys, which made him feel strong and accepted. However, Toby presented as being quite emotionally immature and was sometimes the victim of physical assaults from his peers. When at home, Toby's flashbacks were often strong and he frequently felt overwhelmed by fear and shame, which led to aggression. Toby's feelings for his mother were complex: He was sorry for his violence but he was also angry that she had not protected him in the past.

In order to create safety, stabilisation and space for trauma-processing work, the following elements were put in place: (1) Toby agreed to being electronically tagged by the Youth Offending Team, to allow him to withdraw from delivering drugs without reprisal. (2) He was provided with several clinical sessions focused on dealing with flashbacks, increasing emotional regulation, improving social skills and confidence building. There was a particular focus on dealing with shame and noticing times when he had felt strong and capable without the use of violence, drugs or alcohol. (3) Psycho-education was given to the family and Toby's teachers about the impact of trauma. (4) Toby's school agreed to support Toby in implementing his new skills and came up with a safety plan for managing aggression.

(continued)

Box 8.2 (continued)

(5) Clinical sessions were completed with Toby's mother to explore her experience of domestic violence, help her to understand that Toby's behaviour did not mean he was genetically programmed to be violent like his father and enable her to apologise to Toby for not protecting him from his father.

In the next phase of the work, Toby was able to process some of his most disturbing and intrusive traumas using EMDR. This work was emotionally intense for Toby and led to Toby abusing substances for brief periods. Toby's mother needed additional support from Toby's Social Worker at this time, as she felt she could not cope. A family support worker met with Toby and his mother after therapy sessions, and things settled after a few weeks. After EMDR, Toby worked to develop a coherent narrative of his life and significant experiences and explored alternative narratives and dreams for his future. Toby began to view his father differently and realised that he no longer was able to hurt or humiliate him. Toby stopped blaming himself and appreciated that his mother was struggling to cope with her own trauma. Toby considered that whilst his mother had made a very unwise decision to allow Toby to be cared from by his father, she had always wanted and loved Toby. Toby stopped feeling so worthless and powerless and found that he was able to start thinking more rationally rather than being so overwhelmed by emotion.

Following intervention, Toby's attention difficulties reduced significantly and he no longer required medication for ADHD. Toby was able to engage better in school but continued to struggle with peer relationships and needed some additional support in this area. Toby's relationship with his mum was still difficult at times but they were better able to understand each other's feelings.

Phase 3: Integration, Consolidation and Transition of Treatment Gains

The ISTSS suggest that this phase of the work can take 9–12 months with adults, although sessions are reduced in frequency as changes are consolidated. In this phase of the work, trauma symptoms should be in remission and the individual is working to implement changes in everyday life. There may also be a need to address any additional psychological difficulties. For children, this may mean support to catch up on developmental delay, cognitive development and learning. For parents, there should be a specific focus upon parenting skills and attachment relationships at this stage. The trauma and stabilisation work is likely to have led to an improvement in reflective functioning skills due to a reduction in shame and time spent in a hyper- or hypo-aroused fear response state. Parents should therefore be able to be more attuned and responsive to their child, be in a better position to access and make use of generic parenting or education programmes, develop more healthy adult relationships including more helpful relationships with the professional network around the child and be better placed to deal with new challenges more effectively as they arise. However, they may still require reminders of newly acquired skills and may need support to take new steps and build confidence.

Box 8.3 Recommendations for trauma-focused practice

Professionals working with families on the edge of care need to have an increased ability to recognise and understand traumatic reactions and difficulties including Complex/Developmental Trauma.

Families on the edge of care should have access to trauma-focused assessments and interventions.

Intervention needs to be implemented at a family and systemic level to ensure efficacy and safety. This is likely to require collaboration between agencies but should be tightly co-ordinated by a single professional.

Trauma-focused interventions should include a phased approach, with considerable time and consideration given to the safety, stabilisation and skills building phase of the work to create a safe context for change.

Trauma-processing work can be very powerful and can lead to significant changes in functioning. It should therefore be completed where possible. However, for some families it may not be possible to create sufficient safety to complete this phase of the work.

Conclusion

Trauma is a central feature of the difficulties that needs to be fully explored and understood when working with families at the edge of care. Implementing trauma-focused approaches with children and parents requires evidence-based knowledge, skills and systemic support for working with Developmental/Complex Trauma, in order for associated difficulties to be appropriately identified and addressed. This generally requires multifaceted and phased interventions to be delivered in the context of effective risk management.

References

Adler, L. A., Kunz, M., Chua, H. C., Rotrosen, J., & Resnick, S. G. (2004). Attention-deficit/hyperactivity disorder in adult patients with posttraumatic stress disorder (PTSD): Is ADHD a vulnerability factor? *Journal of Attention Disorders, 8*(1), 11–16.

Banyard, V. L., Williams, L. M., & Siegel, J. A. (2003). The impact of complex trauma and depression on parenting: An exploration of mediating risk and protective factors. *Child Maltreatment, 8*, 334–349.

Blaustein, M., & Kinniburgh, K. (2010). *Treating traumatic stress in children and adolescents*. New York: Guilford.

Booth, P. B., & Jernberg, A. M. (2010). *Theraplay: Helping parents and children build better relationships through attachment-based play* (3rd ed.). San Fransisco: Wiley and Sons.

Brown, R., & Ward, H. (2012). *Decision-making within a child's timeframe: An overview of current research evidence for family justice professionals concerning child development and the impact of maltreatment*. Working Paper No. 16. Childhood Wellbeing Research Centre.

Child Welfare Committee, National Child Traumatic Stress Network. (2008). *Child welfare trauma training toolkit: Comprehensive guide* (2nd ed.). Los Angeles: National Centre for Child Traumatic Stress.

Cloitre, M., Courtois, C. A., Charuvastra, A., Carapezza, R., Stolbach, B. C., & Green, B. L. (2011). Treatment of complex PTSD: Results of the ISTSS expert clinician survey on best practices. *Journal of Traumatic Stress, 24*, 615–627.

Cloitre, M., Courtois, C. A., Ford, J. D., Green, B. L., Alexander, P., Briere, J., et al. (2012). *The ISTSS expert consensus treatment guidelines for complex PTSD in adults*. Retrieved from http://www.istss.org/ISTSS_Main/media/Documents/ISTSS-Expert-Concesnsus-Guidelines-for-Complex-PTSD-Updated-060315.pdf

Dale, G., Kendall, J. C., Humber, K., & Sheehan, L. (1999). Screening young foster children for post traumatic stress disorder and responding to their needs for treatment. *APSAC Advisor, 12*(2), 6–9.

Davis, H., & Day, C. (2010). *Working in partnership with parents* (2nd ed.). London: Pearson.

Dubner, A. E., & Motta, R. W. (1999). Sexually and physically abused foster care children and post-traumatic stress disorder. *Journal of Consulting and Clinical Psychology, 67*, 367–373.

Fonagy, P., Cotterll, D., Phillips, J., Bevington, D., Glaser, D., & Allison, E. (2015). *What works for whom? A critical review of treatment for children and adolescents* (2nd ed.). New York: Guilford.

Ford, J. D., Racusin, R., Ellis, C., Daviss, W. B., Reiser, J., Fleischer, A., & Thomas, J. (2000). Child maltreatment, other trauma exposure, and post traumatic symptomatology among children with oppositional defiant and attention deficit hyperactivity disorders. *Child Maltreatment, 5*, 205–217.

Fusco, R. A., & Cahalane, H. (2013). Young children in the child welfare system: What factors contribute to trauma symptomology? *Child Welfare, 92*(5), 37–58.

Golding, K. S. (2013). *Nurturing attachments training resource. Running parenting groups for adoptive parents and foster or kinship carers.* London: Jessica Kingsley.

Gratz, K. L., Tull, M. T., Baruch, D. E., Bornovalova, M. A., & Lejuez, C. W. (2008). Factors associated with co-occurring borderline personality disorder among inner-city substance users: The roles of childhood maltreatment, negative affect intensity/reactivity, and emotion dysregulation. *Comprehensive Psychiatry, 49*(6), 603–615.

Greeson, J. K. P., Briggs, E. C., Kisiel, C. L., Laayne, C. M., Ake III, G. S., Ko, S. J., et al. (2011). Complex trauma and mental health in children and adolescents placed in foster care: Findings from the National Child Traumatic Stress Network. *Child Welfare, 90*(6), 91–108.

Howe, D. (2005). *Child abuse and neglect: Attachment, development and intervention.* London: Palgrave Macmillan.

Hughes, D. (2004). An attachment-based treatment of maltreated children and young people. *Attachment and Human Development, 6*, 263–278.

Kolko, D. J., Hoagwood, K. E., & Springgate, B. (2010). Treatment research for trauma/PTSD in youth and adults: Moving from efficacy to effectiveness. *General Hospital Psychiatry, 32*(5), 465–476.

Lab, D., Santos, I., & De Zulueta, F. (2008). Treating post traumatic stress disorder in the "real world": Evaluation of a specialist trauma service and adaptation to standard treatment approaches. *Psychiatric Bulletin, 32*, 8–12.

Lambert, J. E., Holzer, J., & Hasburn, A. (2014). Association between parents' PTSD severity and children's psychological distress: A meta-analysis. *Journal of Traumatic Stress, 27*, 9–17.

Lee, D. (2012). *Recovering from trauma using compassion focused therapy.* London: Robinson.

Linehan, M. M. (1993). *Skills training manual for treating borderline personality disorder.* New York: Guilford.

Lyons-Ruth, K., & Block, D. (1996). The disturbed caregiving system: Relations among childhood trauma, maternal caregiving, and infant affect and attachment. *Infant Mental Health Journal, 17*(3), 257–275.

Lyons-Ruth, K., Bureau, J. F., Easterbrooks, M. A., Osbruth, I., & Henninghausen, K. (2013). Parsing the construct of maternal insensitivity: Distinct longitudinal pathways of early maternal withdrawal. *Attachment and Human Development, 15*, 1–28.

Moran, H. (2010). Clinical observations of the differences between children on the autism spectrum and those with attachment problems: The coventry grid. *Good Autism Practice (GAP), 11*(2), 44–49.

Moretti, M. M., & Obsuth, I. (2009). Effectiveness of an attachment-focused manualised intervention for parents of teens at risk for aggressive behaviour: The Connect Program. *Journal of Adolescence, 32*, 1347–1357.

NICE Guidelines. (2005). Post-traumatic stress disorder: Management. National Institute for Health and Care Excellence. Retrieved from https://www.nice.org.uk/guidance/cg26

Parnell, L. (2013). *Attachment focused EMDR: Healing relational trauma.* New York: W.W. Norton and Company.

Robjant, K., & Frazel, M. (2010). The emerging evidence for narrative exposure therapy: A review. *Clinical Psychology Review, 30*(8), 1030–1039.

Siegel, D. J. (2015). *The developing mind: How relationships and the brain interact to shape who we are.* New York: Guilford.

Silver, M. (2013). *Attachment in common sense and doodles.* London: Jessica Kingsley Publishers.

Silver, M., Golding, K., & Roberts, C. (2015). Delivering psychological services for children, young people and families with complex social care needs. *Child and Family Clinical Psychology Review, 3*, 119–129.

Struik, A. (2014). *Treating chronically traumatised children: Don't let sleeping dogs lie.* London: Routledge.

Swenson, C. C., Schaeffer, C. M., Tuerk, E. H., Henggeler, S. W., Tuten, M., Panzerella, P. et al. (2009). Adapting multisystemic therapy for co-occurring child maltreatment and parental substance abuse: The building stronger families project. *Emotional and Behavioral Disorders in Youth, W*, 3–8.

The National Child Traumatic Stress Network. (2003). *Complex trauma in children and adolescents.* White Paper from the National Child Traumatic Stress Network Complex Trauma Task Force. Retrieved from http://www.nctsnet.org/nctsn_assets/pdfs/edu_materials/ComplexTrauma_All.pdf

Van der Hart, O., Nijenhuis, E. R. S., & Steele, K. (2014). *The haunted self: Structural dissociation and the treatment of chronic traumatisation.* New York: Norton.

Van der Kolk, B., Rot, S., Pelcovitz, D., Sunday, S., & Spinazzola, J. (2005). Disorders of extreme stress: The empirical foundation of complex adaptation to trauma. *Journal of Traumatic Stress, 18*(5), 389–399.

9

Multi-family Group Therapy

Elizabeth Mensah and Heleni-Georgia Andreadi

Introduction

"Many Families Grow Together"

It is interaction in the presence of others with similar difficulties that encourages people to help each other, share familiar dilemmas and develop their respective ways of responding and finding solutions. This chapter draws on that premise, in describing and promoting the relevance of Multi-family Group Therapy (MFGT)as used with children and families at the edge of care. A brief theoretical introduction to the model is given, followed by principles, skills and techniques that are adaptable to edge-of-care contexts, in order to achieve positive outcomes.

E. Mensah
London, UK

H.-G. Andreadi (✉)
London, UK

© The Author(s) 2016
L. Smith (ed.), *Clinical Practice at the Edge of Care*,
DOI 10.1007/978-3-319-43570-1_9

As we value users' involvement and voices to ensure successful outcomes from therapeutic interventions, this chapter includes stories and excerpts from the perspective of parents, children and professionals who have participated in multi-family groups (Andreadi and Mensah 2015).

Some of the challenges and opportunities of this approach will also be highlighted. We hope that, in turn, this will encourage and challenge others in their use of multi-family group practices.

MFGT and its Applications to Practice

Multi-family Group Therapy (MFGT) involves working therapeutically with a collection of families in a group setting. It combines the power of group process with the systems focus of family therapy. MFGT is ideally suited to working with families facing similar difficulties. This model of working was developed in the early 1960s by Laqueur and his co-workers (Laqueur et al. 1964) and originally implemented in inpatient units for adolescents and adults with severe mental health difficulties (Laqueur 1973; Wattie 1994).

Since these first groups, the approach has developed and been used successfully in other areas, including the following: outpatient contexts for children and adults presenting with significant mental health disorders (McFarlene 1982; Anderson & Gehart 2007), drug and alcohol abuse (Kaufman and Kaufman 1979), chronic medical illness (Gonsalez et al. 1989), eating disorders (Slagerman and Yager 1989) and non-medical settings such as schools and community projects (Asen et al. 1982; Cooklin et al. 1983). Significantly, MFGT has been usefully applied with families at the edge of care, including its use as a family assessment and intervention tool during care proceedings (Barratt 2012) and with families referred to the Marlborough Family Centre by the courts and social care services due to significant safeguarding concerns (Asen 2002).

As an intervention, MFGT has proven effective for families struggling with multiple difficulties. Sayger (1996) noted that using MFGT with at-risk families increased the opportunity to build a sense of community and social support. In an empirical study, Meezan and O'Keefe (1998) reported that using MFGT was effective in increasing social competence amongst children whose families had been abusive or neglectful, also suggesting that MFGT with these families was more effective than traditional family therapy in fostering changes in parent-child interactions.

Organising Principles

The MFGT model creates a space where important aspects of the family life cycle and structure can be observed and explored. The bringing of many families together and the multiple interactions that occur provide a rich sampling of subsystems and boundary issues, as well as the opportunity for analysing and hypothesising about both intra- and inter-family interactional patterns and communication styles.

Key enduring qualities of MFGT are its versatility and the opportunities it allows to combine or draw from various evidence-based modalities, concepts, skills and techniques (Laqueur et al. 1964; McFarlene 1982; Anderson & Gehart 2007). This provides facilitators with immense scope for creativity in planning and delivery of the model with those who may be described as multi-problem, high-risk or complex families.

In MFGT with families where there are significant safeguarding concerns, theoretical relevance and practice-based experience suggests the usefulness of incorporating principles from systemic and collaborative narrative practices, such as the Tree of Life (Anderson and Goolishian 1992; Epston and White 1995; Denborough 2008; Ncube 2006); resilience-building and positive parenting approaches, including behaviour management skills development; and mentalisation-based therapy (MBT) concepts (Midgley and Vrouva 2012). These will be discussed further below. Whilst acknowledging the need to be versatile and inclusive, the core organising principles of MFGT remain highly relevant (Asen 2002; Asen and Scholz 2010; Asen et al. 1982):

• In a group, the family learns that they are not alone, as other families have similar problems and concerns

- The group gives families hope, as they see other families learn, change and grow and as they receive support and encouragement from each other
- As families find themselves able to care for and help other families, they increase their own sense of competence and agency
- The group becomes a support network, where families can feel accepted just as they are and friendships develop between families that continue outside of and beyond the group
- Families learn through identification with other families and through modelling behaviours observed in other families. This is most possible when families come together who have very similar experiences/difficulties and similarly aged children (or children negotiating similar developmental tasks). It is suggested that the more similarities families can identify, the more influential the group becomes
- The group becomes a safe place to experiment with, practice and get feedback on new skills and ways of relating
- By attending and involving themselves in the group, families are publicly committing themselves to change and exposing themselves to subtle peer pressures.

Each family and each group represents unique perceptions and experiences. MFGT facilitators need to remain open to deconstructing their preconceived assumptions of what is "best for all", so as to create a therapeutic space that is uniquely co-constructed by the participating families in each group. This diversity of backgrounds and experiences allows practitioners and families to explore and enhance their strengths and move away from interactions that are no longer helpful or meaningful.

Establishing a Safe Therapeutic Context

The importance of context, and its recursive influence with all aspects of living and meaning-making, is highlighted within systemic epistemology (Bateson 1972). The need for a positive and safe therapeutic context as a prerequisite for successful outcomes in therapy has been repeatedly highlighted in family therapy literature and elsewhere (Minuchin et al. 2006; Flaskas 1997; Wilson 1993; Mason 2010; Carr 2005).

To this end, an important aspect of systemic practice remains how we prepare ourselves for meeting with the "other" (McAdam and Lang 2009; Andersen 1987; Fredman 2004; Rober 1998). Practices like team hypothesising, inner dialogue, emotional posturing, team reflections and even the use of initial telephone call conversations as the start of our formulation are only a few of the methods that may be used in day-to-day practice.

Organisational contexts may also influence how families are engaged in multi-family group work. For example, within statutory edge-of-care contexts, there may be opportunities to set the tone for how families are invited to attend the groups and how they might be supported to do so, and for this to inform clinical assessment and elimination processes. There may also be opportunities for collaborative working within or across agencies or multidisciplinary teams, comprised of practitioners whose varied experience, knowledge and roles in the families' lives can contribute to creating a therapeutic frame for the work. Through an initial referral, consultation and commissioning process, it is possible to begin reframing linear views of children or family's presentations, extend the systemic paradigm and sow seeds for the possibility of change. It is useful to encourage professionals to maintain the possibility of small shifts that could produce a rippling effect on the family's understandings or behaviours.

The process of "warming the context" (Burnham 2005) via preparing and having the first meetings with families is a significant aspect of the whole MFGT intervention—and usually a predictor of its success. Families at the edge of care often arrive to groups with problem-focused and complaint-saturated narratives, stories of hopelessness, anger and frustration attributed to them by professionals and/or trans-generationally created and held by the families over their lengthy involvement with professional systems (that they may or may not have found helpful). This may position certain family members or whole families in ways that impede their participation and use of the group, unless addressed early on in the process. Likewise, where statutory or legal processes are involved, practitioners need to remain mindful of each family's particular situation and their perceptions and understandings of the remit of the group, which may serve both an assessment and intervention function to inform wider decision-making.

A useful strategy is to organise introductory meetings with each family separately prior to the first group meeting. This space may be used by parents to present some of the problem/complaint-saturated narratives but also to explore their hopes, expectations and past experiences of being part of a group. As well as a beginning to establish the positive alliance required, these meetings provide opportunities to dispel misconceptions and fears. In some cases, preparing for the group also means managing engagement difficulties such as non-attendance, inaccurate referral information or anxieties common to families engaging with statutory child protection services—such as the fear that engaging with professionals will involve being judged or increase the likelihood that children might be removed. Introducing the idea of a preferred future (White 2006) and the use of interventive interviewing (Tomm 1987) offer means of exploring the family's willingness and commitment to making appropriate changes.

Whilst MFGT may involve open or closed group work, the latter is arguably more appropriate when working with families at the edge of care, as it can provide a sense of predictability and familiarity. For families and children who may have experienced multiple changes, movements and uncertainty, environments that provide structure and consistency can be conducive to their experiencing and constructing trustful relationships with others. There is consensus amongst practitioners that such groups are more effective when run with five to eight families (Asen and Scholz 2010), whilst a small-scale evaluation to date suggests that it might be easier for multi-troubled families to sustain their engagement for shorter—around 7–8 weeks—rather than longer periods of time (Andreadi and Mensah 2015).

Although many families at the edge of care will be affected by mental health difficulties, abuse and domestic violence, the nature of the work and context means that MFGT is not suitable for participants with active psychotic presentations or perpetrators of child sexual abuse. Within these restrictions, families may be invited to make decisions about whom they would like to bring along to the group. Engaging fathers can present particular challenges but can add different and useful dimensions to the work if prioritised clinically (Walters 2010). Groups may be carried out in community-based settings, in order to de-stigmatise attendance. Accessibility and continued participation can be supported by the provision of creche facilities and transport to and from sessions.

Group facilitators and families are collectively responsible for planning and ensuring the safety of all participants, children and adults. Encouraging the families to set the "ground rules" in the first meeting, and take responsibility for their implementation throughout the process, is informed by a shared hypothesis that edge-of-care families still have knowledge and ideas about what constitutes safety, which they can meaningfully access if instilled with a sense of agency. The process of co-creation enhances the group's relationships and develops inclusiveness and a sense of group culture. Families repeatedly come up with exhaustive and meaningful lists of what will help everyone remain safe and feel respected when set with this task, which has the potential to be transferred to use in the family home. Children can be especially creative when given the opportunity to contribute to thinking around their and their family's safety. They may have expertise over and above those of the adults in some areas, for example, in creating a set of rules for remaining safe whilst using social media. Parents and children may also work together to create joint "rules", as shown in Fig. 9.1.

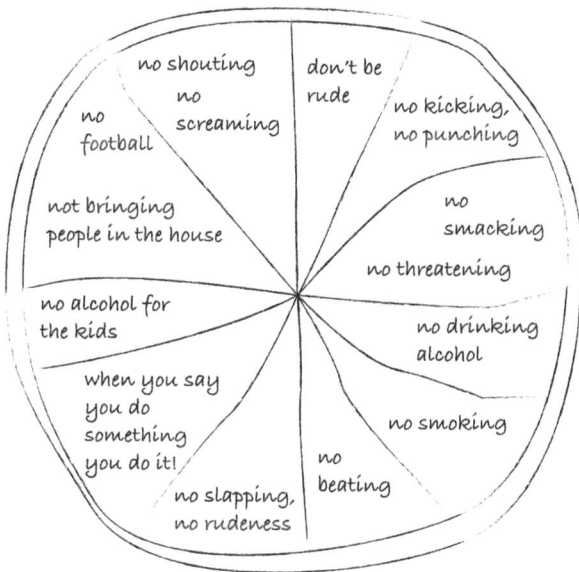

Fig. 9.1 An example of a co-created "pizza for a safer family life"

Establishing an Effective Therapeutic Context

Within systemic thinking, there are multiple views on what constitutes change for a system and how change can be sustained. An important distinction is made between first and second order change (Watzlawick et al. 1974). First order change refers to that which an individual or family can make at the level of behaviour and interaction. This could be suggested and/or imposed by external agents or be the outcome of the individual or family's wish to try something different. For example, a parent may minimise their use of physical chastisement, following professionals' recommendations or fearing the potential consequences if they do not comply. Second order change refers to a substantial shift in an individual's or a system's thinking, beliefs and understandings. For example, a parent may refrain from using physical punishment as they understand that it is having an adverse impact on their child's emotional wellbeing, and they wish to develop more meaningful ways of communicating their wishes to their child. MFGT in edge-of-care contexts is well placed to promote second order change when there is a focus on individuals and families identifying areas in their and their family's life that they would like to be different and developing strategies that will achieve this. For example, participating families might identify "fighting between siblings" as a shared difficulty in the first session; each family unit is then invited to consider their preferred type of sibling relationship and the different factors that might influence those interactions. Each family and the group as a whole can then proceed into finding and trying out ways that will help improve communication and minimise the unhelpful patterns of interaction leading to and maintaining "fighting".

Space may also be created within MFGT for the expectations and perceptions that family members have of themselves and each other to be explored. For example, families where parents have taken up concrete and opposing roles might be invited to reflect on what this role means to them, to other family members and for the overall function of the family, what the expectations, rights and responsibilities are that come with these roles and what would happen if they decided to swap roles for a day. In this way, an increased awareness of interpersonal relating styles is coupled with opportunities to experience new ways of interacting, which makes it more possible for families to make meaningful changes to their circumstances (Thorngren and Kleist 2002).

For some families, the presence of many complex difficulties means the idea of setting and monitoring goals and gaining a sense of achievement might seem very distant. Some families will have had the experience of others—including professionals—telling them what they need to change or do. Helping families identify and share simple things that they would like to change, and which they can focus on achieving within a relatively short space of time, can signify the beginning of reclaiming control of their lives, reconnecting with lost or forgotten hopes and skills and planting seeds of hope for change. Hence, setting simple realistic and clearly defined goals is given priority at the first meeting of an MFGT group. For some, the MFGT group might be their first opportunity to think about change as a family, or to work as a team in the presence of others. As expected, significant dynamics can emerge. Some parents might struggle to give space to their children and go ahead to state what they think should change; some children might set out what they think the adults would like to hear. This provides opportunities for clinicians to consult and support, for example, by facilitating parents revising their pace to encourage and include their children's views. Examples of MFGT goals in edge-of-care contexts are given in Box 9.1.

Box 9.1 MFGT goals in edge-of-care contexts

Working as a team
Getting my children to listen to me
For children not to be nasty to each other
Spend more time with my kids
Stop family members arguing and fighting
Being able to manage the behaviour of my children
For us to listen more to each other
To keep my family safe

Another systemic concept connected to change is an understanding that behaviours and actions (almost always) serve a function according to the context within which they happen. For example, a child who "refuses" to go to school might be "protecting" their parent from an abusive partner. Likewise, problems may be understood as unhelpful patterns of interaction and communication, developed within a family as part of its members' attempted solutions (Cade 1987).

MFGT groups often help families and professionals reframe "bad parenting" and "the child's bad behaviour" as difficulties and challenges shared by many families, often created as intended solutions within the context of long-standing unhelpful patterns of communication. Families are then encouraged to discover other ways of interacting that can be more effective in resolving some of their difficulties. For example, families might decide to hold regular family meetings where they discuss challenges and brainstorm solutions together, instead of reacting in conflictual ways when there is a crisis.

Social learning approaches advocate that children's behaviour is informed by their real life experiences and exposures within their early care giving relationship and environment (Bandura 1977). Accordingly, social learning informed assessment and interventions promote specific parenting behaviours such as positive attention and praise for the desirable behaviour, clear instructions, consistent responses and setting limits to undesirable behaviours in order to achieve the desired change and improve the child's behaviour (O'Connor et al. 2013).

This thinking may usefully translate into MFGT in edge-of-care contexts, where children's behavioural difficulties and parenting issues are often presenting concerns. The group context can support implementation of new parenting practices and subsequent family relationship developments. For example, via the group discussions and experiences shared by other parents, a mother recognises the benefits of having clearly established boundaries and routines in the home and introduces bed time rules. She subsequently observes calmness in the home, more alertness in her children, less frustration in getting up in the morning and some well-needed "me time" for herself after a hectic but satisfying day caring for her children. As she restructures her family subsystems and strengthens boundaries around them (Minuchin 1974), her confidence advances and moves on to allowing more self-caring responsibilities and autonomy to her preadolescent son. As he becomes proud of himself and grows in confidence, their relationship improves with rippling effects on the family and on others in the group as their experience is shared, acknowledged and emulated.

Mentalisation or mentalising is the process by which we make sense of ourselves and each other and our own and the other's actions, thoughts, feelings, intentions and interactions. Rooted in Bowlby's observations and thinking around attachment patterns, mentalisation processes are currently considered important in understanding and working with individuals and families affected by early trauma, difficult attachment histories and ongoing inter-relational difficulties. Consequently, mentalisation-based interventions find a good fit in the work with edge-of-care families and can be effectively applied within a MFGT context (Midgley and Vrouva 2012).

The aim of inviting family members to make sense of their own and others' cognitive and emotional processes in the group context is to identify ways in which their mentalising capacity might be hindered and help them develop reflexivity around their own and others' behaviours and interactions. For example, a parent who interprets their child's repeated detentions as intended to get them into trouble with school professionals might be given tasks that offer alternative understandings of how their children might be feeling and/or what they might be responding to. Similarly, children might be given the task of "looking" with a magnifying glass into their parent's brain and trying to "guess" what they might be thinking and feeling when they are disciplining them for an unwanted behaviour.

Each participating family will be different in terms of their openness and readiness for change, whilst differences might exist between different members of the same family. Some families become more motivated to question and change long-standing beliefs once they have experienced the positive outcomes of a first order level of change, as when a parent's interaction with their child becomes calmer and more effective when they take advice to refrain from raising their voice. There may also be instances where individuals report significant changes in their understanding of their parental role and identity soon after the end of the group process:

I now feel ok about showing how I feel to my kids; before I would hide it all away but I now know that they knew anyway and they'd prefer me to be honest. This whole process made me feel more confident about being a mother and having feelings. (Maria, mother)

Group participants can sometimes experience their interaction with other families as the most helpful aspect of the process:

The best thing was being with the other parents and knowing that they go through what you go through; We are in the same boat. (Pat, grandmother)

This may depend on particular local and cultural contexts. McKay et al. (1995) report similar experiences from their work with groups of inner-city families: "Change is achieved by identification with other families 'who have been there.' … In fact, the presence of other families can be more powerful than the therapist by providing motivation and encouragement for change. The feedback of other families can be less threatening than suggestions offered by the therapists".

MFGT as Collaborative Practice

Systemic and Narrative Therapy practitioners have written extensively about the need for collective methodologies and communal practices that promote meaningful and long-standing change in families, but also in the wider social context (Denborough 2008; Epston and White 1995; Hoffman 2007). As noted above, the presence of multiple families, all sharing similar difficulties, lends itself to the process of re-authoring one's own life and identity narratives and consolidating the new narratives through mutual contribution and appreciative witnessing that the group context can provide. In edge-of-care work, this is especially significant, as most of the families who have been, or are, subject to societal and state intervention have also experienced marginalisation and power differentials in their social position and status.

During MFGT sessions, various techniques, rituals, games and interventions may therefore be used to create a context of mutual learning, developing curiosity about each other and exposure to various skills and competences that serve to develop confidence and enhance relationships within and outside of the family. Families are considered as experts in their lives (Anderson and Goolishian 1992). Professionals and other families therefore become "investigative reporters", trying to find out each family's strengths and aspirations for how they would like their future relationships to be. For example, Appreciative Inquiry (McAdam and Lang 2009) may be used so that the group becomes a space that provides parents and children with more positive experiences and brings forth their abilities and agency. This creates a sense of hopefulness amongst families and the professional systems working with them. Within this paradigm, hope is a significant predictor of change.

Similarly, the Tree of Life approach (ToL) is particularly fitting with the philosophy and intentions of MFGT within edge-of-care contexts. Originally developed as a psychological intervention for children and young people affected by trauma (Ncube 2006), the ToL uses the tree as a metaphor to represent influences, attributes and aspirations as well as significant family and social networks. Used within a narrative therapy framework as a tool for rich story development, it can be adapted and integrated in MFGT groups as a way of helping families reconnect with and share stories of their roots and history, identify and build richer descriptions of their strengths and abilities in the present and express their hopes and wishes for the future. The different elements of the approach also help facilitate a process of externalising problems, rather than situating these in individuals or an individual family. Feedback from families suggests the usefulness and relevance of this approach:

It was nice to do the Trees as it reminded me of the strengths we have as a family and all our networks. (Jessica, mother)

Collective and community approaches rely on and base their effectiveness on the resourcefulness of groups; thus, the appreciative witnessing of improvements made by the participating families in the groups help identify, encourage and reinforce preferred parenting styles and responses, family scripts and patterns of communication (White 2006; Wulff et al. 2011).

To highlight and corroborate changes as they happen, time may usefully be allocated at the beginning of each MFGT session for each family member to feed back to the whole group one behaviour, interaction or family life experience that occurred since the previous sessions that was positive and/or different and they would like to continue building on.

In accordance with narrative collective practices, the last meeting of every MFGT group involves the celebration of the families' journeys and achievements. Each family is encouraged to reflect on their journey. First they are given the opportunity to review their goals and achievements, for example, through the use of scaling questions. They may be invited to present completed Trees of Life to the group, focusing on the values, resilient factors, skills and strengths, as well as some of their hopes and dreams for the future.

Table 9.1 Elements of an MFGT session

Family tea on arrival	This is used as an opportunity to help families develop positive interactions and joint routines—for some families, meal times can be an important focal point, a way of reconnecting, whilst for others, they can be an indicator of disconnection, with some families giving up on ever eating together
Circle and Ball time: checking in and feedback from the week	This is used as an important way for families to reconnect with each other. Usually, sitting in a circle, the ball is thrown by one member to another, with a question which has been agreed by the clinical team. This might include sharing one positive thing that happened to a child or another family member at school or home last week. Through the simple act of others noticing and listening, some children begin to take the steps to speak up with less embarrassment and inhibition and become more eager to identify and share positive stories, whilst negative stories reduce. The applause they receive lightens or brings a sense of happiness and pride. This can also help in reframing parents' views and reports of negative stories about their children. In the case of children who wander away or do not engage, the parent is encouraged—usually by another parent with suggestions—to "gently speak" with the child

(continued)

Table 9.1 (continued)

Joint family activity, as a big group or in single family units	These require families to work together. Clinicians observe, sometimes make suggestions to a particular family or give directions to the whole group, but in the main allow the family to get on with the activity
Parent and child groups: separate activities around the same theme (such as thoughts, feelings, rules and expectations, strengths and skills).	Separate sessions are offered to parents to provide them with the space to air their worries, discuss topics that are not suitable for discussion in the presence of the children and to address aspects of parenting which are problematic. These 40-minute sessions may be used to address issues about setting appropriate boundaries/house rules and how to maintain them, how to manage when emotions get in the way and how to address the legacy of traumatic experiences. Parents tend to present as more relaxed and open in these sessions as they can let their guard down, acknowledge their struggles and learn and support each other in strategies that have worked for them. This also reduces their sense of isolation and frustrations and reinforces the idea that "we are in the same boat".
	During this time, the children are also occupied with activities around the themes discussed by the parents (such as how to express and understand difficult feelings in themselves and in others).
	We have found that some parents venture to raise their frustrations with social care involvement in their lives, sometimes presenting themselves as victims of the system. This can be a useful opportunity for the clinician to intervene and help families consider useful suggestions of how they might reduce statutory intervention in their family through appropriate actions and small but deliberate steps that will bring changes in their and their children's lives
Circle time: feedback and home task	About 20 minutes before the end, the group assembles again in a circle for some reflections and feedback. This is inspired by the "reflecting team" practice (Andersen 1987), but with some adaptation. Families are encouraged by the team to identify their experiences of the day, what they were taking away or what strength they have noticed in their child, themselves or as a family. At times, families are requested to tell each other what they have observed, for example, about interactions as a family and new skills and attitudes they may have noticed.

These are recorded on a certificate provided for this purpose, which each family takes home with them. Other families and the clinical team have the opportunity to comment on one or two qualities they have noticed a particular family have succeeded in developing. Families may bring gifts or shared food and drink to exchange in the last session, which highlights the level of connectedness that has developed and can extend beyond the group. Practice experience suggests that acknowledging improvements for themselves and by others helps families to sustain the changes they have made after the group ends and instils hope for further improvements. Families' growing wish to use their experience and acquired knowledge may translate into a desire to help others:

> *I feel much more confident as a parent. You should run it again and get us to come and help.* (Donna, mother)

This is an outcome often reported by practitioners of collective, community practices. Epston and White (1995) have inspired a lot of this work with their writings on the different positioning of therapists and clients within post-modern therapies. They advocate a practice that de-centres the practitioner and instead positions them as the facilitators of the clients' (individuals, families or whole communities) movement to the position of "expert by experience". This may extend to the use of families who have successfully completed MFGT as co-facilitators for subsequent groups.

Box 9.2 Case example: Kai

Kai was a 35-year-old woman, of African origin, who attended a multi-family group with her four children: M a 9-year-old boy, D a 6-year-old girl and mixed gendered twins (3 years old). She was referred by her social worker who was concerned about the family's isolation, significant physical neglect of the children and Kai's limited skills in managing their difficult behaviour.

At the initial assessment, she reported concerns about her parenting abilities and wanted to expand her skills in managing her children's behaviour more effectively. She was feeling very tired and lacking sleep and opportunities to develop herself. She has not attended a group before, had very

Box 9.2 (continued)

limited social interactions generally and, as a consequence, was anxious about coming.

This is a short extract from an interview with Kai conducted by one of the authors after she had attended a group:

What were your experiences in MGFT?

Very positive! It has been helpful in building relationship with other parents, letting me know that I am not alone, my difficulties were common to other parents and so we were on the same boat. At first, I was very anxious to be in a group, but this disappeared in the first meeting, as I felt very welcome and comfortable. I felt accepted and realised that I was not the only parent struggling with my children. It helped to reduce the isolation of me and my children.

How did it help with your confidence as a parent on a scale of 1 to 10, 10 being the highest you can be?

I would say 9. I am more confident as a parent. Prior to MFGT, first I had no routine, my children would be going to bed at 10 or 12 am or when they are tired and we would have to get up late for school. I was doing everything in the house; I was therefore rushing all the time and very tired, not sleeping well. I was doing everything for my children including cooking, house chores, bathing and dressing all of them. I had gone to my GP complaining of back pains, I was unhappy. This is different now. I have learnt the importance of establishing a routine, boundaries, bedtime. No more late TV. Now my children have an established bedtime and I read them stories before they sleep. My 9-year-old son now bathes and dresses himself, helps with tidying the house and his room, this has increase his confidence. I am teaching the 6-year-old to do the same. I have time to myself when they have all gone to bed. I have a good night's sleep and I feel less tired and less pains in my body.

Before I used to shout but I do not do that anymore.

What helped you in achieving this?

I felt part of the group, I had the opportunity to learn and practice with other parents, I was able to ask questions and felt listened to.

The Role of the MFGT Clinician

It is important to review the context of the role of professionals using the MFGT model, based on the multiple theoretical frameworks and practice implementations described in this chapter. Clinicians and others facilitating multi-family groups in edge-of-care contexts may often be asked to inform decision-making about safeguarding by evidencing of families' capacity to make changes in their interactions and communication within a prescribed time framework. Lang et al. (1990) argue that professionals acting out of this "Domain of Production" can still create space for the development of alternative explanations and possible change, if they adopt a curious and explorative stance towards the family's narrative and presentation. Lang also suggests that practitioners adopt an ethical and graceful position regardless of the actual task in focus, whether writing an informal record of the family's participation to the group to share with colleagues or contributing to a court report—with our formulations about the interactions within a family and with the other families in the group positioned within the context of the "Domain of Aesthetics" that should over-arch all actions in a professional context.

In therapeutic practice, it is well known that the practitioner's role is central to any intervention, whatever the modality, and evidence indicate that the therapeutic relationship is a major contributor to positive outcomes (Hubble et al. 1999). Both the personality and functions of the practitioner are key in MFGT interventions at the edge of care. Working with several families in the room at the same time holds more complexities than providing intervention with one family in the room. The MFGT practitioner has a "multi-positional" role that involves continually shifting positions in terms of physical and mental movement around the room, being temporarily engaged with one family and a distant observer to another in the attempt to facilitate intra- and inter-family connections. The MFGT practitioner has to be ready to intervene in small and larger ways, in an informal context with individual family members or a particular family when they execute a specific task, to direct instructions or comment on team work, to offer observations on the interaction between a parent and child or a whole family, to coach a child or a parent in practicing a skill, to invite thinking of new possibilities or to raise sensitive issues and encourage reflections. When families have complex difficulties and risk issues are present, the level of competence needed to do this requires skills development and ongoing supervisory and peer support.

For example, it may be necessary to intervene with a family whose conflictual interactions raise issues of emotional and physical safety within the group. The solution may be to respectfully but authoritatively advise and support a short "time out" outside the group, which can offer space to ventilate and recalibrate whilst sending a clear message about mutual accountability and the level of concern raised. Such interventions also have implications for the practical aspects of MFGT, including the ratio of therapists to families and the choice of venue. Effective co-working is also paramount, as it can filter down to the families and can function as a model for their developing communication and negotiation patterns. The potential of co-facilitating and sharing tasks between two or three practitioners can also be maximised when roles and responsibilities are allocated in a way that is mindful of each therapist's strengths, limitations and resources. Setting aside time for pre- and post-session team meetings (for planning and debriefing) can prove a useful investment for sustaining reflexive practice.

Conclusion

Multi-Family Group Therapy offers a promising means to effectively address family risk factors and affect meaningful change, identified as key priorities in edge-of-care practice (Brandon et al. 2008; Munro 2011). Likewise, this approach offers a space for fostering dialogue, multiple perspectives and the co-creation of alternative—potentially safer—responses, which are often compromised in situations of high risk, uncertainty and professional and family anxiety (Campbell 2009). The epistemologically collaborative nature of MFGT also supports engagement and a shift from critical and sometimes blaming narratives to more supportive and facilitative interactions between professionals and families in edge-of-care contexts. Further practice development and formal evaluation of the approach in this setting is therefore recommended.

References

Anderson, C. M. (1983). A psycho-educational program for families of patients with schizophrenia. In W. R. McFarlene (Ed.), *Family therapy in Schizophrenia*. New York: Guilford.

Andersen, T. (1987). The reflecting team: Dialogue and meta-dialogue in clinical work. *Family Process, 26*, 415–442.

Anderson, H., & Gehart, D. (2007). *Collaborative therapy: Relationships and conversations that make a difference*. New York: Routledge.

Anderson, H., & Goolishian, H. (1992). The client is the expert: A not-knowing approach to therapy. In S. McNamee & K. Gergen (Eds.), *Social construction and the therapeutic process*. Newbury Park, CA: Sage.

Andreadi, H., & Mensah, E. (2015). *Presenting a pilot of multi-family group therapy with families known to Hackney Children and Young People's Services*. Hackney CYPS Clinical Service Away Day, London.

Asen, K. E. (2002). Multiple family therapy: An overview. *Journal of Family Therapy, 24*, 3–16.

Asen, K. E., & Scholz, M. (2010). *Multi family therapy: Concepts and techniques*. Oxford: Routledge.

Asen, K. E., Stein, R., Stevens, A., McHugh, B., Greenwood, J., & Cooklin, A. (1982). A day unit for families. *Journal of Family Therapy, 4*, 345–358.

Bandura, A. (1977). *Social learning theory*. Englewood Cliffs, NJ: Prentice Hall.

Barratt, S. (2012). Incorporating multi-family days into parenting assessments: The Writtle Wick model. *Child and Family Social Work, 17*, 222–232.

Bateson, G. (1972). *Steps to an ecology of mind: Collected essays in anthropology, psychiatry, evolution, and epistemology*. San Francisco, CA: Chandler.

Brandon, M., Belderson, P., Warren, C., Howe, D., Gardner, R., Dodsworth, J., & Black, J. (2008). *Analysing child deaths and serious injury through abuse and neglect: What can we Learn? A Biennial analysis of serious case reviews 2003–2005*. London: Department for Children Schools and Families.

Burnham, J. (2005). Relational reflexivity: A tool for socially constructing therapeutic relationships. In C. Flaskas, B. Mason, & A. Perlesz (Eds.), *The space between: Experience, context and process in the therapeutic relationship*. London: Karnac.

Cade, B. (1987). Brief/strategic approaches to therapy: A Commentary [education update]. *Australian and New Zealand Journal of Family Therapy, 8*, 37–44.

Campbell, D. (2009). *The best decisions emerge from dialogue*. Presented at Moving Forward for Children and Families Seminar organised by AFT/ Guardian/STP (23rd February 2009).

Carr, A. (2005). *Family therapy: Concepts, process and practice*. New York: John Wiley and Sons.

Cooklin, A., Miller, A., & McHugh, B. (1983). An institution for change: Developing a family day unit. *Family Process, 22*, 453–468.

Denborough, D. (2008). *Collective narrative practice: Responding to individuals, groups, and communities who have experienced trauma.* Adelaide: Dulwich Centre Publications.

Epston, D., & White, M. (1995). Consulting your consultants: A means to the co-construction of alternative knowledges. In S. Friedman (Ed.), *The reflecting team in action.* New York: Guilford.

Flaskas, C. (1997). Engagement and the therapeutic relationship in systemic therapy. *Journal of Family Therapy, 19*(3), 263–282.

Fredman, G. (2004). *Transforming emotion: Conversations in counselling and psychotherapy.* London: Wiley.

Gonsalez, S., Steinglass, P., & Reiss, D. (1989). Putting the illness in its place: Discussion groups for families with chronic medical illnesses. *Family Process, 28,* 69–87.

Hoffman, L. (2007). The art of withness. In H. Anderson & D. Gehart (Eds.), *Collaborative therapies: Relationships and conversations that make a difference.* New York: Routledge.

Hubble, M., Duncan, B., & Miller, S. (Eds.). (1999). *The heart and soul of change: What works in therapy.* Washington, DC: American Psychological Association.

Kaufman, E., & Kaufman, P. (Eds.). (1979). *Family therapy of drug and alcohol abuse.* New York: Gardner.

Lang, P., Little, M., & Cronen, V. (1990). The systemic professional: Domains of action and the question of neutrality. *Human Systems: The Journal of Systemic Consultation and Management, 1,* 34–49.

Laqueur, H. P. (1973). Multiple family therapy: Questions and answers. In D. Bloch (Ed.), *Techniques for psychotherapy.* New York: Grune and Stratton.

Laqueur, H. P., La Burt, H. A., & Morong, E. (1964). Multiple family therapy: Further developments. *Current Psychiatric Therapies, 4,* 150–154.

Mason, B. (2010). Six aspects of supervision and the training of supervisors. *Journal of Family Therapy, 32,* 436–439.

McAdam, E., & Lang, P. (2009). *Appreciative work in schools: Generating future communities.* Chichester: Kingsham Press.

McFarlene, W. R. (1982). Multiple family in the Psychiatric hospital. In H. Harbin (Ed.), *The Psychiatric hospital and the family.* New York: Spectrum.

McKay, M. M., Gonzales, J. J., Stone, S., Ryland, D., & Kohner, K. (1995). Multiple family therapy groups: A responsive intervention model for inner city families. *Social Work with Groups, 18,* 41–56.

Meezan, W., & O'Keefe, M. (1998). Multifamily group therapy: Impact on family functioning and child behaviour. *Families in Society: The Journal of Contemporary Human Services, 79*(1), 32–44.

Midgley, M., & Vrouva, I. (Eds.). (2012). *Minding the child: Mentalization-based interventions with children, young people and their families*. London: Routledge.

Minuchin, S. (1974). *Families and family therapy*. London: Tavistock Publications.

Minuchin, S., Lee, W. Y., & Simon, G. S. (2006). *Mastering family therapy: Journeys of growth and transformation* (2nd ed.). New York: Wiley.

Munro, E. (2011). *The Munro review of child protection: Final report, a child-centred system CM 8062*. London: Department for Education.

Ncube, N. (2006). The tree of life project: Using narrative ideas in work with vulnerable children in South Africa. *International Journal of Narrative Therapy and Community Work, 1*, 3–16.

O'Connor, T. G., Matias, C., Futh, A., Tantam, G., & Scott, S. (2013). Social learning theory parenting intervention promotes attachment-based caregiving in young children: A randomized clinical trial. *Journal of Clinical Child & Adolescent Psychology, 42*(3), 358–370.

Rober, P. (1998). Reflections on ways to create a safe culture for children in family therapy. *Family Process, 37*, 201–213.

Sayger, T. V. (1996). Creating resilient children and empowering families using a multi-family process. *The Journal for Specialists in Group Work, 21*, 81–89.

Slagerman, M., & Yager, J. (1989). Multiple family group for treatment for eating disorders: A short term program. *Psychiatric Medicine, 7*, 269–283.

Thorngren, J. M., & Kleist, D. M. (2002). Multiple family group therapy: An interpersonal/postmodern approach. *The Family Journal, 10*(2), 167–176.

Tomm, K. (1987). Interventive interviewing: Part II. Reflexive questioning as a means to enable self healing. *Family Process, 26*, 153–183.

Walters, J. (2010). *Working with fathers: From knowledge to therapeutic practice*. London: Palgrave Macmillan.

Wattie, M. (1994). Multiple group family therapy. *Journal of Child and Youth Care, 9*, 31–38.

Watzlawick, P., Weakland, J. W., & Fisch, R. (1974). *Change*. New York: Norton.

White, M. (2006). Working with children who have experienced significant trauma. In M. White & A. Morgan (Eds.), *Narrative therapy with children and their families*. Adelaide, Australia: Dulwich Centre Publications.

Wilson, J. (1993). The supervisory relationship in FT training. *Human Systems: The Journal of Systemic Management and Consultation, 4*, 173–178.

Wulff, D. P., St George, S. A., & Besthorn, F. H. (2011). Revisiting confidentiality: Observations from family therapy practice. *Journal of Family Therapy, 33*, 199–214.

10

Understanding and Preventing Re-victimisation

Elly Hanson

Introduction

Re-victimisation following sexual, physical and emotional abuse is a key risk issue for children and young people at the edge of care. Clinical practice in this context therefore offers opportunities to address risk and prevent future harm. To this end, this chapter summarises what is currently known about the factors and processes that underlie re-victimisation and explores promising interventions designed to reduce the problem. There is a focus on interventions relevant to edge-of-care settings (with individuals, families and systems) and on overcoming the challenges to their implementation.

Sexual violence subsequent to child sexual abuse (CSA) is one form of re-victimisation warranting focussed attention, because research indicates that these forms of child and adolescent/adult victimisation are the most closely linked. Child sexual abuse (CSA) is often followed by fur-

E. Hanson (✉)
Bristol, UK

© The Author(s) 2016
L. Smith (ed.), *Clinical Practice at the Edge of Care*,
DOI 10.1007/978-3-319-43570-1_10

ther sexual victimisation in adolescence and adulthood by different per-petrators (Arata 2002; Boney-McCoy and Finkelhor 1995). Prospective longitudinal studies have found that girls sexually abused pre-adolescence were twice as likely to be sexually victimised in adolescence or adulthood compared to matched samples who had not experienced CSA (Barnes et al. 2009; Noll et al. 2003). An extensive review by Classen et al. (2005) further concluded that two out of three women with a history of CSA are likely to suffer subsequent sexual victimisation. This re-victimisation is a problem in and of itself, and because it contributes to psychologi-cal and physical difficulties in adolescence and beyond, adding to the impact of the original sexual abuse (Arata 2002; Green et al. 2000). This is the area where most thinking around practice has developed; and it will therefore be the primary focus of this chapter. However, there are links between most forms of childhood, adolescent and adult interper-sonal victimisations (Widom et al. 2008), and the ideas put forward here are largely relevant to reducing all such forms of re-victimisation. These might include, for example, child sexual exploitation (CSE) and domes-tic abuse following childhood neglect or physical abuse (Hanson 2016; Farmer and Callan 2012).

Guiding principles for the prevention of all types of re-victimisation in edge-of-care contexts are as follows:

- The risk of a child being re-victimised following childhood maltreat-ment should always be thought about and where possible reduced
- Actions to prevent re-victimisation are often the same as those required to improve children and young people's wellbeing and relationships and to tackle the impact of abuse
- Re-victimisation is a risk whether or not a child develops difficulties that fit into diagnostic categories of "mental disorder". Following abuse all children have a right to (United Nations Convention on the Rights of the Child 1989) and may benefit from assessment and sup-port, even if they do not have a mental health diagnosis
- Therapy is only one of a number of vehicles by which the risk of re-victimisation can be reduced; universal education, mentoring, interventions with peers and families, physical and social activities and social justice approaches might all usefully be part of the picture.

It should also be noted that a focus on working with children, young people and their systems to reduce re-victimisation is not meant to imply that they are *responsible* for either its prevention or occurrence. A *both, and* perspective can be taken in which responsibility for abuse is squarely placed with those perpetrating it (and complicit people and organisations), whilst the influence of wider contributory systemic and social factors (such as family and peer group issues) is also attended to. For practitioners in edge-of-care settings, these factors may, at times, be more accessible and amenable to intervention than perpetrator-focussed approaches or individual work with children and young people.

Understanding Re-victimisation

High rates of re-victimisation are accounted for by two types of factors: (1) those that increase the risk of both the initial and subsequent victimisations (e.g., poverty and neighbourhood qualities, parental mental health and substance misuse) and (2) those that are set in motion by the initial abusive experience (e.g., low self-esteem). Table 10.1 outlines key social and psychological factors that research suggests are involved in sexual re-victimisation. Although this highlights a tremendous amount of research, work is still to be done on clarifying which factors are most contributory. More longitudinal studies are needed, along with further exploration of social and systemic factors, developmental trajectories and issues relating to diversity. Most research to date has focussed on the experiences of girls and women. Although many of the factors are also likely to be relevant for boys, at times there will be different dynamics at play linked to gendered patterns of abuse and gender roles (Ruback et al. 2014).

Factors leading to re-victimisation often interact with one another in a variety of ways. Although this adds complexity, it can also create opportunities in support and therapeutic work, as addressing one issue often also impacts another and so on (Briere 2004). Several models of re-victimisation propose the key "mechanisms" at play (e.g., Lynn et al. 2004; Macy 2007; Noll and Grych 2011; Pittenger et al. 2016; Zurbriggen and

Table 10.1 Factors involved in re-victimisation

Factors involved in re-victimisation		Exemplar studies
Post-traumatic stress symptoms (hyperarousal, intrusions and behavioural avoidance)		Messman-Moore et al. (2005), Auslander et al. (2016), Wolfe et al. (2004), Stockdale et al. (2014)
Distress (usually defined in studies as anxiety and depression)		Cuevas et al. (2010), Auslander et al. (2016), Orcutt et al. (2005), Foshee et al. (2004)
Substance misuse		McCart et al. (2012), Messman-Moore et al. (2013), Testa et al. (2010)
Emotional dysregulation (difficulty controlling negative emotions and achieving emotional equilibrium)		Messman-Moore et al. (2013), Ullman and Vasquez (2015)
Difficulties in detecting (often sexual) risk in social relationships and taking subsequent self-protective action		DePrince (2005), Franklin (2013), Gobin and Freyd (2009), Messman-Moore and Brown (2006), Waldron et al. (2015)
Protective factor Post-traumatic growth and positive appraisals following abuse		Irwin (1999), Miller et al. (2011)
Reduced awareness or acknowledgement	Dissociation	Noll et al. (2003)
	Avoidant coping	Fortier et al. (2009)
	Unacknowledged abuse	Littleton et al. (2009)
	Stigma-motivated nondisclosure	Miller et al. (2011)
Self-, other and relational schemas and related emotions and relational patterns	Low self-esteem and low sexual self-esteem	Foshee et al. (2004)
	Non-assertiveness (including in sexual situations)	Ullman and Vasquez (2015), Classen et al. (2001), Vanzile-Tamsen et al. (2005)
	Focussed on the needs of others to the exclusion of one's own	Classen et al. (2001)
	Sensitivity to rejection	Young and Furman (2008)
	Shame, guilt and self-blame	Kessler and Bieschke (1999), Messman-Moore et al. (2013), Tapia (2014)

(*continued*)

Table 10.1 (continued)

Factors involved in re-victimisation		Exemplar studies
Sexual issues	Risky sexual practices (such as less use of contraception, casual encounters)	Bramsen et al. (2013), Miner et al. (2006), Testa et al. (2010), Fargo (2009), Miron and Orcutt (2014)
	Use of sex to reduce negative affect	Orcutt et al. (2005), Miron and Orcutt (2014)
	Sexual preoccupation	Noll et al. (2003)
Social and systemic factors	Family where there is violence, mental health difficulties, substance misuse and/or multiple caregivers	Fargo (2009), Kellogg and Hoffman (1997)
	Protective factor Social support and good friendships	Bender et al. (2003), Collins (1998), Finkelhor et al. (2007)
	Neighbourhood poverty	Drake and Pandey (1996)
	Neighbourhood disorder and lack of cohesion	Obasaju et al. (2009)

Freyd 2004). In practice, this means that there are several likely routes to re-victimisation that may be amenable to intervention.

Post-traumatic stress disorder (PTSD) is one of the strongest and most evidenced risk factors for re-victimisation, and symptoms of hyper-arousal appear to play a particularly important role (Risser et al. 2006). These may compromise a young person's ability to detect real from perceived danger, and their attention may be focussed on inner intrusions (e.g., feelings or images related to the prior abuse) at the cost of attention to their current situation (McCart et al. 2012). A client at Cloitre and Rosenberg's clinic "remarked that her feelings of fear alternated so wildly that she could never trust them to function as a guide to action. She said she had been physically abused so often as a child that her 'danger sensor was smashed'" (Cloitre and Rosenberg 2006).

Emotion dysregulation difficulties may impede a person's ability to detect threat in a similar fashion, as intense and fluctuating emotions may confuse and impair social awareness. They can also prompt defensive and avoidant coping mechanisms that place a person at risk. For example, a young person may regularly and desperately reach to alcohol use or impersonal sex to reduce negative feelings; and their compulsive use of such coping responses may then be exploited by perpetrators. Young people may be more likely to use avoidant coping if they believe their emotions to be harmful, overwhelming or a reflection of weakness, "madness" or deficiency.

> I get into cars with men I don't know, take drugs and do bad things because I'm depressed.
> "P" aged 16, quoted in Pearce (2002).

Risky sexual practices (such as multiple sexual encounters with different people and the infrequent use of contraception) are also associated with re-victimisation. Girls are more likely to engage in risky sexual practices if they have a large number of male peers, though good friendships with boys and older females can be protective (Noll et al. 2000). Risky sexual behaviour is also more likely if experiences of sexual abuse led to experiencing sexual feelings early on, if consensual sexual activity began early relative to peers or if young people experience high levels of sexual preoccupation (Noll et al. 2011; Simon and Feiring 2008). It appears that sexual abuse may contribute to the use of sex to manage emotions partly via its impact on the early development of the sexual arousal system.

Turning to strategies that children may use to cope with the abuse itself, a passive and submissive approach is often necessary in abusive situations but can create subsequent vulnerability. If abuse is inescapable, active resistance can increase danger, as abusers may respond to it by being increasingly forceful. However, submissiveness becomes maladaptive in situations where the person does have more control. As articulated by McCollum (2015), "one way in which children who are abused survive is by learning how to tolerate, rather than to escape from, dangerous situations ... they make themselves more vulnerable to re-victimisation ... because they respond to danger not by getting out of it but by staying in it and confirming the survival strategies that made them feel safe throughout their childhood". Some research suggests that sexual abuse survivors may be particularly vulnerable to reverting to this coping strategy when intoxicated (Staples et al. 2015).

Dissociation is a closely related coping strategy and involves children reducing their awareness of the abuse whilst it is happening or their emotions or memories about it afterwards (often on into adulthood). Children and young people may be more likely to dissociate from their abuse-related memories and feelings if there is no available framework to help them to make sense of it and no-one to help them manage otherwise overwhelming feelings and understandings; for example, "I am damaged, defective, worthless" (Talbot et al. 2004). When faced with a contradiction between their experiences and the social narratives around them, children may dissociate from their abuse-related memories and feelings in order to avoid the confusion that would otherwise result. Lynn et al. (2004) argue that, alongside dissociation, survivors however retain an intact sense of a different, abusive social world and may seek to "match" their current social world to this reality to find coherence. They suggest that some survivors "may find potential abusers subjectively 'more real' than non-abusers who do not and cannot inhabit the dissociated social world shared so intimately by perpetrators".

> So much of my life is just sectioned off. And it had to be while I was a kid. I mean, I couldn't be going to school and remembering all that stuff. Y'know, there was two worlds.
> "Darren", adult survivor of organised sexual abuse (Salter 2012).

This social narrative model of re-victimisation complements Betrayal Trauma Theory developed by Jennifer Freyd and colleagues, for which there is now a wealth of evidence (DePrince et al. 2012). In a nutshell, this theory posits that children reduce their awareness of abuse by a person they depend on in order to maintain relationships crucial to their survival. It is more adaptive to be able to act as if everything is "normal" than to face the abuse and the threat it holds. It would be hard to keep functioning with the full knowledge that the people who are meant to be one's source of safety are also the source of danger (or collude with it). DePrince (2005) and others find evidence that survivors of betrayal trauma often have reduced awareness of social rules, which, whilst highly adaptive for surviving abuse, makes it harder for them to detect and escape from social threat in adolescence and adulthood.

A tendency to dissociate in response to abuse-related triggers may also lead some survivors to lose awareness of the present in sexual situations, undermining their ability to exert agency (whether it be consent, escape, or resistance).

> I realise now looking back that even as a little girl I was hiding my own feelings, doing things that I didn't really want to do so as not to upset others, making decisions based on what I thought other people wanted me to do, and basically thinking/feeling that every other person was better than me and I was inferior.

> These fixed beliefs come to us at a very young age and getting rid of them or even going against them is really really hard. I find saying no and putting myself first almost physically uncomfortable. I get this horrible feeling in the pit of my stomach that I'm doing something wrong and I'm going to get told off (Internet forum discussion between women who have experienced domestic abuse; accessed via http://www.womensaid.org.uk, 06/2012).

All forms of child abuse can lead a child to develop negative schemas (or core beliefs) about themselves, others and social relationships. They may come to believe that they are bad, powerless or unworthy of unconditional love; that others are typically more powerful and malevolent; that social relationships typically conform to dominant-submissive patterns; and that sex is a means to be valued and primarily about meeting the other person's needs. Such beliefs can contribute to risk of revictimisation in a variety of ways. For example, young people may comply with sexual coercion, believing that they are powerless to resist it, that they deserve it or that it is necessary to retain desperately sought after love and commitment (Young and Furman 2008).

> *It's only possible to protect yourself if you think you're worth protecting. "R", victim of CSE (Pearce 2002).*

There are few studies that specifically examine the impact of family relationships and behaviour on re-victimisation. Trust between parents and young people and parental monitoring can reduce risky sexual behaviour (Borawski et al. 2003; DiClemente et al. 2001), possibly in turn reducing re-victimisation. Jankowski et al. (2002) found that parental caring did not protect children from re-victimisation, although other research indicates that supportive responses to disclosure may help to do so (Casey and Nurius 2005). This concords with a wider literature demonstrating that caregiver validation and support following abuse can reduce difficulties such as PTSD and distress (Hong and Lishner 2016), thereby likely also reducing re-victimisation.

Tied to this, denial and dissociation in parents and caregivers may encourage dissociative problems in children, (thereby also increasing risk), because they reduce the opportunities for children to adaptively make sense of and integrate their experiences. More straightforwardly, these tendencies can impede parents' ability to acknowledge and recognise abuse and so protect children from it (McCollum 2015). The difficult emotions parents may struggle with after they find about sexual abuse can also undermine protection and support (Cahalane et al. 2013; Tavkar and Hansen 2011), which in turn increases risk of further abuse. There can be particular complexities in edge-of-care contexts where family breakdown results from parents disbelieving or denying children's disclosures of abuse or where parents respond in accordance with loyalties to both the child and perpetrator. A variety of relational and psycho-social processes within the family are likely to be at play in such situations, which need to be explored and understood whilst risks are managed.

Turning to peer group and wider social influences, it would appear that good friendships reduce risk of re-victimisation (Collins 1998), whereas societal pressures to sexually objectify oneself and others increases it (Franklin 2013; Brown and L'Engle 2009). Cultural products such as pornography may reinforce to female survivors messages communicated by previous sexual abuse, such as their value being bound up in their sexuality and sexual submission and sex primarily being about male (other people's) gratification.

It is worth emphasising that no factor discussed here *causes* re-victimisation and that the only thing necessary for re-victimisation is a person who behaves abusively. Clearly the risk a young person faces is most closely related to the number of people in their social worlds willing or predisposed to abuse and the degree to which others collude.

Towards Effective Interventions

Promising approaches to preventing re-victimisation are now emerging in clinical practice, with many being particularly relevant to at-risk children and young people at the edge of care. Those discussed here are by necessity a limited set of suggestions, to be taken as points of reference and focus, rather than as a constricting list. For other approaches, and evidence of effectiveness, see Lindsey et al. (2014) and Bolton-Oetzel and Scherer (2003).

Disclosure

When no-one else beyond the perpetrator(s) and victim is aware that abuse has occurred/is occurring, telling someone else what has happened/is happening can lead to support and protection. However, children usually face many barriers to disclosure, put in place by the person(s) abusing and wider systems (Collin-Vézina et al. 2015). Children are attuned to how family members are likely to respond and adapt their decision to tell accordingly (Hershkowitz et al. 2007). They may fear what the abusive person will do, the impact on their family, what will happen to them, and blame themselves and/or feel ashamed. They may also lack a formal understanding of the abuse being "wrong", may not have the vocabulary to help them tell or may not have someone they can turn to. Furthermore, when children do try to tell someone (often through behaviour and "testing the water" with small details), their disclosures frequently go unheard (Allnock and Miller 2013). Such issues can be heightened for children and young people at the edge of care, who may lack trusted and reliable confidantes and may be in situations where they fear being removed from their families and/or be concerned that making disclosures will affect contact with parents and siblings.

Both universal and specialist services should be alive to the barriers to children telling others about abuse and proactively attempt to reduce them. Positive actions might include:

- Giving all children knowledge and principles to help them understand that abuse is not okay, ways to articulate to others any experiences of abuse and means to get help if their friends disclose. Examples include NSPCC schools work and their "Underwear Rule" campaign, which can be adopted by local areas (nspcc.org.uk)
- Training for all those who work with children and young people about potential indicators of abuse, as well as how to speak to children about it—including foster carers, youth justice practitioners, sexual health nurses and other professionals who may come into contact with the most vulnerable children and young people
- Universal services such as schools including regular wellbeing checks for all children by trusted adults (such as their class teacher, teaching assistant or learning mentor), with clear multi-agency arrangements for any concerns to be reflected and acted upon
- Where abuse is suspected or risk is heightened, undertaking work to shift power structures and collusive practices that may be impeding any disclosures and educating families and communities about abuse, so that if a child does disclose, they are heard, affirmed and protected

Disclosure is a gradual process. Children are often able to say more after they are kept safe; feel cared for and accepted by someone; and appreciate that what happened was abusive and they were not to blame.

The process of labelling and articulating abuse can reduce a young person's risk of re-victimisation. Practitioners working with children and young people at the edge of care therefore need to be thoughtful about the significance of children developing or losing trust in adults (such as family members and foster carers), the quality of key attachment relationships and children's strategies for managing conflicting feelings and loyalties—particularly within alternate care arrangements. These can all influence whether disclosures are possible and manageable for the child.

Engagement

A significant proportion of young people and their families do not engage with, or drop-out of, support and therapy offered following abuse (Saxe et al. 2012). People may fear negative consequences of support (such as stigma, blame, exposure, intrusion or psychological problems worsening) or see it as irrelevant, ineffective or unfeasible. Services should therefore actively work to provide options that address these concerns and offer discussions and information that enable people to make decisions in their best interests. This can usefully involve starting from an explicitly strengths- and solutions-based approach, for example, by sharing positive assumptions about the family and child and communicating an understanding of difficulties as adaptations (that is, as normal responses to abnormal experiences). It is also important that services and practitioners prioritise developing strong therapeutic relationships with those who have experienced abuse; key qualities being empathy, compassion, hope and validation (Ackerman and Hilsenroth 2003).

Models of practice that are most likely to be effective in preventing re-victimisation have engagement as a core component. For example, Trauma Systems Therapy aims to enhance engagement of children and families in trauma-focussed work through a blend of methods, including education about trauma, co-ordination of all help through one lead provider, problem-solving and explicitly and collaboratively mapping out the therapeutic journey. Initial evidence suggests this can increase engagement by 80% (Saxe et al. 2012). Another promising approach is that of the London-based charity MAC-UK. Working with young people who are typically offending, in gangs, and experiencing mental health difficulties, they are engaged (via outreach conversations) in projects of interest (involving music or sport) and offered "street therapy" alongside, often in small chunks and as where and when young people feel comfortable. A first evaluation found that 90 % of the young people that the charity worked with, who had not previously received help, engaged to the fullest extent possible, and high proportions desisted from crime and engaged in employment, education and training (Chakkalackal and Cyhlarova 2013). It is plausible that the approach of MAC-UK helps many young people to escape from patterns of re-victimisation (given the extent of victimisation in such groups) (Ruback et al. 2014). Other flexible, co-ordinated and strengths-based approaches to working with families whose children are at risk of sexual exploitation include the Relational Safeguarding Model (PACE 2014) and Barnado's Families and Communities Against Sexual Exploitation (FCASE; D'Arcy et al. 2015).

Assessment

Clinical assessments that seek to identify risks of re-victimisation need to explore individual, family and systemic factors. These may include identifying "latent" psychological vulnerabilities (such as shame, negative working models of self and others, sexual preoccupation) as well as more overt difficulties, such as anxiety, depression, post-traumatic stress, family conflict and issues within peer groups.

Beyond reflective and conversational interviews with parents, children, teachers and others (depending on developmental stage and context), useful questionnaires include those that holistically assess a variety of common consequences of abuse (such as the Trauma Symptom Checklists: TSCC, Briere 1996, and TSCYC, Briere et al. 2001) and those that explore often hidden but relevant issues such as shame, dissociation, coping strategies and understandings of the abuse (such as the Trauma Appraisal Questionnaire, DePrince et al. 2010, for adolescents, and the Child Dissociative Checklist; Putnam et al. 1993). Validated story stem approaches, in which children's representations of family and peer relationships are explored by asking them to complete stories using doll vignettes, are a useful addition to the assessment of pre-adolescent children (Robinson 2007).

Working with Parents and Caregivers

All (non-abusive) parents deserve support following the discovery of their children's abuse, and this will likely benefit both themselves and their children (Corcoran and Pillai 2008). Even the most loving parents may struggle to provide their children with what they need following abuse, given that they will be dealing with many intense feelings (such as shock, rage, fear, self-blame, stigma and sometimes divided loyalties; Tavkar and Hansen 2011) and may well not have a complete understanding of the impact of abuse, its dynamics and children's needs going forwards. Clinical work with parents and caregivers should explore the impact on the wider family of finding out about the abuse and their feelings and attitudes about abuse in general, relationships with the perpetrator(s) and their children's emotions and narratives. Well-meaning but potentially harmful approaches parents and caregivers may take include placing too much responsibility on children to avoid future abuse, minimising (or indeed exaggerating) its impact, avoiding discussion about the abuse and expressing aggressive intent towards the abuser(s), which can leave children feeling isolated (Allnock and Miller 2013; Deblinger and Runyon 2005). These can be particularly significant issues for children in alternate care arrangements—such as those placed with members of their extended family or in foster care—or for those who are reunified with their families following a period of time in care.

Parental and caregiver interventions may be group or individual, stand-alone or interwoven with their child's treatment, one or two sessions or longer courses and focussed only on the abuse or a wider set of relevant issues (van Toledo and Seymour 2013; Galloway and Hogg 2008; Smith 1994, 2012; and Corcoran 2004). All of this will depend on the issues at play for a particular family or caregiving context and what is available and needed locally. Where possible, other significant adults should be included to create a support network. At a minimum, parent- and caregiver-focussed interventions should interweave two core components:

- *Psycho-education directly aimed at strengthening constructive parental/ caregiver support.* Information should be provided to parents/carers about the dynamics and impact of abuse (including grooming of children and families when the abuse is sexual) and what children need following abuse: protection from further abuse, belief in what they say, explicit non-blame, validation of their emotions and spaces to work out and express them. Children also need to sensitively hear messages from their parents and carers that will help them to reduce or avoid self-blame, shame, negative schemas about themselves and narrow sexualised identities. Online written information (e.g., Hanson 2015) can provide an initial starting point for conversations. A balance is necessary between sharing ideas and information and helping parents and carers apply all of their existing strengths to this new situation. Many will have previously drawn on skills in helping children and others deal with stress and difficulty, which can be used in this context.
- *Space to process and reflect on their feelings about the abuse.* Reflective listening and sensitive questions can help parents and carers express their feelings about the abuse and how it appears to have affected the child and to begin to adaptively make sense of it in ways that help themselves and their child. This can help negative emotions to reduce in strength so that they do not compromise offering child-centred support (as well as being a goal in and of itself).

In relation to older children, parents and carers may also benefit from support around positive parenting of adolescents, especially focussed on balancing supervision and monitoring with building trust and empowerment. Authoritative (versus authoritarian or permissive) parenting helps build resilience and reduce risky behaviours (Chan and Koo 2010; Oberlander et al. 2011).

Where parents have difficulties such as mental health problems, substance misuse or their own ongoing victimisation, or where their child's abuse has triggered distress related to their own childhood experiences (Hébert et al. 2007), it may be necessary to offer individual therapeutic support. This is also the case when parents appear to deny, dissociate from or minimise their children's abuse, potentially linked to how they coped with abuse towards themselves (McCollum 2015). This therapy might interweave direct guidance on support for their child, or this could follow. The South Essex Rape and Incest Crisis Centre early offer programme is a good example of a blend of the above support options applied in practice. This service offers therapy, information about abuse and keeping one's child safe and parenting support to all mothers who have experienced abuse themselves in childhood and have a child known to children's social care. Narrative and systemic therapies have also been identified as a means to deal with the complexities of disrupted family dynamics and to promote the protective capacities of non-abusing parents (Smith 2012).

Therapeutic Interventions With Children and Young People

Group and individual therapeutic support for children and young people can effectively tackle the psychological difficulties that increase vulnerability to re-victimisation. Although there are few studies delineating the impact of interventions on further rates of abuse specifically, there is reason to believe that if they can reduce problems such as PTSD, sexual risk-taking, distress, dissociation, negative schemas, emotion dysregulation and substance misuse, then they will also help to protect children from further abuse (Trask et al. 2011; Sánchez-Meca et al. 2011). A discussion of the full range of psychological interventions with proven efficacy in these areas is beyond the scope of this chapter. The treatment approach developed for a particular child should be developmentally appropriate and driven by an evolving and collaborative understanding of a young person's (and their families' and wider systems') particular strengths and difficulties (a formulation-based approach). Within this context, trauma-focussed interventions are likely to be most relevant, including trauma-focussed cognitive behavioural therapy for older children and adolescents (TF-CBT; Cohen et al. 2000; Deblinger and Runyon 2005); game-based CBT, a group-based approach for children between 5 and 13 years old and their parents (Springer and Misurell 2010; Misurell and Springer 2013); eye-movement desensitisation and reprocessing (EMDR); which some research suggests may be more efficient than TF-CBT (Jaberghaderi et al., 2004; Jarero, Roque-López and Gomez, 2013) and the related approach of Brainspotting (Grand, 2011; Grixti and Dean, 2015). Dialectical Behaviour Therapy (DBT) adapted for adolescents also has potential to address correlates of complex developmental trauma (Linehan 2014). Offered as either a group or individual approach, this focusses on developing emotion regulation, distress tolerance, mindfulness and interpersonal skills. Studies indicate it reduces self-harm and suicidal behaviour in young people (Fleischhaker et al. 2011; Mehlum et al. 2014). A shared (and evidence-based) asumption underlying a variety of therapies is that the post-traumatic stress symptoms of hyper-arousal and intrusions (such as nightmares and flashbacks) are maintained by avoidance of abuse-related memories and emotions. Therapies such as TF-CBT, EMDR, art and drama therapies and brainspotting (BSP) all help children and young people to mentally revisit the trauma without feeling emotionally overwhelmed or unsafe (often following an emotion-regulation skills building phase). They differ in how directive they are: at one end, TF-CBT explicitly guides a young person through recalled trauma memories, at the other, BSP enables a young person to connect with gaze-spots that correspond to trauma-related bodily sensations and emotions (EMDR asks young people to follow therapists' hand movements with their eyes whilst mentally focussing on trauma memories). Across them all, how much of the trauma is "processed" is likely to depend on how safe the young person feels, which in turn is closely linked to their degree of perceived control and the attunement between therapist and client.

At times, focussing on trauma memories may result in young people feeling stuck in negative abuse-related feelings about themselves or others (e.g., feeling that they are damaged, disgusting or worthless). In these moments, therapists may direct clients' attention to evidence of alternatives and explore whether other "parts" of the child may feel different and may offer self-compassion. Opening up conversations between different parts of a person (Schwartz 1997) may assist them in developing their own adaptive understandings of self, others and relationships. Additionally, EMDR and BSP may be particularly suited to young people with lower levels of verbal skill or with high levels of shame, as they do not depend on articulation of abuse-related events and emotions. For younger children, art based approaches may be helpful, such as Santen's (2015) body map approach—which uses drawn figure outlines in which children can explore their emotions and bodily feelings. All such approaches develop children's ability to tolerate emotions whilst reducing the need for dissociative and other coping strategies.

Interventions that promote body awareness and connection, including yoga and mindfulness, may also be particularly relevant where somatic symptoms and sexual arousal-related issues are identified (Tylka and Augustus-Horvath 2011). Virtual reality interventions can also help young people develop protective strategies in affectively arousing but safe situations (Jouriles et al. 2009).

A rare study that explored the impact of treatment specifically on re-victimisation (DePrince et al. 2015) found that two 12-session group interventions both reduced the risk of further abuse in adolescents where there were existing child protection concerns. One (termed "risk detection/executive functioning", RD/EF; DePrince and Shirk 2013) taught mindfulness, problem-solving and the recognition of social threat, whereas the other (termed "social learning/feminist", SL/F; Wolfe et al. 1996) focussed more on developing healthy relationship skills and teaching young people about societal influences on abuse. Young people in the RD/EF group were nearly five times less likely to report sexual re-victimisation in the six months following compared to a control group, and those in the SL/F group were three times less likely to report physical violence re-victimisation. In statistical analyses, both groups performed equally well. These are important results, not least because other research suggests that more generic, universal abuse prevention programmes are less successful with young people who have already experienced abuse (e.g., Rothman and Silverman 2007).

When abuse has left a child with a poor sense of self and self-worth (including a narrow sexualised identity), work to build self-esteem and a positive, holistic identity is a gradual process, usually occurring in the context of various relationships in which the child feels validated and cared about. Inidividual therapy can provide one such relational setting.As a therapist proves themselves over time to be trustworthy, and interested in the child's thoughts, feelings and concerns, the child is likely to disclose more, providing further opportunities for the therapist to offer validation and develop conversations that shift negative beliefs (in a positive spiral). Psycho-education that challenges myths about abuse can help to dismantle the "rationale" the child may have for negative self-appraisals, especially when matched with relational acceptance and validation (Linehan 1997). Structured activities that develop children's awareness of their range of strengths and qualities (such as the Tree of Life exercise; O'Dea and Abraham 2000) may also prove useful starting points.

At times, a young person may hold on self-blame in an attempt to assuage the feelings of powerlessness that they (subconsciously) fear might otherwise surface (as to be to blame for the abuse at least implies that they had some agency and control). Exploring this dilemma, for example, through an imagined conversation between parts of the young person holding different views or between two imagined friends, can help the child to resolve it for themselves. Ultimately, powerlessness at the time of the abuse may need to be accepted, alongside an awareness of greater control and agency in the present and future. This dual perspective is a good basis for discussions about the difference between what was adaptive then and now (e.g., passivity then and assertiveness now). Feelings of powerlessness may be further diminished through opportunities for young people to discover that they can positively influence both their own and others' lives. Taking part in social justice activities or politics may be one such avenue (Wolfe et al. 1996) and furthermore could fuel post-traumatic growth. Children may also usefully be taught to develop a compassionate inner voice or inner "perfect nurturer", which amplifies and gives weight to emerging positive self-appraisals and self-acceptance (Bowyer et al. 2014). This experiential approach can be effective at diminishing self-denigrating and attacking inner voices and thoughts. Also of benefit are techniques that help young people develop a holistic appreciation of their body. One effective approach directs young people to reflectively write about their body's health, creativity, senses, and physical, self-care and communicative skills (Alleva et al. 2015). Collaboratively developing self-care and body nurturing routines with young people as well as raising their awareness and active resistance to objectifying messages from society are further promising strategies (Tylka and Augustus-Horvath 2011). Facilitating positive relationships between young people and their family members could arguably be the most effective means to developing self-esteem. Other relationships that can have a powerful impact include those with peers, mentors, peer-mentors and animals.

All of the above strategies would arguably leave young people better able to detect and adaptively respond to sexual threats, such as attempts at grooming. Such skills may be developed further through the extensive use of role-play alongside teaching about healthy relationship dynamics (see the RD/EF intervention mentioned above). Even when people mentally know how to act protectively towards themselves, putting this knowledge into practice can be difficult when they are unexpectedly in a threatening situation and old patterns learnt during abuse feel most familiar and comfortable. Role-plays can create new behavioural tendencies that young people feel confident about applying and which take forward their developing self-efficacy and esteem.

Working with the Wider System

Group interventions with peer groups and training with professionals who work with children (e.g., teachers and sports club leaders) can help to create safer contexts for young people, for example, by developing school cultures in which sexual aggression and conducive cultural messages are not tolerated (Gidycz et al. 2011). Effectively such interventions reduce the number of peers and other individuals susceptible to exploiting a young survivor's abuse-related difficulties. If, on the other hand, such interventions are not possible, providing an at-risk young person with options of safer environments to move to (such as other schools, clubs, etc.) may be indicated.

Conclusion

The best thing for children and young people is that they live lives free from abuse from the outset. Work towards this goal needs to continue to develop and grow—with those who abuse or are at risk of doing so and with families, communities and across society. In tandem, when children do sadly experience abuse, efforts should always be made to protect them from further abuse and harm. Such efforts should be responsive towards a particular child and their situation and form part of a broader safeguarding approach that develops once a child has been immediately protected from abuse by the initial perpetrator(s).

Understanding vulnerability to re-victimisation provides many clues as to what might help to reduce risk and build resilience following abuse. This chapter has outlined a number of promising approaches, and the task for future research is to clarify their (and others') effectiveness. In the meantime, there is enough knowledge to spur action across social care, education, health and voluntary sectors—all of which have both responsibilities and opportunities to affect change. There can be particular challenges to supporting children and young people at the edge of care who are at risk of re-victimisation, but there are also interventions that are relevant and applicable to this cohort. Across all types of intervention, with child (and adult) survivors, their families and the other systems in which they reside and interact, similar principles of effectiveness apply. In essence, when we help children and young people to enjoy and develop positive relationships, a rich sense of self and identity and the skills with which to experience and process their emotions and memories, we not only help them achieve wellbeing but also help to protect them.

References

Ackerman, S. J., & Hilsenroth, M. J. (2003). A review of therapist characteristics and techniques positively impacting the therapeutic alliance. *Clinical Psychology Review, 23*(1), 1–33.

Alleva, J. M., Martijn, C., Van Breukelen, G. J., Jansen, A., & Karos, K. (2015). Expand your horizon: A programme that improves body image and reduces self-objectification by training women to focus on body functionality. *Body Image, 15*, 81–89.

Allnock, D., & Miller, P. (2013). *No one noticed, no one heard: A study of disclosures of childhood abuse.* London: NSPCC.

Arata, C. M. (2002). Child sexual abuse and sexual revictimization. *Clinical Psychology: Science and Practice, 9*(2), 135–164.

Auslander, W., Myers Tlapek, S., Threlfall, J. M., Edmond, T. & Dunn, J. (2016) Mental health pathways linking maltreatment to interpersonal revictimization during adolescence for girls in the child welfare system. *Journal of Interpersonal Violence* (page numbers not yet specified).

Barnes, J. E., Noll, J. G., Putnam, F. W., & Trickett, P. K. (2009). Sexual and physical revictimization among victims of severe childhood sexual abuse. *Child Abuse and Neglect, 33*(7), 412–420.

Bender, M., Cook, S., & Kaslow, N. (2003). Social support as a mediator of revictimization of low-income African American women. *Violence and Victims, 18*(4), 419–431.

Bolton-Oetzel, K., & Scherer, D. G. (2003). Therapeutic engagement with adolescents in psychotherapy. *Psychotherapy: Theory, Research, Practice, Training, 40*(3), 215–225.

Boney-McCoy, S., & Finkelhor, D. (1995). Psychosocial sequelae of violent victimization in a national youth sample. *Journal of Consulting and Clinical Psychology, 63*(5), 726–736.

Borawski, E. A., Levers-Landis, C. E., Lovegreen, L. D., & Trapl, E. S. (2003). Parental monitoring, negotiated unsupervised time, and parental trust: The role of perceived parenting practices in adolescent health risk behaviours. *Journal of Adolescent Health, 33*(2), 60–70.

Bowyer, L., Wallis, J., & Lee, D. (2014). Developing a compassionate mind to enhance trauma-focused CBT with an adolescent female: A case study. *Behavioural and Cognitive Psychotherapy, 42*(2), 248–254.

Bramsen, R. H., Lasgaard, M., Koss, M. P., Shevlin, M., Elklit, A., & Banner, J. (2013). Testing a multiple mediator model of the effect of childhood sexual abuse on adolescent sexual victimization. *American Journal of Orthopsychiatry, 83*(1), 47–54.

Briere, J. (1996). *Trauma symptom checklist for children*. Odessa, FL: Psychological Assessment Resources.

Briere, J. (2004). Integrating HIV/AIDS prevention activities into psychotherapy for child sexual abuse survivors. In L. J. Koenig, L. S. Doll, A. O'Leary, & W. Pequegnat (Eds.), *From child sexual abuse to adult sexual risk: Trauma, revictimization, and intervention*. Washington, DC: American Psychological Association.

Briere, J., Johnson, K., Bissada, A., Damon, L., Crouch, J., Gil, E., et al. (2001). The trauma symptom checklist for young children (TSCYC): Reliability and association with abuse exposure in a multi-site study. *Child Abuse and Neglect, 25*(8), 1001–1014.

Brown, J. D., & L'Engle, K. L. (2009). X-rated sexual attitudes and behaviors associated with US early adolescents' exposure to sexually explicit media. *Communication Research, 36*(1), 129–151.

Cahalane, H., Parker, G., & Duff, S. (2013). Treatment implications arising from a qualitative analysis of letters written by the non-offending partners of men who have perpetrated child sexual abuse. *Journal of Child Sexual Abuse, 22*(6), 720–741.

Casey, E. A., & Nurius, P. S. (2005). Trauma exposure and sexual revictimisation risk comparisons across single, multiple incident, and multiple perpetrator victimisations. *Violence Against Women, 11*(4), 505–530.

Chakkalackal, L., & Cyhlarova, E. (2013). *Evaluation of music and change: A new mental health intervention for young people involved in gangs.* London: Mental Health Foundation http://www.mac-uk.org/wped/wp-content/uploads/2013/03/20130708_Music-and-Change_Executive-Summary.pdf.

Chan, T. W., & Koo, A. (2010). Parenting style and youth outcomes in the UK. *European Sociological Review, 27*(3), 385–399.

Classen, C. C., Palesh, O. G., & Aggarwal, R. (2005). Sexual revictimisation: A review of the empirical literature. *Trauma, Violence and Abuse, 6*(2), 103–129.

Classen, C., Field, N. P., Koopman, C., Nevill-Manning, K., & Spiegel, D. (2001). Interpersonal problems and their relationship to sexual revictimization among women sexually abused in childhood. *Journal of Interpersonal Violence, 16*(6), 495–509.

Cloitre, M., & Rosenberg, A. (2006). Sexual revictimization. In V. M. Follette & J. L. Ruzek (Eds.), *Cognitive-behavioural therapies for trauma.* New York: Guilford Press.

Cohen, J. A., Mannarino, A. P., Berliner, L., & Deblinger, E. (2000). Trauma-focused cognitive behavioural therapy for children and adolescents an empirical update. *Journal of Interpersonal Violence, 15*(11), 1202–1223.

Collins, M. E. (1998). Factors influencing sexual victimisation and revictimisation in a sample of adolescent mothers. *Journal of Interpersonal Violence, 13*(1), 3–24.

Collin-Vézina, D., De La Sablonnière-Griffin, M., Palmer, A. M., & Milne, L. (2015). A preliminary mapping of individual, relational, and social factors that impede disclosure of childhood sexual abuse. *Child Abuse and Neglect, 43*, 123–134.

Corcoran, J. (2004). Treatment outcome research with the non-offending parents of sexually abused children: A critical review. *Journal of Child Sexual Abuse, 13*(2), 59–84.

Corcoran, J., & Pillai, V. (2008). A meta-analysis of parent-involved treatment for child sexual abuse. *Research on Social Work Practice, 18*(5), 453–464.

Cuevas, C. A., Finkelhor, D., Clifford, C., Ormrod, R. K., & Turner, H. A. (2010). Psychological distress as a risk factor for re-victimisation in children. *Child Abuse and Neglect, 34*(4), 235–243.

D'Arcy, K., Dhaliwal, S., Thomas, R., Brodie, I., & Pearce, J. (2015). *Families and communities against child sexual exploitation (FCASE) final evaluation report*. Bedfordshire: University of Bedfordshire.

Deblinger, E., & Runyon, M. K. (2005). Understanding and treating feelings of shame in children who have experienced maltreatment. *Child Maltreatment, 10*(4), 364–376.

DePrince, A. P. (2005). Social cognition and revictimisation risk. *Journal of Trauma and Dissociation, 6*(1), 125–141.

DePrince, A. P., Brown, L. S., Cheit, R. E., Freyd, J. J., Gold, S. N., Pezdek, K., & Quina, K. (2012). Motivated forgetting and misremembering: Perspectives from betrayal trauma theory. In R. F. Belli (Ed.), *True and false recovered memories*. New York: Springer.

DePrince, A. P., Chu, A. T., Labus, J., Shirk, S. R., & Potter, C. (2015). Testing two approaches to revictimisation prevention among adolescent girls in the child welfare system. *Journal of Adolescent Health, 56*(2), S33–S39.

DePrince, A. P., & Shirk, S. R. (2013). Adapting cognitive-behavioural therapy for depressed adolescents exposed to interpersonal trauma: A case study with two teens. *Cognitive and Behavioural Practice, 20*(2), 189–201.

DePrince, A. P., Zurbriggen, E. L., Chu, A. T., & Smart, L. (2010). Development of the trauma appraisal questionnaire. *Journal of Aggression, Maltreatment and Trauma, 19*(3), 275–299.

DiClemente, R. J., Wingood, G. M., Crosby, R., Sionean, C., Cobb, B. K., Harrington, K., et al. (2001). Parental monitoring: Association with adolescents' risk behaviours. *Paediatrics, 107*(6), 1363–1368.

Drake, B., & Pandey, S. (1996). Understanding the relationship between neighbourhood poverty and specific types of child maltreatment. *Child Abuse and Neglect, 20*(11), 1003–1018.

Fargo, J. D. (2009). Pathways to adult sexual revictimisation: Direct and indirect behavioural risk factors across the lifespan. *Journal of Interpersonal Violence, 24*(11), 1771–1791.

Farmer, E., & Callan, S. (2012). *Beyond violence: Breaking cycles of domestic abuse*. London: The Centre for Social Justice. Retrieved from http://www.centreforsocialjustice.org.uk/core/wp-content/uploads/2016/08/DA-Full-report.pdf

Finkelhor, D., Ormrod, R. K., & Turner, H. A. (2007). Re-victimisation patterns in a national longitudinal sample of children and youth. *Child Abuse and Neglect, 31*(5), 479–502.

Fleischhaker, C., Böhme, R., Sixt, B., Brück, C., Schneider, C., & Schulz, E. (2011). Dialectical behavioural therapy for adolescents (DBT-A): A clinical trial for patients with suicidal and self-injurious behaviour and borderline symptoms with a one-year follow-up. *Child and Adolescent Psychiatry and Mental Health, 5*(3), 1–10.

Fortier, M. A., DiLillo, D., Messman-Moore, T. L., Peugh, J., DeNardi, K. A., & Gaffey, K. J. (2009). Severity of child sexual abuse and revictimisation: The mediating role of coping and trauma symptoms. *Psychology of Women Quarterly, 33*(3), 308–320.

Foshee, V. A., Benefield, T. S., Ennett, S. T., Bauman, K. E., & Suchindran, C. (2004). Longitudinal predictors of serious physical and sexual dating violence victimisation during adolescence. *Preventive Medicine, 39*(5), 1007–1016.

Franklin, C. A. (2013). Anticipating intimacy or sexual victimisation? Danger cue recognition and delayed behavioural responses to a sexually risky scenario. *Feminist Criminology, 8*(2), 87–116.

Galloway, S., & Hogg, N. (2008). Non-abusing parents and their role in risk management. In J. Houston & S. Galloway (Eds.), *Sexual offending and mental health: Multidisciplinary management in the community* (Vol. 28). London: Jessica Kingsley Publishers.

Gidycz, C. A., Orchowski, L. M., & Berkowitz, A. D. (2011). Preventing sexual aggression among college men: An evaluation of a social norms and bystander intervention program. *Violence Against Women, 17*(6), 720–742.

Gobin, R. L., & Freyd, J. J. (2009). Betrayal and revictimisation: Preliminary findings. *Psychological Trauma: Theory, Research, Practice, and Policy, 1*(3), 242–257.

Grand, D. (2011). Brainspotting a new brain-based psychotherapy approach. *Trauma and Gewalt, 3*, 276–285.

Green, B. L., Goodman, L. A., Krupnick, J. L., Corcoran, C. B., Petty, R. M., Stockton, P., & Stern, N. M. (2000). Outcomes of single versus multiple trauma exposure in a screening sample. *Journal of Traumatic Stress, 13*(2), 271–286.

Grixti, M., & Dean, R. (2015). *Brainspotting with young people: An adventure into the mind.* Sussex: Sattva.

Hanson, E. (2015). *If you find out your child has been sexually abused or exploited.* Parentinfo.org. http://parentinfo.org/article/if-you-find-out-your-child-has-been-sexually-abused-or-exploited

Hanson. (2016). Exploring the relationship between neglect and child sexual exploitation: Evidence Scope One. Dartington: Research in Practice. Retrieved from https://www.rip.org.uk/resources/publications/evidence-scopes/child-neglect-and-its-relationship-to-sexual-harm-and-abuse-responding-effectively-to-childrens-needs

Hébert, M., Daigneault, I., Collin-Vézina, D., & Cyr, M. (2007). Factors linked to distress in mothers of children disclosing sexual abuse. *The Journal of Nervous and Mental Disease, 195*(10), 805–811.

Hershkowitz, I., Lanes, O., & Lamb, M. E. (2007). Exploring the disclosure of child sexual abuse with alleged victims and their parents. *Child Abuse and Neglect, 31*(2), 111–123.

Hong, P. Y., & Lishner, D. A. (2016). General invalidation and trauma-specific invalidation as predictors of personality and subclinical psychopathology. *Personality and Individual Differences, 89*(1), 211–216.

Irwin, H. J. (1999). Violent and nonviolent revictimisation of women abused in childhood. *Journal of Interpersonal Violence, 14*(10), 1095–1110.

Jaberghaderi, N., Greenwald, R., Rubin, A., Zand, S. O., & Dolatabadi, S. (2004). A comparison of CBT and EMDR for sexually-abused Iranian girls. *Clinical Psychology and Psychotherapy, 11*(5), 358–368.

Jankowski, M. K., Leitenberg, H., Henning, K., & Coffey, P. (2002). Parental caring as a possible buffer against sexual revictimisation in young adult survivors of child sexual abuse. *Journal of Traumatic Stress, 15*(3), 235–244.

Jarero, I., Roque-López, S., & Gomez, J. (2013). The provision of an EMDR-based multicomponent trauma treatment with child victims of severe interpersonal trauma. *Journal of EMDR Practice and Research, 7*(1), 17–28.

Jouriles, E. N., McDonald, R., Kullowatz, A., Rosenfield, D., Gomez, G. S., & Cuevas, A. (2009). Can virtual reality increase the realism of role plays used to teach college women sexual coercion and rape-resistance skills? *Behaviour Therapy, 40*(4), 337–345.

Kellogg, N. D., & Hoffman, T. J. (1997). Child sexual revictimisation by multiple perpetrators. *Child Abuse and Neglect, 21*(10), 953–964.

Kessler, B. L., & Bieschke, K. J. (1999). A retrospective analysis of shame, dissociation, and adult victimisation in survivors of childhood sexual abuse. *Journal of Counselling Psychology, 46*(3), 335–341.

Lindsey, M. A., Brandt, N. E., Becker, K. D., Lee, B. R., Barth, R. P., Daleiden, E. L., & Chorpita, B. F. (2014). Identifying the common elements of treatment engagement interventions in children's mental health services. *Clinical Child and Family Psychology Review, 17*(3), 283–298.

Linehan, M. M. (1997). Validation and psychotherapy. In A. C. Bohart & L. S. Greenberg (Eds.), *Empathy reconsidered: New directions in psychotherapy*. Washington, DC: American Psychological Association.

Linehan, M. M. (2014). *DBT® skills training manual*. New York: Guilford Publications.

Littleton, H., Axsom, D., & Grills-Taquechel, A. (2009). Sexual assault victims' acknowledgment status and revictimisation risk. *Psychology of Women Quarterly, 33*(1), 34–42.

Lynn, S. J., Pintar, J., Fite, R., Ecklund, K., & Stafford, J. (2004). Toward a social-narrative model of revictimisation. In L. J. Koenig, L. S. Doll, A. O'Leary, & W. Pequegnat (Eds.), *From child sexual abuse to adult sexual risk: Trauma, revictimization, and intervention.* Washington, DC: American Psychological Association.

Macy, R. J. (2007). A coping theory framework toward preventing sexual revictimization. *Aggression and Violent Behaviour, 12*(2), 177–192.

McCart, M. R., Zajac, K., Kofler, M. J., Smith, D. W., Saunders, B. E., & Kilpatrick, D. G. (2012). Longitudinal examination of PTSD symptoms and problematic alcohol use as risk factors for adolescent victimisation. *Journal of Clinical Child and Adolescent Psychology, 41*(6), 822–836.

McCollum, S. E. (2015). Multigenerational dissociation: A framework for building narrative. *Journal of Trauma & Dissociation, 16*(5), 563–576.

Mehlum, L., Tørmoen, A. J., Ramberg, M., Haga, E., Diep, L. M., Laberg, S., et al. (2014). Dialectical behaviour therapy for adolescents with repeated suicidal and self-harming behaviour: A randomised trial. *Journal of the American Academy of Child and Adolescent Psychiatry, 53*(10), 1082–1091.

Messman-Moore, T. L., & Brown, A. L. (2006). Risk perception, rape, and sexual revictimisation: A prospective study of college women. *Psychology of Women Quarterly, 30*(2), 159–172.

Messman-Moore, T. L., Brown, A. L., & Koelsch, L. E. (2005). Post-traumatic symptoms and self-dysfunction as consequences and predictors of sexual revictimisation. *Journal of Traumatic Stress, 18*(3), 253–262.

Messman-Moore, T. L., Ward, R. M., & Zerubavel, N. (2013). The role of substance use and emotion dysregulation in predicting risk for incapacitated sexual revictimisation in women: Results of a prospective investigation. *Psychology of Addictive Behaviours, 27*(1), 125–132.

Miller, A. K., Canales, E. J., Amacker, A. M., Backstrom, T. L., & Gidycz, C. A. (2011). Stigma-threat motivated nondisclosure of sexual assault and sexual revictimisation: A prospective analysis. *Psychology of Women Quarterly, 35*(1), 119–128.

Miner, M. H., Flitter, J. M. K., & Robinson, B. B. E. (2006). Association of sexual revictimisation with sexuality and psychological function. *Journal of Interpersonal Violence, 21*(4), 503–524.

Miron, L. R., & Orcutt, H. K. (2014). Pathways from childhood abuse to prospective revictimisation: Depression, sex to reduce negative affect, and forecasted sexual behaviour. *Child Abuse and Neglect, 38*(11), 1848–1859.

Misurell, J. R., & Springer, C. (2013). Developing culturally responsive evidence-based practice: A game-based group therapy program for child sexual abuse (CSA). *Journal of Child and Family Studies, 22*(1), 137–149.

Noll, J. G., & Grych, J. H. (2011). Read-react-respond: An integrative model for understanding sexual revictimisation. *Psychology of Violence, 1*(3), 202–215.

Noll, J. G., Haralson, K. J., Butler, E. M., & Shenk, C. E. (2011). Childhood maltreatment, psychological dysregulation, and risky sexual behaviours in female adolescents. *Journal of Paediatric Psychology, 36*(7), 743–752.

Noll, J. G., Horowitz, L. A., Bonanno, G. A., Trickett, P. K., & Putnam, F. W. (2003). Revictimisation and self-harm in females who experienced childhood sexual abuse results from a prospective study. *Journal of Interpersonal Violence, 18*(12), 1452–1471.

Noll, J. G., Trickett, P. K., & Putnam, F. W. (2000). Social network constellation and sexuality of sexually abused and comparison girls in childhood and adolescence. *Child Maltreatment, 5*(4), 323–337.

Obasaju, M. A., Palin, F. L., Jacobs, C., Anderson, P., & Kaslow, N. J. (2009). Won't you be my neighbour? Using an ecological approach to examine the impact of community on revictimisation. *Journal of Interpersonal Violence, 24*(1), 38–53.

Oberlander, S. E., Wang, Y., Thompson, R., Lewis, T., Proctor, L. J., Isbell, P., et al. (2011). Childhood maltreatment, emotional distress, and early adolescent sexual intercourse: Multi-informant perspectives on parental monitoring. *Journal of Family Psychology, 25*(6), 885–894.

O'Dea, J. A., & Abraham, S. (2000). Improving the body image, eating attitudes, and behaviors of young male and female adolescents: A new educational approach that focuses on self-esteem. *International Journal of Eating Disorders, 28*(1), 43–57.

Orcutt, H. K., Cooper, M. L., & Garcia, M. (2005). Use of sexual intercourse to reduce negative affect as a prospective mediator of sexual revictimisation. *Journal of Traumatic Stress, 18*(6), 729–739.

Parents against child sexual exploitation (PACE). (2014). *The Relational Safeguarding Model: Best practice in working with families affected by child sexual exploitation.* Leeds: PACE.

Pearce, J. (2002). *It's someone taking a part of you: A study of young women and sexual exploitation.* London: National Children's Bureau.

Pittenger, S. L., Huit, T. Z., & Hansen, D. J. (2016). Applying ecological systems theory to sexual revictimisation of youth: A review with implications for research and practice. *Aggression and Violent Behaviour, 26*(1), 35–45.

Putnam, F. W., Helmers, K., & Trickett, P. K. (1993). Development, reliability, and validity of a child dissociation scale. *Child Abuse and Neglect, 17*(6), 731–741.

Risser, H. J., Hetzel-Riggin, M. D., Thomsen, C. J., & McCanne, T. R. (2006). PTSD as a mediator of sexual revictimisation: The role of re-experiencing, avoidance, and arousal symptoms. *Journal of Traumatic Stress, 19*(5), 687–698.

Robinson, J. L. (2007). Story stem narratives with young children: Moving to clinical research and practice. *Attachment and Human Development, 9*(3), 179–185.

Rothman, E., & Silverman, J. (2007). The effect of a college sexual assault prevention program on first-year students' victimisation rates. *Journal of American College Health, 55*(5), 283–290.

Ruback, R. B., Clark, V. A., & Warner, C. (2014). Why are crime victims at risk of being victimized again? Substance use, depression, and offending as mediators of the victimisation-revictimisation link. *Journal of Interpersonal Violence, 29*(1), 157–185.

Salter, M. (2012). *Organised sexual abuse.* London: Routledge.

Sánchez-Meca, J., Rosa-Alcázar, A., & López-Soler, C. (2011). The psychological treatment of sexual abuse in children and adolescents: A meta-analysis. *International Journal of Clinical and Health Psychology, 11*(1), 67–93.

Santen, B. (2015). Treating dissociation in traumatised children with body maps. In C. A. Malchiodi (Ed.), *Creative interventions with traumatised children.* New York: Guilford Press.

Saxe, G. N., Ellis, B. H., Fogler, J., & Navalta, C. P. (2012). Innovations in practice: Preliminary evidence for effective family engagement in treatment for child traumatic stress–Trauma systems therapy approach to preventing dropout. *Child and Adolescent Mental Health, 17*(1), 58–61.

Schwartz, R. C. (1997). *Internal family systems therapy.* London: Guilford Press.

Simon, V. A., & Feiring, C. (2008). Sexual anxiety and eroticism predict the development of sexual problems in youth with a history of sexual abuse. *Child Maltreatment, 13*(2), 167–181.

Smith, G. (1994). Parent, partner, protector: Conflicting role demands for mothers of sexually abused children. In T. Morrison, M. Erooga, & R. C. Beckett (Eds.), *Sexual offending against children: Assessment and treatment of male abusers.* London: Routledge.

Smith, G. (2012). *Working with trauma: Systemic approaches.* London: Palgrave Macmillan.

Springer, C., & Misurell, J. R. (2010). Game-based cognitive-behavioural therapy (GB-CBT): An innovative group treatment program for children who have been sexually abused. *Journal of Child and Adolescent Trauma, 3*(3), 163–180.

Staples, J. M., George, W. H., Stappenbeck, C. A., Davis, K. C., Norris, J., & Heiman, J. R. (2015). Alcohol myopia and sexual abdication among women: Examining the moderating effect of child sexual abuse. *Addictive Behaviours, 41*(2), 72–77.

Stockdale, M. S., Logan, T. K., Sliter, K. A., & Berry, S. A. (2014). Interpersonal violence victimisation and sexual harassment: A prospective study of revictimisation. *Sex Roles, 71*(1-2), 55–70.

Talbot, J. A., Talbot, N. L., & Tu, X. (2004). Shame-proneness as a diathesis for dissociation in women with histories of childhood sexual abuse. *Journal of Traumatic Stress, 17*(5), 445–448.

Tapia, N. D. (2014). Survivors of child sexual abuse and predictors of adult revictimisation in the United States: A forward logistic regression analysis. *International Journal of Criminal Justice Sciences, 9*(1), 64–73.

Tavkar, P., & Hansen, D. J. (2011). Interventions for families victimised by child sexual abuse: Clinical issues and approaches for child advocacy center-based services. *Aggression and Violent Behaviour, 16*(3), 188–199.

Testa, M., Hoffman, J. H., & Livingston, J. A. (2010). Alcohol and sexual risk behaviours as mediators of the sexual victimisation-revictimisation relationship. *Journal of Consulting and Clinical Psychology, 78*(2), 249–259.

Trask, E. V., Walsh, K., & DiLillo, D. (2011). Treatment effects for common outcomes of child sexual abuse: A current meta-analysis. *Aggression and Violent Behaviour, 16*(1), 6–19.

Tylka, T. L., & Augustus-Horvath, C. L. (2011). Fighting self-objectification in prevention and intervention contexts. In R. M. Calogero, S. Tantleff-Dunn, & J. K. Thompson (Eds.), *Self-objectification in women: Causes, consequences, and counteractions*. Washington, DC: American Psychological Association.

Ullman, S. E., & Vasquez, A. L. (2015). Mediators of sexual revictimisation risk in adult sexual assault victims. *Journal of Child Sexual Abuse, 24*(3), 300–314.

United Nations Convention on the Rights of the Child. (1989). Treaty Series. *1577*, 3. Retrieved from http://www.refworld.org/docid/3ae6b38f0.html

van Toledo, A., & Seymour, F. (2013). Interventions for caregivers of children who disclose sexual abuse: A review. *Clinical Psychology Review, 33*(6), 772–781.

Vanzile-Tamsen, C., Testa, M., & Livingston, J. A. (2005). The impact of sexual assault history and relationship context on appraisal of and responses to acquaintance sexual assault risk. *Journal of Interpersonal Violence, 20*(7), 813–832.

Waldron, J. C., Wilson, L. C., Patriquin, M. A., & Scarpa, A. (2015). Sexual victimisation history, depression, and task physiology as predictors of sexual revictimisation: Results from a 6-month prospective pilot study. *Journal of Interpersonal Violence, 30*(4), 622–639.

Widom, C. S., Czaja, S. J., & Dutton, M. A. (2008). Childhood victimisation and lifetime revictimisation. *Child Abuse and Neglect, 32*(8), 785–796.

Wolfe, D. A., Wekerle, C., Gough, R., Reitzel-Jaffe, D., Grasley, C., Pittman, A. L., et al. (1996). *The youth relationships manual: A group approach with adolescents for the prevention of woman abuse and the promotion of healthy relationships.* Thousand Oaks: Sage Publications.

Wolfe, D. A., Wekerle, C., Scott, K., Straatman, A. L., & Grasley, C. (2004). Predicting abuse in adolescent dating relationships over 1 year: The role of child maltreatment and trauma. *Journal of Abnormal Psychology, 113*(3), 406–415.

Young, B. J., & Furman, W. (2008). Interpersonal factors in the risk for sexual victimization and its recurrence during adolescence. *Journal of Youth and Adolescence, 37*(3), 297–309.

Zurbriggen, E. L., & Freyd, J. J. (2004). The link between child sexual abuse and risky sexual behavior: The role of dissociative tendencies, information-processing effects, and consensual sex decision mechanisms. In L. J. Koenig, L. S. Doll, A. O'Leary, & W. Pequegnat (Eds.), *From child sexual abuse to adult sexual risk: Trauma, revictimisation, and intervention.* Washington, DC: American Psychological Association.

11

Safe Returns from Care

Caroline Pipe

Introduction

The most common outcome for children who have entered the care system is a return home (Farmer et al. 2011). Therefore, developing robust and focussed policy and practice to support this process is of central importance to ensuring good outcomes for children and their families. Significant attention has been paid to assessing parental capacity, in order to establish whether children's interests are best served by removing them from their parents' care (Howarth 2001; Williams et al. 2015). However, little in the way of research and practice guidance have been generated regarding assessment, planning and support for reunification.

Research regarding reunification generally is in its infancy (Farmer et al. 2011). Nonetheless, that which has been undertaken, along with anecdotal evidence and practice experience, indicates several identifiable

C. Pipe (✉)
London Borough of Hammersmith and Fulham, London, UK

© The Author(s) 2016
L. Smith (ed.), *Clinical Practice at the Edge of Care*,
DOI 10.1007/978-3-319-43570-1_11

229

factors appearing to contribute to positive outcomes (Thoburn et al. 2012; Wade et al. 2011). These include:

- Factors leading to children coming into care (such as domestic violence, parental drug use, relationship breakdown) being successfully addressed
- Evidence of improved parental capacity to regulate emotions and to hold the child in mind
- Evidence of motivation throughout family and professional systems for reunification to succeed
- Consistent and constructive contact between parents and children whilst they are in care
- Respectful and compassionate relationship-based practice with children and their families
- The creation and implementation of collaborative family-focussed support plans
- The active presence of a skilled and coordinated professional network working in partnership with parents and children
- Involvement and validation of the family's own support network
- Intensive, targeted support (including practical and financial) over an extended period of time
- Tolerance of setbacks and defined contingency plans.

It is critical to consider how key elements that contribute to successful reunification may be effectively actioned and supported. Central to this process is the quality of relationships between family and professional networks and how these are shaped and defined by contextual factors, specifically those relating to power and difference. With this in mind, this chapter aims to utilise ideas from systemic theory to consider how approaches to reunification work may be fairer and more family focussed, building on existing strengths and generating a greater sense of collaboration. By adopting a systemic lens, opportunities are created to deconstruct existing patterns of interactions, thus facilitating a more open and inquisitive stance.

Several key systemic ideas and frames of reference will be considered. As anxious and distrusting relationships within families are often isomorphically replicated in professional systems (Liddle and Saba 1983), it is useful to consider dialogical processes, as a means to generate richer shared understandings amongst family and professional networks (Bakhtin 1981). Ideas from the work of Seikkula and Arnkil (2006) also bear consideration in relation to how unhelpful patterns of interaction may be reconstructed, allowing newer and more constructive pathways to emerge. These will be discussed further below.

Throughout consideration of these ideas, I aim to remain connected to my experiences of working with children at the edge of care and their families and mindful of my position of privilege in terms of my race and educational and employment opportunities. My intention is to hold in mind the concept of voice entitlement (Boyd 2010) and consider how the following ideas may contribute to a culture of ethical and effective practice when working with families in need.

Precursors to Reunification

In order to consider how successful reunifications may be achieved, it is salient to consider how returns home may come about. A percentage of young people gravitate home following multiple placement breakdowns and high levels of absconding. Others return from care because foster or residential placements appear unable to meet the needs of the child (Sinclair et al. 2005). Such situations generate a curious predicament where children and parents whose relationships are likely to be strained and lacking in resources attempt to re-establish a workable pattern of caregiving and care seeking with minimal preparation and support. Stable and dynamic risks of significant harm to children are often present in these circumstances.

In many instances, these kinds of returns home end in re-entries into care, leading to a process described by Farmer et al. (2011) of "oscillations" between home and care, identified as being extremely detrimental to the welfare of the child. Therefore, it is imperative that more effective analysis of such cases and tighter and timelier interventions may interrupt such patterns at an earlier stage, thus promoting better outcomes.

In other cases, family reunification is much more considered, either as a consequence of the outcome of a specific assessment and monitoring process (such as during care proceedings) or due to mutual agreement between families and local authorities following the use of a Section 20 agreement. Substantial evidence exists that the appropriate use of Section 20 accommodation is more likely to facilitate successful returns home, as opposed to court mandated entries into care, due primarily to families being more able to work collaboratively with professional agencies outside the auspices of the court process (Wade et al. 2011).

A substantial proportion of families at the edge of care have long histories of connections with statutory services, often including transgenerational patterns of children living in care. In addition, experiences of social marginalisation (through such factors as racism, poverty and poor educational attainment) may encourage families to "see the outside world as threatening, unreliable and antagonistic" (van Lawick and Bom 2008). Engaging families in more collaborative ways aims to interrupt life-limiting patterns of disempowerment and generate possibilities for newer and more helpful narratives to evolve.

By adopting a more curious stance regarding the family's relationship with professional services, practitioners may elicit new stories about a family's intent, their values and aspirations (Mason 2010). Likewise, by engaging in a process of reflexive questioning, opportunities emerge for parents to consider how their identities have been constructed and how they may wish these to be revised to ensure more useful narratives are available.

By using reflexive questions, we are encouraged into "thinking aloud and getting to know one's own thoughts" (Seikkula and Arnkil 2006). This promotes consideration of positioning (Davies and Harre 1990), as we are invited to consider the perspectives of others and how we may be viewed and perceived, as in the examples below:

You've attended all of the planned contact sessions this month and the feedback has been really good, what do you think this tells you about the kind of Mum you are?

If I were to come back in ten years' time and ask Bryony what she thinks you did to support her when she was out of education, what you think she'd say?

An emphasis on relational processes not only contributes to the generation of shared meanings between professional and parents but also increases one's capacity to see the world through the eyes of another. For parents who have been separated from their children for extended periods of time, many of whom who have struggled to sustain consistent emotional connections, the ability to hold the child in mind is of crucial importance in terms of successfully meeting their emotional needs.

Addressing difficulties in parents' emotional availability and ability to mentalise in relation to their children may involve interventions over an extended period of time. Generating opportunities to think differently about themselves as parents are useful here, in order to initiate recursive processes of trust and confidence building between parents and professionals. In turn, these allow parents to adopt a more self-reflexive stance, developing their capacity for warmer and more appreciative connections with their children. In this context, reflexivity can be conceptualised as engaging in an awareness of our prejudices and belief systems and how these inform our relational experiences (Hedges 2010). By considering the way in which we position ourselves and are positioned by others, opportunities emerge to think and do differently, thus creating a generative process of change.

Generating opportunities for reflexive thinking contributes to beginning the process of "second order" change (Hoffman 1985), a process in which "the focus of change is in the meaning and the ideas which are held about the behaviour, rather than the behaviours themselves" (Gross 1991). In terms of improving parental capacity, the concept of "second order" change is of considerable importance, as it indicates that change has occurred at the level of thinking, belief and action (Pipe and Richardson 2015). In identifying examples of this type of progress, professionals may then be reassured that observed changes are more likely to be embedded and internally motivated, thus promoting sustainability and replication in varying contexts. "First order" changes, by comparison, are characterised by changes only in behaviours, rather than the belief systems that underpin them, and are therefore less likely to be sustained once external motivators—such as social work monitoring—cease. In addition, through developing opportunities for families to engage in "second order" change, relationships are enhanced due to an increased appreciation of the experiences and viewpoints of others and the opportunity to think more constructively about one's own contribution to shaping and determining interactional patterns. In embedding "second order" change, capacity to tolerate challenges and uncertainty is increased, thus strengthening the likelihood of the successful management of the reunification process by both professional and families.

Dialogical Processes: Shared Meanings, Shared Endeavours

A significant number of Serious Case reviews have highlighted how relational difficulties between families and professionals have contributed to catastrophic breakdowns in the management of risk (Reder and Duncan 1999) or mistaken levels of optimism stemming from collusive and uncritical practice (Laming 2009). Families who have experienced long-term involvement from statutory services will hold narratives regarding their experiences that are seldom voiced, creating a lack of coordination between meanings and beliefs held by families and professionals (Pearce and Pearce 2000). Given the intensity of public surveillance of edge of care practice (Nielsen 2002), there is also a risk that a climate of risk adverse practice may become established, contributing to a culture of distrust and hostility between families and professionals, wherein the motives and capacities of each are viewed with suspicion and pessimism.

Systemic theories offer an opportunity to deconstruct these positions and consider how family and professional systems may re-imagine their relationships and reposition themselves in relation to each other. The work of Seikkula and Arnkil (2006)—in which the concept of dialogism (Bakhtin 1981) is combined with themes of social constructionism—offers an opportunity to diminish defensive practices to evoke a sense of sharing and openness amongst the professional and familial system. This is proposed to occur through lessening the value and centrality of monologues, in which a specific "voice" may be privileged. The aim of the approach is to generate dialogical processes, in which shared languages and meanings are generated. Dialogism is defined as the process by which communication is generated in response to and anticipation of what has gone before and what will follow. Seikkula (2011) therefore writes that "intersubjectivity is the basis of human experience and dialogue the way we live it". In edge-of-care contexts, the aspiration is that these processes lead to decisions and planning based on the family's strengths and priorities, with professionals adopting a "flexible, organised and versatile" stance (Seikkula and Arnkil 2006) to support and embed changes. Particular attention is paid to the activity of professionals and families engaging in network meetings, in order to share information and generate plans.

Key to the use of such meetings is the notion of positioning and attending to power differentials between families and professionals. Dialogical approaches attempt to address these by considering what might be created in determining who speaks first. Therefore, attempts are made to privilege families' voices in the opening moments of conversations, perhaps by asking:

If we (the professional network) were to be helpful to your family today and in the future, what would you notice us doing?
Or:
If I could ask for some advice regarding how we can make this meeting a success, what would you say?

Whilst the concept of working in partnership is consistently endorsed (HM Government 2015), the level to which families are genuinely trusted and the level of trust they can afford professionals often remains limited, creating tension and misunderstandings (Aggett et al. 2011). Therefore, professionals need to actively create opportunities for transparency regarding this issue. An example of a parent's position being explored is detailed in Box 11.1.

> **Box 11.1 Case example: Danielle**
>
> Danielle: *I hate the idea of you all talking about me behind my back, I mean I know you've got to discuss stuff, but I feel like I'm always the last to know and everything's been decided before I even get here.*
>
> Caroline: *I'm wondering what we need to do to shift that a bit—one thing I try and say is, "If Danielle was listening to us, what do you think she'd say?" It's just an idea to try and remind everyone this is about you and your family, to keep you in the room so to speak.*
>
> Danielle: *But I'm not, am I?*
>
> Caroline: *So, I'm wondering how we can make sure you know more of what was said—and how we can ask you to give your opinions on our ideas, rather than deciding without you.*
>
> Danielle: *Yes, you did do that once before and it was good: You said, "This person had this idea, but this person said this, and we wondered what you'd think". I felt you hadn't all decided stuff without me.*

Undertaking this kind of work can be a challenge in the context of difficult dynamics in professional and family systems. Given that reunification will involve risk management, expenditure and the investment of time, services and practitioners may be keen to shift responsibilities to their colleagues from other disciplines, may invite others to take on a higher level of activity or may attempt to control the network to comply with their position (Laming 2009; Munro 2011). Potential then emerges for competitive or controlling interplays where participants "fight to be right", rather than adopting more open and less defensive postures. During such episodes, networks risk losing their curiosity and compassion and rush instead to positions of "unsafe certainty", in which agencies adopt an assumptive and illusionary stance of "knowing", particularly in relation to risk management (Mason 1993). In such circumstances, networks may become entrenched in repetitive patterns of unsuccessful activity, at the very time that creativity, trust and openness are most crucial.

In order to address this, Seikkula and Arnkil developed the practice of "Anticipation Dialogues" (Seikkula and Arnkil 2006), with the intention of centralising the family's resources and supporting their endeavours by generating "polyphonic" dialogues where shared understandings are established, thus unifying and coordinating future activity. Central to this sequenced approach is the process of "recalling the future" (Seikkula and Arnkil 2006), an approach used by facilitators in meetings to shift participants from the restrictions of problem-defining monologues. The key aims of this approach are to separate the tasks of listening and speaking (thus growing away from the need to justify, respond, correct) and to focus on the near future by generating a joint action plan. In order to liberate family members from their current situations, which may feel stuck or overwhelming, the facilitator uses a future-orientated question (Tomm 1987) to generate possibilities. Seikkula and Arnkil express their reluctance to "prescribe" questions, but a general opening question would be formulated along the lines of:

> *It is a year from now and things are working out pretty well for your family. How is this from your point of view? What in particular do you notice?*

After conversation has been initiated, the stance of the facilitator is key to the process that follows. They are tasked with repeating key phrases verbatim as part of a summary and avoiding offering comments or judgements. The intention behind this is for participants to "hear back" their own story and think about their relationship to it. This process of "thinking aloud" encourages an understanding that all utterances are subjective, thus diminishing the opportunities for certain accounts to be privileged.

Whilst engaged in this process, the facilitator will attend closely to creating a sense of intimate and respectful connection with the speaker, in an attempt to fade away the wider audience. In doing so, interest is given to each individual's account, ensuring chances for reflection and consideration. Participants are thus less inclined to adopt "postures of mobilization" (Fredman 2004), which focus on an outward gaze and the responses of others, and instead enjoy an opportunity to consider their own ideas and perspectives in a non-competitive and judgemental frame.

The second part of the "Anticipation Dialogues" sequence invites a sense of agency and the recognition of the roles others may play in processes of change, for example, by asking:

> *What made these changes possible, what did you do and who supported you and how?*

A central tenet here is the simultaneous activation of agency and attending to detail. In processes of change, plans may fail due to a lack of detail and an inadequate focus on active engagement. By thickening stories with more detail and depth, participants are invited to bring alive their ideas and envisage them in reality. Motivation and purpose are ignited by the articulation of action and an opportunity is given to think what "help" may look like and how it might be achieved.

The third phase of "Anticipation Dialogues" connects directly with the presenting issues by asking the participant to recall what they were concerned about a year ago and what had decreased their worries. The purpose of this question is to create a context in which complexities can be viewed from a position of resolution, rather than one of stuckness—thus encouraging possibilities and a sense of hope. This is of particular significance when family members may feel speaking of their difficulties in the present tense positions them poorly in terms of how professional view them. By being able to publicly share ideas regarding how they intend to lessen worries, newer perspectives are invited and opportunities to change begin to emerge. The process then moves to asking professionals two similar questions, namely:

A year has passed and you hear the family are doing really well. What did you do to support this and who was helpful to you?
And then:
What were you worried about a year ago and what lessened your worries?

Of particular note here is that professionals are asked to name who and what helped them, highlighting the need for collaboration and reducing notions of isolation or omnipotence. The concept of help becomes a mutually held theme, rather than being a linear process from professional to family.

Seikkula and Arnkil describe a process of scribing the process above by recording key phrases on flip chart paper or boards, thus creating a shared narrative in which the family's language is privileged. This creates the basis for the final stage of the process, the generation of a plan. The plan is activity lead, focussing on "who does what with whom next" (Seikkula and Arnkil 2006).

The inclusive, dialogical nature of this approach to network meetings moves participants away from entering meetings with their minds made up and instead opens space for repetitive patterns to alter and, most crucially, allows planning and intervention to become a joined process as the network unites in a collaborative exploration of hopes and ideas. By creating an environment in which competitiveness and binary positions can be relinquished, new possibilities emerge which place the family centre stage, with the professional network providing strong supporting roles in which respective talents and strengths are recognised and appreciated. An organising theme of many network discussions at the edge of care is an intolerance of uncertainty, both in terms of the process of the meeting and in terms of the plan. The structure and pacing of "Anticipation Dialogues" seek to address this issue by providing a clear and managed pattern in which attention is paid to each participant. The process leads to the generation of a shared and detailed plan, where individuals are invited to take responsibility for their unique contributions.

To engage in dialogical processes may be an alien experience for families and practitioners alike, and one viewed with scepticism and doubt. It is the role of the facilitator to acknowledge this and positively connote participants' efforts to invest some trust in the process. Indeed, it is helpful to remind the network of the value of their scepticism, in terms of ensuring that plans made are relevant, achievable and supported by participants and the organisations they represent.

Whilst dialogical network meetings may involve a number of family members, many factors—including practicalities and ways in which families might experience shame (Hardy and Laszloffy 1995)—mean that meetings involving a large number of professionals may not be the most fertile terrain to draw upon the resources of a family's personal network. Therefore, it is necessary to consider how statutory services may respond in culturally competent ways to ensure valuable resources are secured and nurtured, in a manner that families can relate to and make use of.

It is the responsibility of practitioners to ensure that stories regarding deficit and loss are not privileged when asking families to consider their existing networks. Skilled and sensitive discussions may allow families to offer ideas regarding non-traditional and peripheral helpers whose roles might developed with endorsement from professionals able to shift from prescribed notions of "family" and "support". By using core principals of dialogical processes in such conversations, resources may reveal themselves in unexpected ways. An example of this process is given in Box 11.2.

> **Box 11.2 Case example: Gifty**
>
> Caroline: *Gifty, I'm really aware that when we spoke about holding Family Group Conference, you told me there was no point, because all your family are in Ghana except your sister—who you don't speak to at the moment.*
> Gifty: *That is correct.*
> Caroline: *I wondered if we'd asked about this in a way that didn't really fit, and if perhaps I'd said, "Who is helpful to you right now?", it might have made more sense?*
> Gifty: *What do you mean?*
> Caroline: *Well, I was thinking about that lady you talk about called Aunty, the one who lives opposite you.*
> Gifty: *Oh, Aunty! She's great. She always says, "Bring Joshua around and he can make cakes with me". She goes to my church too.*
> Caroline: *Does she? I didn't even know that—tell me a bit more ...*

Direct Work with Families: Preparing for Successful Returns

Having discussed relationships between parents and professionals, attention now turns to how relationships between parents and their children may be strengthened to a point where rehabilitation home is a viable plan. Multiple factors will contribute to the way in which parents and children perceive each other and the quality of their current relationship, including reasons for becoming looked after, the family's experiences and current care arrangements.

A central aspect of reunification will be working with children and their parents to actively address relational issues and the family's experience of loss and separation. The basis for such interventions will be contact between children and their parents, an issue of notable complexity. Whilst infrequent and poor-quality contact has been linked to lower incidents of successful reunification (Wade et al. 2011), contact alone appears insufficient in itself to promote positive outcomes (Cleaver 2000). In cases where the child resides in a long-term placement, and in cases involving the revocation of care orders, contact may be highly infrequent and a plan for increasing frequency will need to be established in the first instance. Alterations to existing contact plans often present challenges for families, carers and the professional network. The planning and logistics of contact may be complicated and frustrating. Carers may feel displaced by the increasing presence of the child's parent in their lives and hold anxieties regarding the placement being undermined either deliberately or inadvertently. For children and their parents, changes to contact plans may be emotionally demanding and confusing. The expectation that a family/child/carer network will simply adapt to new contact arrangements is unrealistic. In order to build quality contact, it is imperative that professionals adopt a proactive stance in terms of working with participants to promote good outcomes. This includes attention being paid to the relationship between birth families and current carers (e.g. foster carers) and how they are positioned in relation to each other.

Regardless of the nature and duration of care arrangements, it is likely parents and carers will hold beliefs about each other. In some cases such relationships may be experienced as collaborative and sustaining, in others, resentment and hostility may be present. Two accounts of parent's viewpoints from my own practice are detailed below:

> She was absolutely lovely. She always said to me, they're your children, you know them best. She couldn't have done more for them.
> I could not believe what they let her get away with in that place. They let her get her nails done, she'd cuss at them. It was disgusting.

Whilst it is unrealistic to imagine that significant differences in approaches to caring for children may always be resolved, it is helpful for professionals to promote respectful connections between parents and carers where possible. The dialogical approaches to network meetings discussed earlier may be built on in smaller encounters between parents and carers, with parties agreeing to a collaborative plans that endorse parental authority without undermining the role and position of the carers. For children and young people, the opportunity to experience their parents and carers as a united and complimentary team is likely to generate a sense of consistency, minimising opportunities for splitting and the challenges this generates.

The process of reunification requires parents to reclaim their identity *as* parents, an identity which may have been poorly formed initially, and further diminished by experiences of judgement, failure and criticism, particularly in cases involving care proceedings. In an attempt to connect parents with their intentions regarding the resumption of the care of their children, the use of reflexive questioning may promote newer thinking regarding their potential, along with an increased capacity to appreciate their children's perspectives and experiences of events. An example of this process is detailed in Box 11.3.

Box 11.3 Case example: Chantelle

Chantelle was a Black British 14-year-old girl who had been placed in care due to her mother Simone's addiction to crack cocaine. Following Simone's successful engagement with substance misuse services, Chantelle's return home was being considered.

Caroline: *Simone, can you remember back to when Chantelle was a baby? What ideas did you have about how you'd look after her; what were your dreams?*

Simone: *I thought about her going to school, having friends, us doing stuff together, her doing well, learning…*

Caroline: *And you as a Mum, what did you think you'd do to make that happen?*

Simone: *I was going to get a job, stay out of trouble and just be there for her really.*

Caroline: *So now, getting clean, doing your volunteer work, what's that telling you about who you might be as a parent?*

Simone: *That I can stick to things, that I can help other people.*

Caroline: *… and what do you think Chantelle needs to know about you as her Mum?*

Simone: *That I've caused her grief.*

Caroline: *What else?*

Simone: *That I've learnt from my mistakes and I'm going to do it differently this time.*

Caroline: *Who's going to help you?*

Simone: *Sandra, I can talk to her anytime. You. The social worker perhaps …*

In attending to parents' experiences of reunification processes, the theme of ambivalence is often present. Regardless of the precipitating factors of the plan for reunification, resuming care of a child or children necessitates significant lifestyle changes. Paradoxically, the pressure that some parents experience when children return to their care may threaten the positive changes they have made during their absence. Parents who have been required to "prove" their fitness to resume care of their children may, quite appropriately, have reservations regarding expressing ambivalence to professionals, leading to the suppression of doubts and worries regarding future plans. These are significant in relation to parents' capacity to cope and the management of risk issues.

Therefore it is essential that explicit permission is granted for the expression of such doubts, beginning with dialogues regarding current levels of trust and transparency in the relationship between parents and professionals. An example from my practice is given in Box 11.4 to illustrate this process.

Box 11.4 Case example: Julie

Julie was a White Irish woman in her thirties whose three children had come into care a year ago, as a result of their exposure to a violent relationship between Julie and her ex-partner.

Caroline: *Can I ask you one of those scaling questions?*

Julie: *Go on.*

Caroline: *On a scale of one to ten, one being not at all and ten being completely, how open do you think you can be with me regarding the kids coming home?*

Julie: *Now? Nine, ten, I've got nothing to hide. How open can you be with me?*

Caroline: *Good question! Maybe I should go for a nine too. So, here's my question: What's your biggest fear about the kids coming home?*

Julie: (long pause, Julie is crying) *That you'll take them back off me.*

Caroline: *Say more?*

Julie: *I'm worried that something will go wrong, I'll mess up.*

Caroline: *How might you mess up?*

Julie: *Shouting at them, you know, not being able to handle them.*

Caroline: *Okay, so thinking back to when you have messed up as you say—what are you going to do different now?*

Julie: *Just not let it build up, talk to someone.*

Caroline: *... and what do I need to do to help you?*

Julie: *Just talk to me really.*

Caroline: *I'm thinking about how much pressure you might feel you are under for it all to be perfect. You've waited so long for them to come home.*

Julie: *I know. Now it is happening and I want it to, but I know it's going to be so hard. One day I think it will be ok and then the next I'll be like this, crying and worrying.*

Caroline: *... and is the crying and worrying ok?*

(continued)

> **Box 11.4** (continued)
>
> Julie: *No, because you'll think I'm not up to it.*
> Caroline: *I've got another idea—I'm thinking how useful it is you've been able to let me know about this, so we can think together about this, rather than pretending it's not there.*

Another aspect of achieving successful reunification is the process of parents and children developing accounts of their experiences together. This requires parents to acknowledge the difficulties they have encountered and the impact this has had on their children. For many parents this is a painful process.

Whilst the ability to sit with discomfort is required of both parents and professionals, it is essential for attention to be given to the co-existence of additional stories, so that parents are not caught in conversations of blame and regret. These are unlikely to encourage reflexivity or open opportunities for change. It is the importance of being able to transform accounts of failure that offer hope. Once a parent can connect with their child's experiences of pain and loss in such a way that allow them to move on, scope exists to work with children and parents together to build connections and envisage a future where they live together successfully. For example, a parent whose severe depression contributed to their parenting becoming emotionally and physically abusive may be supported in developing a narrative which acknowledges the impact of mental health difficulties on children's welfare whilst generating a commitment to recognise future triggers and indicators enabling timely support seeking.

The nature of direct work with children and their parents will depend on the ages of the children and the circumstances of their return. With smaller children, the creation of a shared narrative through pictures, a story board or story-telling involving characters may work well, particularly as narrative approaches focus strongly on utilising the family's own language (Wilson 1998). For older children a more traditional, conversational approach may be appropriate, although it is to be considered that many children will refrain from speaking about aspects of their relationships with their parents for fear of being disloyal or jeopardising chances of reunification. In such cases, inviting hypothetical ideas or asking a young person to provide advice to a family in similar situations might be appropriate (White and Epston 1990). For other young people, speaking with their parents in the company of a mediating third party can be a useful way to dissolve unhelpful patterns of interaction that impact significantly on relational functioning. These kinds of sessions require careful preparation and skilled facilitation, ideally using evidence-based models of relationship-focussed practice (Pendry 2012).

Research indicates that successful reunifications are likely to require these kinds of thoughtful, intensive and targeted clinical interventions over an extended period of time (Farmer et al. 2011). The minutiae of support packages (including the allocation of specific tasks, financial arrangements, respite provision and contingencies) need significant attention in order for families to feel respected and contained as they commence their future lives together. By demonstrating their commitment to the support plan, the professional network models a sense of respectfulness and value to the family. Preparation and planning cannot ensure the reunification process does not falter at some stage. Therefore, it is the responsibility of the professional network to cultivate resilience and tolerance, working alongside the family to overcome setbacks in constructive and timely ways. Explicit acknowledgment of the likelihood of such events becomes an integral aspect of network discussions, for example, by asking questions to develop coping narratives:

> *Given the newness of this situation, it's likely we might all experience some difficulties. What stories and ideas might we hold in mind when we find ourselves struggling or losing hope?*

Conclusion

Successful reunification processes are contingent on the existence of collaborative and transparent relationships between professionals and families, in which meaningful and strengths-based plans can be established and actioned. By engaging in systemic practice to assist us in addressing issues of power and difference, professionals are enabled to develop a more flexible and coherent stance, promoting attentiveness to both risks and possibilities.

Reunification remains a complex and emotive process that demands a great deal of commitment, trust and courage from all involved. By drawing on research, clinical theory, practice examples and input from families, professional networks can thereby attempt to develop more thoughtful practices, which productively combine risk management with the rights and wishes of families to reconnect and experience a constructive and positive future together.

References

Aggett, P., Swainson, M., & Tapsall, D. (2011). Seeking Permission: An interviewing stance for finding connection with hard to reach families. *Journal of Family Therapy, 37*(2), 190–209.

Bakhtin, M. (1981). *Dialogic imagination.* Austin, TX: Texas University Press.

Boyd, E. (2010). "Voice entitlement" Narratives in supervision: Cultural and gendered influences on speaking and dilemmas in practice. In C. Burck & G. Daniel (Eds.), *Mirrors and reflections: Processes of systemic supervision.* London: Karnac.

Cleaver, H. (2000). *Fostering family contact.* London: TSO.

Davies, B., & Harre, R. (1990). Positioning: The discursive production of selves. *Journal for the Theory of Social Behaviour, 20*(1), 43–63.

Farmer, E., Sturgess, W., O'Neil, T., & Wijedasa, D. (2011). *Achieving successful returns from Care. What makes reunification work?* London: British Association for Adoption and Fostering (BAAF).

Fredman, G. (2004). *Transforming emotion: Conversation in counselling and psychology.* London: Karnac Books.

Gross, V. (1991). Systemic thinking and the practitioners Dilemma in child sex abuse: Smooth travelling between domains. *Human Systems: The Journal of Systemic Consultation and Management, 2*, 263–277.

Hardy, K. V., & Laszloffy, T. A. (1995). The cultural genogram; Key to training culturally competent family therapists. *Journal of Marital and Family Therapy, 21*, 227–237.

Hedges, F. (2010). *Reflexivity in therapeutic practice.* London: Palgrave Macmillan.

Hoffman, L. (1985). Beyond power and control: Towards a "Second Order" family systems therapy. *Family Systems Medicines, 3*, 381–396.

HM Government. (2015). *Working together to safeguard children. A guide to interagency working to safeguard and promote the welfare of children.* London: TSO.

Howarth, J. (Ed.). (2001). *The child's world. Assessing children in need and their families.* London: Jessica Kingsley Publications.

Kendrick, A. (Ed.). (2008). *Residential child care: Prospects and challenges.* London: Jessica Kingsley Publishers.

Laming, L. (2009). *The protection of children in England: A progress report.* London: TSO.

Mason, B. (1993). Towards positions of safe uncertainty. *Human Systems: The Journal of Systemic Consultation and Management, 4,* 189–200.

Mason, B. (2010). Six aspects of supervision and the training of supervisors. *Journal of Family Therapy, 32,* 436–439.

Munro, E. (2011). *The Munro review of child protection: Final report. A child centred system.* London: Department for Education.

Nielsen, J. (2002). Working in the grey zone: The challenge for supervision in the area between therapy and social control. In D. Campbell & B. Mason (Eds.), *Perspectives on supervision.* London: Karnac.

Pearce, W. B., & Pearce, K. (2000). Extending the theory of the coordinated management of meaning ("CMM") Through a community dialogue process. *Communication Theory, 10*(4), 405–423.

Pendry, N. (2012). Systemic practice in a risk management context. In S. Goodman & I. Trowler (Eds.), *Social work reclaimed: Innovative frameworks for child and family social work practice.* London: Jessica Kingsley Publishing.

Pipe, C., & Richardson, K. (2015). The challenge of collaborative practice in parenting assessments. In B. Williams, E. Peart, R. Young, & D. Briggs (Eds.), *Capacity to change: Understanding and assessing a parent's capacity to change within the timescale of the child.* London: Family Law.

Rahilly, T., & Hendry, E. (2014). *Promoting the wellbeing of children in care: Messages from research.* London: NSPCC.

Reder, P., & Duncan, S. (1999). *Lost Innocents: A follow-up study of fatal child abuse.* New York: Routledge.

Seikkula, J. (2011). Becoming dialogical—Psychotherapy or a way of life? *The Australian and New Zealand Journal of Family Therapy, 32*(3), 179–193.

Seikkula, J., & Arnkil, T. E. (2006). *Dialogical meetings in social networks.* London: Karnac Books.

Sinclair, I., Baker, C., Lee, J., & Gibbs, I. (2005). *Foster children: Where they go and how they get on.* London: Jessica Kingsley Publishers.

Tomm, K. (1987). Interventive interviewing: Part II. Reflexive questioning as a means to enabling self-healing. *Family Process, 26,* 167–183.

Thoburn, J., Robinson, J., & Anderson, B. (2012). *Returning children home from public care.* Research Briefing 42: Social Care Institute for Excellence.

van Lawick, J., & Bom, H. (2008). Building bridges: Home visits to multi-stressed families where professional help reached a deadlock. *Journal of Family Therapy, 30,* 504–516.

Wade, J., Biehal, N., Farrelly, N., & Sinclair, I. (2011). *Caring for abused and neglected children: Making the right decisions for reunification or long term care.* London: Jessica Kingsley Publishers.

White, M., & Epston, D. (1990). *Narrative means to therapeutic ends.* New York: W.W Norton.

Williams, B., Peart, E., Young, R., & Briggs, D. (2015). *Capacity to change—Understanding and assessing a parent's capacity to change within the timescale of the child.* London: Family Law.

Wilson, J. (1998). *Child-focused practice: A Collaborative systemic approach.* London: Karnac Books.

Index

© The Author(s) 2016
L. Smith (ed.), *Clinical Practice at the Edge of Care*,
DOI 10.1007/978-3-319-43570-1

Printed in Great Britain
by Amazon

65662226R00159